Praise for *Original Sins*

'What a frightening and funny book, full of shocking, memorable scenes. I'm glad Matt Rowland Hill lived to tell the tale' Adam Foulds

'Matt Rowland Hill has gone to the depths of himself and emerged with something unique, graceful, piercingly smart, and devilishly funny. Many books have been written about addiction. *Original Sins* is unlike all of them, and stands among the very best' Rob Doyle

'Matt Rowland Hill guides us to the edge of devastation, and doesn't flinch from the ache of addiction, family anguish and inward despair. But this is a book that's optimistic to the core, as honest about grief as it is about joy. I won't forget it' Jessica J Lee

'Hill's surviving his journey through religious fundamentalism into hardcore drug addiction is an accomplishment. His writing this memoir—unflinching, heart-rending, funny, insightful as hell—is a triumph. This is a phenomenal book' Antoine Wilson

'This book is a scorching, relentless, absolutely essential read about the roots of addiction and what it takes to save yourself. Hill writes like he has nothing to lose, and like he was born to create this harrowing, utterly transfixing, beautifully wrought portrait of a young man tortured by the twin horrors of family and religion. I couldn't put it down and when I finished reading, I realized I've been waiting for someone to tell the brutal truth about all this. To go all the way into the deepest dark of it, to break my heart in exactly this terrifying way. To take that darkness and make a brilliant, forceful work of literature from it is the holiest alchemy, and is itself Hill's masterful and unbelievably hard-won answer to the question: What will save us? Only art' Merritt Tierce

'Matt Rowland Hill probes, mercilessly, the ways extreme religion and extreme addiction intersect. But there is no simplistic placing-of-blame here. At the center of this stunning memoir is a beautiful, painful irony: though the hellfire and brimstone Christianity of his childhood undoes him, it's his adult encounter with authentic Christianity – love, grace, forgiveness, radical surrender – that also begins to rescue him. What most impressed me about this addiction memoir was its staunch refusal to become an addiction memoir, with the pat journey-into-the-abyss-and-out-again trajectory. Instead, Hill allows his story to be precisely what all our stories are: a series of days, and hours, and moments in which we are given, over and over, the profound responsibility to choose life over death' Jamie Quatro

'Matt Rowland Hill's marvellous debut, by turns excruciatingly anguished and elatingly funny but always engrossing, is an essential experience for anyone interested in family dynamics, adolescence, class, psychology, theology, or English prose' Leo Robson

ORIGINAL SINS

ORIGINAL SINS

MATT
ROWLAND HILL

A Memoir

Chatto & Windus
LONDON

1 3 5 7 9 10 8 6 4 2

Chatto & Windus, an imprint of Vintage, is part of the
Penguin Random House group of companies whose addresses
can be found at global.penguinrandomhouse.com

Penguin
Random House
UK

First published by Chatto & Windus in 2022

penguin.co.uk/vintage

A CIP catalogue record for this book is available from
the British Library

ISBN 9781784743826

Epigraph on p. ix from *Young Man Luther* by Erik H. Erikson, reprinted
courtesy of W. W. Norton & Company.

Typeset in 10.5/14.5 pt Sabon LT Std
by Integra Software Services Pvt. Ltd, Pondicherry

Printed and bound in Great Britain by Clays Ltd, Elcograf S.p.A.

The authorised representative in the EEA is Penguin Random House Ireland,
Morrison Chambers, 32 Nassau Street, Dublin D02 YH68.

Penguin Random House is committed to a sustainable future for
our business, our readers and our planet. This book is made from
Forest Stewardship Council® certified paper.

MIX
Paper from
responsible sources
FSC® C018179

For Jonathan Rhys Hill

For our light affliction, which is but for a moment, worketh for us a far more exceeding and eternal weight of glory;

While we look not at the things which are seen, but at the things which are not seen: for the things which are seen are temporal; but the things which are not seen are eternal.

2 Corinthians 4:17–18

The crisis in a young man's life comes when he half-realises that he is hopelessly overcommitted to what he is not.

Erik Erikson, *Young Man Luther*

Contents

ORIGINAL SINS

Is there anything more lovely than the sight of clean works, fresh from the pharmacy in the morning?

There's a knock at the door, but I don't answer. Staring back at me from the bathroom mirror is a thirty-year-old man wearing a charcoal-grey suit and a black tie clipped neatly into place. Laid out on the toilet lid are three aluminium spoons in blister packs, six yellow sachets of citric acid, four orange-capped 1ml syringes in sealed plastic wrappers, eight antiseptic swabs in miniature white envelopes, a tube of cigarette filters and three lighters. I know by the end of the day I'll be rifling through pockets of blood-soiled litter for a needle that isn't bent and clogged beyond use. But for now, looking at my tools in the rhomboid light cast by the window above the sink, I feel inspired, like a gifted painter standing before a blank canvas.

The knocking's louder this time, and a Welsh-accented male voice calls through the door: 'What yew doing in there, mun?'

'I'll just be a minute!' I shout. There's no reply, and it occurs to me with satisfaction that my strangled tone might, under the circumstances, be mistaken for grief.

As far as bathrooms to shoot up in go, this one – clean, spacious, well lit – is close to the ideal. I once thought myself a connoisseur of bathrooms, these sanctuaries where I can leave the world unseen and be alone with my favourite hobby. I relished the nefarious glamour of injecting heroin in an upholstered lavatory with palm fronds and gleaming brass taps. I even had a pervert's fondness for a reeking public bog scrawled with felt-tip cartoon dicks. But as you grow older, you increasingly come to appreciate what really matters. And, as they say, it's the little things that count: a decent light to help find a vein, a flat surface on which to carry out the sacrament of cooking up, a reassuringly heavy door. If I absolutely had to find fault with this bathroom – if I could change one thing – it would be the fact that it's in a church filled with mourners at the funeral of a friend of mine who died last week from an overdose of the same drugs I'm about to mainline into my bloodstream.

Oh well, I think, as the knocking starts again and I kneel over the toilet, slowly opening a pea-sized plastic wrap of chalky brown powder: you can't have everything.

When the call came ten days ago, I almost didn't pick up. I was waiting for Armani in a piss-scented stairwell in Hackney's Downs Park Estate, and the sight of Joanna Sidhu's name on my phone made me feel embarrassed, caught out. The floor looked as though the detritus of a shipwrecked crew of junkies and crackheads had washed in with the tide: shattered glass, crushed beer cans, a single bloodied ballet pump, a headless plastic doll. It was hard to imagine a world where this scene and Joanna Sidhu – kind, benign Jo, with her emphatic North-American smile – could both exist.

'Hey, stranger,' said the voice on the line. 'Long time.'

Normally, once I'd known someone a while, a wariness would hatch in my mind and begin to infect all our interactions, until I felt sure that somehow I'd thoroughly disgraced myself and that my humiliation was an open secret, like a repulsive crime equally impossible to mention or forget. But Jo, though I'd known her since university, had always been exempt from this rule. She never showed any sign she was aware of my real or imagined sins. Which is why I accepted her call, even though I usually never answered the phone while waiting to score. I lit a cigarette with my free hand.

'Jo, I don't have long,' I said. 'Work's crazy right now.'

'Oh man, tell me about it. Work's crazy here too. Actually I'm about to go into an eleven o'clock. But listen up a minute, ok?'

From the stairwell's wire-mesh window I could see Armani peddling laboriously up the main road on a kid's BMX. It was summer, but the sky was overcast and his shoulders were hunched against the spitting rain. I watched him turn right into the estate and I knew that in three minutes he'd have cycled through the car park, locked his bike, walked across the courtyard and climbed the four flights of stairs to where I was standing. I'd waited here so many times that my brain had learned to count down those three minutes with remarkable precision. My guts loosened with anticipation, and I realised I hadn't heard a thing Jo had said.

'Sorry Jo, the line's terrible. What was that?'

Two minutes and fifteen seconds.

'Can you hear me now? I said I got a call this morning, about Gareth Lloyd. I know you guys used to be close, so I wanted to tell you. I'm so sorry, Matt. He died yesterday.'

'Wait, what?'

One minute and fifty seconds.

'They won't know till after they've run tests, but they think it had something to do with drugs.'

A hundred seconds. Under a hundred seconds.

'Jesus Christ, Jo. I don't know what to say.'

'I know. It's like – I don't think it's sunk in for me yet either.'

I pulled on my cigarette. My hand was trembling with excitement. I tried to think of something to say, tried to imagine what I was supposed to be saying.

Sixty seconds.

'It just – it doesn't seem real,' I finally said, and at that moment the door downstairs clattered open. I heard Armani's breathing grow heavy as he began climbing the stairs.

'Jo, I'm really sorry. I have to go.'

'Wait, you're coming to the funeral, right? A week on Saturday?'

'Of course! Look, I'll call you later, ok?'

'Wagwarn Mark!' said Armani breathlessly, turning the last corner. Six months ago Armani had been a young man whose black hoodie almost swallowed his wiry frame. Now he was about forty and too big for the green velour tracksuit he wore with a string vest and fake gold necklace. The Caribbean accent was new, too. But I was used to Armani's sudden metamorphoses. In the past he'd been an Irish traveller with a gold earring, a crop-haired Ghanaian with a lazy eye, and a gang of Bengali youths. I'd bought drugs from a number of different Armanis before I understood that a single phone with its precious list of contacts was being sold from one dealer to another. In this way, whenever one Armani disappeared – having been shanked or gone to prison – another soon arrived to take his place, and all his previous incarnations were instantly forgotten. Some customers probably didn't even notice.

'Hi Armani,' I said, bumping his offered fist.

'Yo white boy!' said Armani. 'It's on top out there, man! Feds everywhere, innit.' He fished around in a pouch strapped inside his waistband. There must have been a hundred wraps in there – the blue ones containing heroin and the white, crack – and I tried not to stare, feeling like a poor man at the bank as the teller opened a till stuffed with notes. 'Just findin' you some nice big ones. You wantin' two and two, right?'

'Better make it three dark and five light.'

Armani grinned, familiar with my impulsive orders. I stared at his skull while he counted the items, wondering if desperation could ever lead me to smash a brick down onto it and take the pouch. I'd feel terrible: I was fond of Armani, we'd developed a real camaraderie since he'd morphed into an affable Jamaican earlier this year, even if he never could get my name right and I couldn't be bothered to correct him. But then again, the contents of that pouch would keep me going for at least a week: an eternity in junkie time. He took my twenty and four tens, glancing at them to check they were correct before slipping them into his pocket.

'So wagwarn, bruv?' said Armani, half turning as he made his way down the narrow staircase. 'You good?'

'I dunno, man,' I said to Armani's back. 'To be honest, I'm kind of spun out at the moment. I just heard a guy I know died.'

Armani paused, turned to look at me, frowned. 'Friend a yours?'

'Yeah. I think it was an OD.'

'That's deep, fam.'

Outside, the rain had stopped and I was hit by the damp chalky smell of the pavement scalding in the sun.

Concentrating on rolling a cigarette, Armani sucked his teeth in disgust. 'Can't trust nobody out on road, bruv! Mandem slingin' all kinds a shit! Rat poison, brick dust, paint stripper, you get me?' Looking genuinely saddened by the unscrupulousness of some people, he ran his tongue along the edge of the paper. 'Fuckin' criminals, innit!'

'Anyway, see you, Armani.' I felt calmer now with the gear in my pocket, but I was eager to begin the walk home, which I knew would take exactly twelve and a half minutes.

'Yo, hold up, fam,' he said. I offered him my fist but, instead of bumping it, he took hold of my hand and pressed something inside. 'Sorry about your bredren, yeah?'

It was a perfect summer morning and the estate's towers threw huge shadows across the road as I strode home. I cut through Hackney Downs, where kids were playing tennis and Turkish mums pushed toddlers on swings. I knew my heart would be pounding hard when I entered my building's front door, walked up the seventeen steps to my flat, let myself in and began cooking up. My mind was so fixed on that moment that I was three minutes from home before I remembered to look in my clenched fist and found, with a surge of gratitude that almost brought tears to my eyes, two tokens of Armani's sympathy, one white and one blue.

'You look like death,' I say now to the face in the mirror, framed by the apricot bathroom wallpaper. My skin is clammy and pale and there are violet-grey rings around my eyes, one of which is twitching and seems to have burst a blood vessel. But it isn't quite true, of course. At least when you die, you get a haircut, a clean suit and a session with a makeup artist. I hold the spoon under the tap, adding a few drops of water to the little mound of powder. Well, the grass is always greener, isn't it?

'Yew all right in there?' calls the Voice from Beyond, which is how I've begun to think of the man outside.

'I'll be absolutely fine, if you could please just give me a fuck-ing minute!' I snarl, flushing the toilet to drown out the sound of the lighter, which I hold now under the spoon, the flame tonguing the metal. The powdery liquid hesitates for a moment, simmers, and then erupts in a little rapture of froth, bubbles winking at the brim, before resolving into an espresso-dark pool.

Christ, I'm half in love with it: the burnt-syrup smell of freshly cooked heroin. Like returning from a long journey and opening your front door to the comforting waft of home. I'm well aware that all right-thinking people would look at me now – here of all places, on today of all days, bent over the cistern, tearing off a strip of filter with my teeth and placing it in the spoon – with downright revulsion. But at some point in the morbid GIF file of my life – cluck, score, use; cluck, score, use – I must have given up caring about the opinions of right-thinking people.

In any case, maintaining a steady flow of opiates through my body has long ceased to be a reckless indulgence or even a treatment for emotional malaise. With a habit like mine, shooting up five or six times a day is simply a medical necessity. Without it I'd soon descend into the inferno of withdrawal, and then I'd struggle to make it from my bed to the bathroom to puke, let alone all the way to north Wales to pay my respects to the dearly departed. Rolling up my sleeves, I say out loud, 'I'm afraid the condition of the patient leaves us with no choice but to operate!'

'Pardon me?' calls the Voice from Beyond.

'Never mind!' I shout. I really must stop talking to myself; people are going to start thinking there's something wrong with me.

Anyway, it's not as though I didn't exhaust all other options before showing up here loaded with crack and heroin. I even hauled myself down to the methadone clinic and sat in the waiting room, which – with its public health notices, easy-wipe chairs and atmosphere of stifled dread – might have been mistaken for a badly dilapidated dental practice, except that several of my fellow clients visibly had no need for a dentist, since they had no teeth. When my name was called I went into a small room and sat opposite a 'substance misuse worker' who, before giving the go-ahead for a doctor to write me a prescription for methadone, insisted on delivering a pep talk on the benefits of abstinence. Leaning over the desk, she gave me an earnest look.

'Now, uh,' she said, glancing down at her notes, '*Matthew*. What I'd like you to do is imagine I could hand over all the money you've ever spent on heroin and give it to you in one nice big lump sum. Can you do that for me?' She helpfully mimed placing a heavy bag of cash on the desk. 'Now, if you could walk out of here and take it home with you right now, what would you spend it on? Go ahead, anything at all! Use your imagination!'

'Well—' I began, rapidly losing patience with this idiotic thought experiment.

She nodded encouragingly. 'Go on! There are no wrong answers!'

'If I could only choose one thing—'

'Yes?' Her head was nodding so hard it seemed about to fall off.

I stared at her blankly. 'I suppose I'd probably buy a fucking enormous quantity of heroin. And then I'd go home and start taking it all.'

Fifteen minutes later I was in the pharmacy with a methadone script – '60ml to be administered daily' – but my resolve lasted all of twenty-four hours. The moment I choked down the first mouthwash-flavoured gulp of the unnaturally green liquid I recalled why I hated methadone: it arrests the physical symptoms of withdrawal, but it does nothing about the craving in the pit of your stomach or the hyena-like jabber in your brain. The next day I was back at the same counter, requesting yet another supply of needles. The thing about smack is that it just *works*, that's what people don't realise.

Others might see me as an extremist, a fanatical member of a chemical death-cult. But the way I see it, I'm simply a pragmatist. When you strip away the bullshit, life is pain management: nothing more, nothing less. And heroin is, by far, the most effective painkiller I've ever found.

I open one of the white wraps, the crumpled plastic an oyster shell with its dirty-white pearl. Now, the crack, I have to admit, isn't, strictly speaking, a medical necessity. But doing heroin without its twin is unthinkable. Dark and light, the dealers call them. Yin and yang. They're like a perfectly balanced equation, a fiendish problem turned into a gorgeously elegant solution. Heroin is the sonorous bass, and crack the sweet airy treble. Besides, man can't live by bread alone. You've got to have at least *some* fun.

But the situation raises an interesting question of etiquette: exactly how much crack is it appropriate to add to a speedball at a friend's funeral? I tip the whole of one bag into the spoon and decide to open another. There's only one thing worse than doing too much crack, and that's doing too little: that's my philosophy. I pour in another half wrap, pause for a moment and then, what the hell, add the rest. It's going to be an emotional day, after all. And I'm pretty sure this is, if not exactly what Gareth would have wanted, at least what Gareth would have gone ahead and *done* if the roles were reversed.

The Voice from Beyond is thumping on the door but I don't even reply, I'm so close now, so close, thrumming with adrenaline, mouth so dry I couldn't even speak if I wanted to. Using the syringe's orange cap, I pestle the crack until the spoon is brimming with brown sediment. Then I remove the lid, press the needle into the filter and draw back the plunger, slowly filling the chamber. It's thrillingly dark; I can almost taste the mixture of drowsy numbness and searing ecstasy contained in it. I hold the syringe in my teeth while I clench my left bicep and pump my hand, scouting for a vein. 'This is my body,' I say to myself as I dig the needle under my epidermis. It slides straight through the vein, so I pull out again, prodding around for the slight pucker of resistance that means I'm safely in. Then there's the tell-tale plume of blood in the barrel, a tiny dark supernova, which means – thank *fuck* – I'm good to go. 'And this is my blood,' I intone as I press the plunger down, watching the barrel empty, until its contents have disappeared into my arm and a dark red bead rolls down my wrist. I have a few seconds to brace myself before the speedball hits, and in that interlude, as I gently pull the needle out of my arm, the truth strikes me with utter clarity: I will never, ever be able to live without this.

And why the hell would I want to?

'Where have you been?' whispers Jo when I find her in the church. 'I was getting worried.'

'I'm fine now,' I gasp, collapsing into the pew.

It's a relief to have made it to my seat next to Jo. And it's a relief I didn't die back there in the bathroom. To show up at another man's funeral only to kill yourself in the bog would go down as the worst kind of attention seeking. When I regained consciousness – the needle still in my right hand and my cheek on the floor in a puddle of drool – I had no idea how long I'd been out cold. A minute? An hour? I barged out the door past a flushed man with military badges in his lapels before realising, thanks to the anxiety pouring through my adrenal system like electricity through a jump cable, that the second bag of crack had been a foolish miscalculation. For a minute I paced around the vestibule among stacks of Bibles and wreaths of lilies experiencing sheer terror – terror about nothing, terror in its pure physical form – before the solution came to me like an epiphany. *More smack*! My rational mind saw at once that my plan, in solving the immediate problem, would instantly create another, more serious one by stranding me in north Wales with only one more hit to last all day. But my legs seemed to have other ideas: they were already carrying me back to the bathroom. And anyway, once you started giving proper consideration to the consequences of your actions, where would that sort of thinking lead?

Jo slips her arm through mine as the organ begins playing a new hymn and the congregation rises to its feet. I can still feel the flurry and shimmer of the smack in my veins, and I wonder if that's why I have the overpowering sense of having wandered into a waking dream. But no, it isn't just the drugs. Scattered around the church are the faces of people I know, mutual friends of Gareth's and mine from university, but as in a dream they are mixed up with details from another time and place. The varnished pews, the olive-green hymn books, the arched windows filling the hall with dull light: these are all straight out of the churches of my youth.

Stranger and more dreamlike still, when the singing begins, is the sound of Welsh, the second language of my childhood. I wasn't expecting that. The melodic vowels and rasping fricatives are stored in my tongue's muscle memory, and I find myself singing along. But as the words come out of my mouth I notice they have no meaning. With a shock I realise the language I spoke every school day until I was eleven has become foreign to the man I am now.

When I take my seat, a familiar-sounding voice begins speaking in English from the front of the hall. But when I look up, half-expecting to see my father as I saw him in the pulpit every Sunday for sixteen years, in his place is another preacher: shorter, clean-shaven, middle-aged.

The man begins to list Gareth's virtues: he was the life and soul of every occasion; he never lost his sense of child-like wonder; he was the most curious and intelligent young man you could hope to meet. This portrait bears only the faintest resemblance to the Gareth I knew at university: a brash, anarchic figure with a wild grin and shaggy hair, always the last to accept the party was over. Or the second-to-last. My mind begins to drift, and after a while all I hear is the rhythmic thud of a single word: *was, was, was.*

This is the real burial, I think to myself. This is how they'll turn you from a living person into a memory. They'll seal you in a coffin of cliché, lower you into a hole, and cover you with half a tonne of platitudes. The preacher's voice grows slower and louder as he reaches his peroration. 'And above all,' he says, 'Gareth believed in the Lord. He never flinched from asking hard questions of his faith. But he knew in his heart that Jesus was his Saviour.'

Talk about a deathbed conversion. If they don't get you before you stop breathing, they'll convert you the minute you can't argue back. Yes, it's a very good job I didn't die when I overdosed back there in the bathroom. Any more smack in that speedball and I'd have wound up as a rhetorical device in one of my father's sermons.

'Gareth knew that Christ died for our sins, that he was resurrected for us to rise again. Oh, heavenly father,' says the preacher, closing his eyes. 'Even as we gather here today, Gareth is yours. And we know that one day we will meet him again, if only we ask you to forgive our transgressions. May you come into our hearts now, sweet Lord Jesus.'

He begins declaiming the Lord's Prayer, the congregation murmurs along, and by the end I'm involuntarily reciting the words that are scored into me like a tattoo: *for thine be the kingdom, the power and the glory, forever and ever. Amen.*

Sure, I think, sitting down again. Thine be the kingdom. Thine be the hypocrisy of this whole asinine affair. Thine be the infantile attempt to give death the slip through wish fulfilment. Thine be the make-believe, the collective delusion.

Thine be the fallacy and the taboo. Thine be the paedophile priest and the suicide vest. Oh, and for that matter, thine be the gas chamber, thine be the gulag, thine be the famine. Thine be the fairy tale of heaven and hell, good and evil, angels and demons, the simple-minded dualism of it all. Thine be the fear. Thine be the broken home. Thine be my brother Jonathan hating himself all his life for desiring other men. Thine be my friend Gareth, dead at thirty because he couldn't handle the world you made without blotting out his agony. Thine be the irredeemable fucking mess of my own life. Sometimes I wish the whole repulsive story *were* true, just so I could say these things to you once at the end, face to face, instead of raging through a glass darkly. Yes, you bastard, thine be the needle, thine be the crack pipe, thine be the early grave, forever and ever and ever and ever and ever and ever and ever.

Jo looks over at me and squeezes my arm again. The force of my rage surprises me. It's been well over a decade since I put away childish things and turned my back on my parents' dogma. Long ago I learned to see church services for what they are: cheap spells and charms, like chants performed at an ancient fireside to ward off the terrifying dark. I had an overdose of the opiate of the masses and decided I preferred the real thing. I shook the dust off my feet at eighteen and tried to forget my childhood faith, just as I've seemingly forgotten one of my childhood languages. Ever since then the rituals of evangelical Christianity have meant no more to me than the annual rigmarole at Mecca.

So why, when the pianist begins playing and the congregation stands to sing an old Welsh hymn, do I find myself sobbing? It's a simple gospel tune in a major key, a series of melodic phrases rising and falling away without resolution. Although I'm not sure I've ever heard the song before, I feel as though its chords have been hidden inside me somewhere deeper than memory, waiting for precisely this moment to be called out. I try to resist the wail rising in my chest, I clench my jaw and clamp my mouth shut, but when the tune lands on a minor chord a dam breaks inside me and tears begin streaming down my cheeks. Reaching back into my dormant Welsh, I try to translate the words, but only fragments come to me. *Arglwydd, dyma fi* . . . Here I am, Lord . . . *Ar dy alwad di* . . . something at your call . . . *Golch fi'n burlan yn y gwaed.* . . something something something blood . . . *A gaed ar Galfari* . . . No, I have no idea what the fuck it means. I just know, as another moan rises up through my throat and I notice the alarmed expression on Jo's face, that I have to get out of here.

I hurry out through the vestibule to the street. It's Saturday afternoon in this quiet town, and normal people are doing normal weekend things: shopping, pushing buggies, walking dogs. I stand on the pavement, allowing myself to weep. Instinctively I reach for the inside pocket of my suit jacket and, with a jolt of panic, recall I have only half a bag of smack left. Dealing with whatever's going on inside me right now with half a bag is comically hopeless, like trying to put out a house fire with a water pistol. I wipe my face with the cuff of my shirt. My tears have a pleasurable salty flavour. Voices reach me from inside the church. Above me, gulls circle in the screaming air.

'What I want to know,' says Amy Howerska above the murmur of conversation in the air-conditioned hall, 'is what's with the fancy bloody dress?'

Amy's levity is a relief. Since composing myself after the service and making my way into the reception I've struggled to maintain the tone of solemn conviviality the occasion requires. I'm feeling both too high and too desolate. Now, as I lean against the handrail of the wood-panelled bar, the sonic boom of my last hit of heroin is fading to a dull synaptic tingle. And I'm already experiencing the first threat of another sensation: withdrawal. It feels as though there's a baby crab scuttling around inside me, trying to claw its way out through my intestines.

'Some of the boys decided Gareth would have wanted a celebration-of-life,' I say, 'which apparently means getting dressed up for a pub crawl in Honolulu.' Amy and I look out over the room, full of black suits and frocks with the odd young man standing awkwardly in a tropical shirt and shorts. 'I suppose only a few people got the memo.'

Emboldened by Amy's conspiratorial laugh, I say, 'Well, they got him in the end, didn't they?'

'Who?'

'Gareth. I mean, they turned him into a believer just in time for a good Christian burial.'

'It's a *funeral*, sweet cheeks. What did you expect?' A serious note enters her voice. 'Anyway, he *was* a believer. He talked about it all the time.'

'Did he?' I say, surprised. 'He never said anything to me about it.'

'That's because you boys never stopped getting messed up long enough to have a proper conversation.' Amy stops, looks abashed. 'Sorry, Matt. Look, I didn't mean—'

As I'm waving away her apology, Micky Spall passes by, weaving through the crowd in a floral shirt. 'Mick!' Amy says, drawing him by the arm towards us. 'We were just discussing burial options. When it's his turn Matt wants to be left in a ditch by the highway with the horse thieves and the – oh, sweetheart.'

Only now she notices Micky's face, punch-drunk with grief. 'Come here,' she says. He allows himself to be pulled into an embrace and starts quietly convulsing against Amy's shoulder.

Across the room, Jo appears among the crowd of strangers and starts making her way over. Just the sight of her seems to calm the crab in my gut. Jo belongs to a species of capable, serious, professional people I've always openly disdained and secretly revered. When I imagine her life, I picture air-conditioned rooms with huge windows overlooking towers of sun-struck glass and steel. And she has the good-natured sexiness of a daytime TV presenter. Is it my imagination, or has she been hanging around me all day, linking our arms and rubbing my shoulder flirtatiously? Her face brightens as she approaches, but then she notices Micky weeping in Amy's arms.

'Oh, *Mick*,' she says, as though he's a wayward but infinitely forgivable child, and clasps his hand.

Deprived of the spotlight of Jo's attention, I find myself saying, 'Do you know what I really can't stand?'

Nobody says anything.

'*Wales*,' I continue. 'At the end of the day, we're just a province of England with delusions of nationhood. We're pathetic.'

Amy and Jo stand there letting me talk, holding on to Micky by the arms like he's a boxer out on his feet. I wonder if I should change the subject to something more appropriately funereal, but I can't help it.

'I mean, the Scots are finally getting their act together. The Irish have got the Hunger Strikes and the Easter Rising. What have we got? Inflatable daffodils and Tom Jones singing "Delilah" before kick-off at the rugby. Even the countryside's only nice because English capitalists haven't thought of a way of making money by digging it up yet. If you ask me—'

As I've been talking, the agitation in my stomach has become harder and harder to ignore. Now it feels as though a trapdoor inside me has been kicked open. I scan the hall for a bathroom.

'Sorry,' I manage to say. Jo's still smiling, but when I slip past her I notice the expression that's been in her eyes all day: pity.

As I set out on the journey towards the disabled bathroom at the far end of the hall – past the coats and blouses, the cuff-links and pearls, the sausage rolls on paper plates – I know I must do two things. First, I must keep placing one foot in front of the other until I've reduced the distance between the door and my body to zero. Second, I must never – not for a single moment – stop applying the full force of my will to gripping my guts. I successfully cover twenty, thirty, forty feet. With just eight or nine to go, I allow myself to believe I've made it. But the thought leads to a fractional relaxation of my will, and before I have time to consider what's happening, I feel my pants filling up with viscous, warm shit. Hitching them into a sling to hold their contents in place, I limp the rest of the way and shut the door.

It's only after I've pulled off my suit trousers and my pants – unleashing shit everywhere, shit all over the tiled floor, shit all the way down my bare thighs and calves – and stood barefoot in just my shirt and jacket, washing first my hands and then my legs and then my hands again; only after I've balled up my underwear and shit-stained socks and flung them as far as possible out of the little window; only after I've used three rolls of toilet paper and an entire bottle of soap dispenser to remove as much of the shit as possible from the floor and the toilet, discovering that my efforts have only spread the shit more widely, forcing me to go back and repeat each action a second or third time; it's only then, after I've spent half an hour methodically return-ing the room to its original state, that I find, behind the toilet plinth, the blue wrap of heroin – my only defence against withdrawal, of which diarrhoea is just the first symptom – open and half-submerged in a little puddle of shit.

Horrified, but seeing that I have no choice, I scoop up the solution of smack and shit into an aluminium spoon, and repeat the formula: water, citric, lighter, filter, needle. Five trochees: a perfect line of poetry. Gasping with relief, I pull the syringe out of my vein and notice that, although my hands are clean, my nails are ten crescents of filth.

When I emerge sockless from the bathroom and begin striding towards the exit, nobody looks over at me. Nothing has changed; the room looks and sounds precisely as it did before. 'Of course,' a man in a hot-pink shirt is saying to the Voice from Beyond, 'the Varsity rugby match isn't the national spectacle it used to be, more's the pity.'

'No, I don't suppose it is,' says the Voice from Beyond.

Just before I make it outside, a woman, fiftyish, her flint-grey hair pulled back from a face raw with crying, grips my arm, peers up into my eyes and says: 'It's just a terrible shame. A terrible, terrible shame.'

'Look, I can't – I'm so sorry,' I say, removing her hand and breaking for the door.

Shame, I think, stepping out into the sunlight and inhaling the tang of the fresh sea air. Well, that's one word for it.

Genesis

My mother was at her wit's end.

'I'm at my wit's end,' said my mother, twisting in the passenger seat to face my siblings and me. The sun was bright in the hazy blue sky and the car smelled of warm plastic and vinyl. 'What time did I tell you all to be ready?'

My brother put his hand up. 'Eight o' clock at the absolute latest,' he said, pleased to know the right answer.

'That's right, Jonathan. And can anyone tell me what time it is now? Rachel?'

'Quarter to eleven,' said my big sister from the third row of the seven-seater.

'Exactly! Which means we're nearly three hours behind schedule, and we haven't even left yet. I'm absolutely at my wit's end with all of you!'

'Right,' said my father brusquely. 'Let's not waste any more time then, shall we? Everybody close your eyes while I pray.'

'Play!' shouted Abigail, strapped into her car seat between my brother and me.

'Heavenly father,' said my father. 'Thank you for this opportunity to spend time together as a family. Thank you for Mummy, and all the hard work she does for us.'

Catching Jonathan's eye in the rear-view mirror, I poked my tongue out at him.

'We pray you will hold us safe in your loving arms as we make our way to Guernsey today. Help me to drive safely, Lord. We pray that traffic conditions will be favourable, particularly at Junction 33 on the way into Cardiff, which can get very congested, especially during the school holidays. And may we be a witness unto your Son, Christ Jesus, for his name's sake. Amen.'

'Amen!' five voices shouted back, my father shifting into first gear.

As the car nosed into the stream of passing vehicles on Sketty Avenue, my mother let out an exhausted sigh and opened her eyes. Blinking, as though waking from a holy trance, she took in her surroundings. When her gaze came to rest on my father, an appalled look came over her face.

'Phil,' she said, looking down at his lap. 'What are those?'

'Those are my legs, dear. I believe you've seen them before.'

'I mean those shorts. What are you doing in those shorts?'

My father was wearing khaki shorts, out of which he burst at both ends like a tube of toothpaste that had been squeezed in the middle. His belly strained against the steering wheel, his big fleshy thighs were grey-white and hairless, and on his feet he wore sandals over white socks.

'What I'm doing in these shorts, dear, is taking my beloved wife and children on their annual summer holiday.'

'Please Phil. You look absolutely ridiculous. I told you to go on a diet. Either go on a diet or buy some new summer clothes. Isn't that what I said? You'll have to stop at the next services and change into something more suitable for a man of your – your figure.'

'Daddy?' I called out, looking up from the game of Tetris I was playing on my Gameboy.

My father, staring straight ahead, concentrated on driving.

'*Phil*,' said my mother, 'are you listening to a word I'm saying? You are *not* wearing those shorts.'

'That's peculiar,' said my father after a long pause.

'What is?'

In the sarcastic English accent my father reserved for when he was in a bad mood with my mother, he said: 'It rarely is most peculiar. Rarely, rarely peculiar. You insist I'm not whirring these shorts. And yet only twenty minutes ago I looked in the mirror, and as far as I can recall these shorts were *exactly* what I was whirring.'

'Daddy!' I shouted.

'What is it, Matthew?' My father was speaking in his normal voice now, but his knuckles were white where they gripped the steering wheel.

'Jonathan had his eyes open when you were praying,' I said nonchalantly.

'Playing!' said Abigail.

'I did not!' Jonathan squealed.

I slotted an L-shaped tile neatly into its place. 'He did.'

'I didn't! Daddy, he's lying!'

'Do you promise you didn't have your eyes open?' I said.

'I promise!'

I savoured the moment before producing my checkmate move. 'But do you promise *on your word-as-a-Christian?*'

I knew Jonathan wouldn't dare utter an untruth on his word-as-a-Christian. To break your word-as-a-Christian was not only to lie, but to do so before God himself. The fact that my parents had never revealed what divine punishment awaited those who committed this sin had only increased its fearsome aura in our minds. Perhaps the offender would be transformed into a pillar of salt, like Lot's wife when she took a final glance at the home she was leaving forever.

Rachel's face appeared between the headrests. 'And how do you know,' she said archly, 'that he had his eyes open while Daddy was praying?'

'Yes, quite,' said my father.

'Kite!' said Abigail.

My father shifted gear. 'Stop winding your little brother up please, Matthew.'

'I'm at the end of my tether with these children,' muttered my mother.

'Dear me,' said my father. 'You've reached the end of your wit *and* your tether already. And we're not even on the M4 yet.'

I tried to flip a long tile through a gap but it was moving too fast and suddenly blocks were raining down, filling the screen, until the perfect wall I'd constructed was a chaos of crazy paving and the music stopped and it was Game Over.

The A483 out of Swansea was tailed back for miles. Up ahead, the smokestacks and cooling towers of Port Talbot steelworks were wreathed in steam. My father edged the car forward a few feet, stopped; edged forward, stopped. The ducts on the dashboard seemed only to be circulating warm, stale air. Even with all the windows down the heat in the car was stifling.

'I knew this would happen,' said my mother.

'Did you now?' said my father mirthlessly.

'This is why I said I wanted everybody ready by eight o'clock at the absolute latest.'

To be ready: this was the great struggle of my mother's life. Every morning she woke up at 6am, lay down in a scalding bath for twenty minutes while listening to a cassette tape of her favourite hymns, and then went to war against an ever-mounting state of unreadiness. Whenever she scored a small victory – cleaning, sweeping, hoovering, dusting or polishing the enemy into retreat – the forces of unreadiness only seemed to regroup in ever more cunning formations. Over the past week, as the day approached when we'd swap homes with a preacher's family from Guernsey, my mother's usual domestic routines had reached a pitch of almost vindictive intensity. Each item of silver cutlery in the velvet-inlaid mahogany box in the lounge cabinet was taken out and polished. The floral net curtains in the front windows were removed, washed and rehung. The bone china plates mounted in the hallway were taken down and dusted, not once but twice. So were the family portrait photographs in the dining room, captured each year in a professional studio, all Sunday best and awkward smiles against a backdrop of weeping willows. When, in church, we sang a hymn called 'Jesus is Coming: Are You Ready?' I sometimes thought of my mother, imagining that her greatest fear was for the Lord to return and find dusty fingerprints on the mantelpiece over the gas fire in the lounge.

'Have you boys got your seatbelts on?' said my mother, turning to my brother and me.

'I have!' said Jonathan eagerly.

'Matthew?'

'But we're not even moving.'

'We'll be moving in a minute. Put that seatbelt on *now*, please. I'm not telling you again.'

I decided to risk ignoring her. 'Daddy?'

'Yeeee-ees?' said my father, the word dipping in the middle and rising at the end, like a slack rope.

'Why do we have to wear seatbelts?'

My mother answered for him. 'Because if Daddy crashes this car, you'll go flying head-first through that windshield, that's why!'

Jonathan looked concerned. 'But if we crash we'll go straight to heaven, won't we?'

'Only if you've accepted Jesus Christ as your Lord and Saviour, fat face,' I told him.

'That's right, Matthew,' said my father. 'If we ask Jesus to forgive our sins and invite him into our hearts, one day we'll go to heaven to be with him for eternity.'

'And if you haven't, you'll go to hell,' said Rachel in a bored voice.

I considered this for a moment. 'But why do we have to wear seatbelts if we've already prayed for God to protect us?'

'He'll only protect you if you're wearing your seatbelt!' said my mother.

'Because God wants us to wear seatbelts?'

'Exactly.'

'But why?'

'Because it's the law! That's why! It's the law! Do you want the police to come and take Mummy and Daddy away? And you know what will happen then, don't you? You'll be put in a *home*. A home for children who don't have a Mummy or Daddy. Is that what you want?'

'No,' I said resentfully.

'Jonathan! *What are you doing?*' said my mother.

My brother had his head between his knees and his hands clamped over his ears. He looked up. 'I'm asking the Lord Jesus to come into my heart as my Lord and Saviour!'

'Right,' said my father, growing irritated. 'Has everyone asked Jesus to come into their hearts? Rachel?'

'I did it ages ago,' she said.

'Good. Matthew?'

'Yes,' I said sullenly.

'Abigail?'

'Geezers!' said Abigail, clapping her hands.

'Angela?'

My mother simply glared at him.

'Right, that's everyone then.'

For a moment, the cars in our lane seemed to pick up speed, like a current through a slow river. As we inched forward the speedometer on the dashboard fluttered upward. Then the tail lights in front glowed red, my father braked, and the little orange pointer swooned to zero.

The steel skeleton of the Severn Bridge rose up with its huge rigging of girders and zigzagged suspension cables. Down below, meadows subsided into mudflats and tawny water.

My brother was clutching the Gameboy, gazing reverentially into its little screen from under his bowl of brown hair.

'Jonathan,' said my mother into her sun visor's mirror. 'You're going to make yourself carsick like that.'

My brother bit his lip in concentration. 'I'm fine.'

'What are you playing?' I said, leaning over Abigail.

'*Mortal Kombat II.*'

'Which one are you?'

Jonathan attempted a flykick but was blocked by his opponent, who retaliated with an uppercut blow to the head. 'Liu Kang.'

'You should do an Instant Air Fireball. Nobody can defend against an Instant Air Fireball.'

'I don't want to, thanks.'

'Do you even know how to do an Instant Air Fireball?'

'Leave your brother alone, please, Matthew,' said my mother. 'Why don't you give Abigail some attention?'

Abigail pivoted expectantly towards me in her car seat. Hovering in front of her, I made a curtain of my hands and opened them suddenly. 'Boo!'

My sister looked unimpressed. I tried tickling her chin. 'What's the matter?'

'Angry,' said Abigail.

'Yes, I think we're all a little hungry,' said my father. 'Why don't we stop for lunch at the next Little Chef?'

'*Phil*,' hissed my mother. 'Do you want to spend all our money before we even get to Guernsey?'

My father breathed in slowly through his nose. 'All right then, how about some music? Let's all listen quietly and be alone with our own thoughts, shall we?'

My father rotated the radio dial until, from the snowstorm of white noise, a woman's voice emerged. In my mind the vocals were a fluorescent pink strobe against a sheen of golden chords. My father drummed the steering wheel in time to the beat. The woman's voice whipped around the car like a lasso: *Girls just want to have fuuuu-uun!*

My mother snapped the radio off. 'That's quite enough of that.'

'Mummy!' I wailed in protest. 'I *like* that one!'

'*Angela*.' My father's voice was halfway between a question and a warning.

'Phil, please don't *Angela* me.'

My father groaned. 'Go on then, dear. Tell us what's the matter.'

'Oh, nothing. It's just that I thought we were supposed to be *Christians*, that's all.'

'And Christians can't listen to the radio, I suppose? I must have missed that bit in scripture. Which gospel was that again?'

'*You* might be happy with your daughters thinking all girls want to do is have *fun*.' This final word my mother spat out like a piece of rotten food. 'But some of us have *morals*, Phil. Christian morals.'

'It's a pop song, dear. You remember pop music, don't you? The Carpenters, the Bee Gees, Simon and Garfunkel?'

'Please don't patronise me. And if you ask me, they shouldn't be listening to anything as ungodly as Simon and Garfunkel either.'

'Would it be too much for us to try and be a little light-hearted? Couldn't we, once in a while, maybe not take everything quite so seriously? Would it be entirely outside the bounds of possibility for us to go on a *family holiday* without starting off with a good old-fashioned *family row*?'

'I see. So I'm a party pooper. A stick-in-the-mud. Well, if it's my job to be a stick-in-the-mud for the sake of the Lord Jesus Christ, so be it.'

'Angela, please don't start.'

'I'm not starting, Phil. And please don't take that tone with me. As far as I recall, Titus 2 verses 4 and 5 tell us to *teach the younger women to be discreet, chaste, keepers at home, that the word of God be not blasphemed.* It doesn't say anything about teaching them that *girls just want to have fun.*'

'And to be obedient to their husbands.'

'Pardon me?'

'You missed a bit. *To be discreet, chaste, keepers at home and obedient to their husbands.*'

'All I'm saying is that maybe some of us should give a bit more thought to what kind of messages we're sending our children. Maybe then, when I told them to be ready for eight o'clock, they'd be ready for eight o'clock. Maybe they'd do as they're told and wear their seatbelts without arguing back.'

'Angela, *please.*'

'*A child left to himself bringeth his mother to shame.* Proverbs 29 verse 15.'

'Dear, we've been in this car for under two hours. We'll be here for another five. Can we *please* not argue all the way to Guernsey?'

'I'm not arguing, Phil. You're the one who's arguing. I'm just not prepared to sit idly by and listen to the works of the devil being glorified.'

My father inhaled sharply. 'My darling wife,' he said through his teeth. 'I'm sure you're not insinuating that by allowing my children to listen to the radio I'm acting as an agent of Satan. You didn't mean that, did you?'

My mother smiled thinly. '*He that committeth sin is of the devil.* 1 John 3 verse 8.'

My father stared straight ahead, saying nothing. Spores of tension wafted backwards from the front seats and attached to everything in the car. I wound down my window, letting in the thrashing noise of wind and traffic. Sticking my arm out, I tilted my hand into the blasting airstream.

'Matthew,' said my mother. 'Have I ever told you the story of the little boy who had his arm out of the car window when a lorry drove past and took it right off? Do you want to go walking around Guernsey with one arm?'

My father, who'd been driving silently, suddenly seemed to jolt awake.

'Don't you ever, *ever*,' he said, his voice rising from a growl to a shout, 'SPEAK TO ME LIKE THAT IN FRONT OF MY CHILDREN AGAIN! DO YOU HEAR ME?'

My mother gave a look that said my father had proved her point by raising his voice. She closed her eyes. 'Lord, forgive my husband. If my father could hear him now, speaking to me like this—'

'LORD, FORGIVE MY WIFE FOR BEING A NAG-GING, PIG-HEADED, NASTY PIECE OF WORK! AND PLEASE TELL HER IF SHE WANTS TO GO BACK TO HER FATHER IN PONTYPRIDD, SHE CAN BE MY GUEST!'

My mother looked out of the window. 'And you call yourself a *minister*.'

'Who wants to play I-Spy?' said Rachel anxiously. 'Mummy, Daddy, do you want to play?'

'Pray!' said Abigail.

'And *another* bloody thing,' said my father.

'Don't you dare swear at me!'

'If we're playing memory verses, here's one for you. *It is better to dwell in the wilderness than with a contentious and an angry woman*! Proverbs 21 verse 19!'

'I spy with my little eye, something beginning with—'

'1 Timothy 3 verse 5,' countered my mother.

My father looked at her, stumped.

'*For if a man know not how to rule his own house, how shall he take care of the church of God?*'

'Oh, fuck off,' said my father.

In the mirror, I saw my mother turn pale. 'What did you just say?'

'You heard me.'

For a moment she was silent. Then a low moan rose from her, and she began weeping. A few moments later Jonathan began wailing, followed by Abigail.

'Mummy, Daddy! Stop it! We're playing I-Spy!' shouted Rachel over the sounds of sobbing that filled the car. 'I-spy-with-my-little-eye-something-beginning-with—'

'You're a horrible man,' said my mother. 'A horrible, dirty, ugly man. How *dare* you call yourself a Christian! How *dare* you! I'm sorry I ever married you. I wish you'd just – just – go away and leave me alone. I'd rather be *dead* than hear my husband speak to me like that. You'd be happier then, wouldn't you? You'd probably all be happier! Admit it! You'd all be a lot happier if I just died!'

My father seemed to be gnawing at the inside of his cheek. Then, in a level voice, he said: 'Woman, if you died tonight, I'd *dance on your grave.*'

As we exited the Severn Bridge, leaving Wales behind, England's green, flat fields were quilted in late summer light. Rachel called out the letter *f*. I scanned the scenery outside the window: an overtaking lorry, an orange windsock bellyflopping in the breeze like a fish on land, a blue sign that read LONDON 121. I thought about the word *fireball*. I pictured the car crashing, a huge explosion, the whole surrounding scene burning up in white devouring flames until there was nothing left, except the ash of cars and bones on the road like fallen snow, everything calm and quiet like sleep.

When my mother, siblings and I entered Guernsey Baptist Chapel, a crowd of curious faces turned to watch. The church was dim and musty, the only decoration a wooden cross on the front wall next to the fanned brass pipes from which organ music droned. I followed my mother to the front pew, conscious of the congregation's gaze. I'd always enjoyed the special status of belonging to the minister's family, the sense of being the elect among the elect, as though we were somehow closer to God by virtue of my father's work. On one side of me was Rachel, who sat with her back straight and hands in her lap, and on the other was Jonathan, whose legs I entertained myself by kicking.

My father appeared and, as he made his way down the central aisle, the organ music stopped and everyone stood up. There was a solemn hush when he climbed the six steps to the pulpit. I had to resist the urge to wave, to remind everyone that he was *my* father, we had the very same surname, and when the other boys and girls went home later with their unspecial parents, I'd be going home with *him*. At the lectern, he began to pray.

'Heavenly father, we come to you in the mighty name of Jesus. May you bless this time as we worship you together. May you guide us, teach us, and heal us by your blood. Amen.'

I'd never quite been able to shake the feeling that I had two fathers. On weekdays there was the taciturn, sad-eyed figure who made me breakfast and helped get me ready for school; on Sundays he seemed a different personality altogether. In the pulpit he bristled with holy energy and his voice was made of rich and contrasting colours like stained glass. Watching him speak before a silent church filled me with awe, and I'd never succeeded in thinking about God without picturing my father in the pulpit, his brown beard, thinning hair, tulip-bulb nose, pouched eyes and long ears intricately whorled like seashells. Was it in order to test if that God-like man was really the same one who tied my shoelaces each morning that, at the age of three or four, I used to wait until the congregation was bowed in prayer before clambering up the steps and wrapping myself around his ankles? When, at home after the service, my furious mother would demand I be punished for invading the pulpit – *spare the rod and spoil the child* – my father's stricken look as he undid his belt would sting me more than his half-hearted blows while he bent me over his knee. It was always that look I pictured when I thought of God sending his son to be nailed to the cross. And in God's right hand was my father's belt, made from the same black leather as the cover of his Bible.

'Please be seated,' he said when the first hymn had finished. His face brightened. 'Now then, can all the children come to the front? Don't be shy!' Nobody moved, and he smiled patiently. Then one girl about my own age skipped down the aisle, followed by other children alone or in twos.

My father stepped down from the pulpit, balancing on the balls of his feet before his young audience. 'I knew you were hiding somewhere!' Addressing a boy with curtained blond hair, he said: 'Well then! What's your name?'

'Joshua,' said the boy.

'Well, that's a wonderful biblical name. And how old are you, Joshua?'

'I'm six,' he said proudly.

'Are you now? And tell me something, Joshua. Do you know the story of Abraham?'

He glanced behind him as if searching for the answer from a parent. 'I – I'm not sure.'

My father chuckled. 'That's quite all right. Can anyone else tell me who Abraham was?'

Jonathan, still sitting beside me in the pew, put his hand up.

'Well, I don't need to ask *your* name. What can you tell me about Abraham, young man?'

'He was very, very old!' said Jonathan, a little breathlessly. 'And his son was called Isaac.'

'That's right! Abraham was one hundred years old when Isaac was born.'

'My granny's nearly a hundred!' shouted a girl with brown plaits.

My father shook his head in amazement. 'Well, that's marvellous. That's really marvellous. Now then, listen quietly boys and girls, and let me tell you a story.

'One day, Abraham heard God speaking to him, telling him to go to a mountaintop the next morning and sacrifice his son, Isaac, as an offering to the Lord.

'Now, for many years, Abraham had prayed to God, pleading to be blessed with the birth of a son. When at last Isaac was born, Abraham was overjoyed. So when God commanded him to sacrifice Isaac, his heart was broken.

'The next day, Abraham, Isaac and their servants set out together. All day they walked, father and son, side by side. When at last Abraham saw the mountaintop in the distance, he told his servants to wait behind.'

Here my father paused, looking out over the church. Everyone's attention, child and adult, was fixed on him. When he began talking again, his eyes were moist and his voice was beginning to crack.

'So they approached the place where the sacrifice was to be made. Isaac, who had walked on ahead, turned and called out: *Father!*

'*Here I am, my son*, said Abraham.

'*We have the wood and the fire*, said Isaac, *but where is the lamb to be sacrificed?*

'Abraham could barely speak. His son was the most precious thing in the world to him. Fighting back tears, he said, *God himself will provide the lamb.*

'Then, praying for strength to do what needed to be done, Abraham pounced on Isaac.'

In my mind's eye I saw the man wrestling his terrified son to the ground. I imagined myself in Isaac's place, my father binding my hands and feet, obedient to some murderous voice I couldn't hear. I struggled, but he was too strong. I could barely breathe as I felt myself pressed against the stone, my arms and legs trussed up behind me, the blade cold at my neck, ready to open my flesh, to saw through my windpipe, to soak the hillside in my blood.

'And then the Lord spoke to Abraham, commanding him to spare his son. So he untied Isaac and they stood embracing each other on the mountaintop, weeping together for a very long time.

'In this way, Abraham showed his obedience to the Lord. And because he proved he was willing to sacrifice even the thing he loved most in the world, God promised his descendants would be known as the nation of Israel, and that through them all the world would be blessed.

'Then Abraham and Isaac found a ram, caught in a thicket nearby, and they sacrificed it joyfully together.

'And that, boys and girls, is how much God loves us. Because, just like Abraham, God was willing to give up his only son, sending him to die on the cross for us. All we have to do is give our lives to him, and our sins will be forgiven. Isn't that amazing?'

My father crouched lower, looking straight into the eyes of the kneeling and sitting children. 'Do you know something? You're never too young to ask God for his forgiveness. You're never too young.'

Almost whispering, his voice hoarse with emotion, he continued: 'Jesus is standing at the door and knocking, boys and girls. He promises that if you hear his voice and open the door, he will come in. Can you hear Jesus knocking on the door of your heart now? Will you turn away? Or will you open the door and let him in?'

He paused, closing his eyes, and the church was absolutely still. I strained my ears, almost expecting to hear a knocking in the distance. But all I heard was the hum of traffic and, further off, the sound of the ocean like a giant rasping lung.

The next day my parents took us to a beach on the island, a narrow curve of whitish sand enclosed by coral-studded scarp and fringed with wild grass. I wandered off to explore the rock pools, climbing over lichen-furred stones until I was high above the sea, which roiled and slapped below. Among broken shells and bone-white crisp packets I found a live starfish, its body pale and webbed, and experienced a sickening urge to stamp my spade through one of its scaly arms. From the crest of the rocks I looked over the crowded beach, feeling a twinge of worry when I realised I couldn't pick out my family among the sunbathers on serried mats, surfers in wetsuits, and children on their backs making sand-angels. I made my way carefully down the stones, over piles of beach scree, and hurried along the folded dunes. Weaving between bodies with their smell of cooking skin and sunscreen, I finally found my parents on their striped deckchairs. My mother wore a navy one-piece bathing suit and my father was in his khaki shorts and a button-down shirt. Abigail was helping Rachel bury Jonathan up to his neck.

'Where have you been?' said my mother, squinting into the sun.

She seemed more curious than annoyed, so I relaxed. 'I was exploring the rock pools. I found a starfish!'

'A starfish,' said my father without looking up from his book, which was called *Calvin's Geneva* and had a stern-faced man on the cover. 'Did you now?'

Jonathan craned his neck from where he was buried. 'Can starfishes live outside of water?'

'Of course they can't,' I said. 'Not for long anyway. And, by the way, dumbo, the word for more than one starfish is starfish, not starfishes.'

'You be careful you don't go anywhere I can't see you,' said my mother. 'Now, who'd like to go and have a dip in the sea?'

'I need a wee before I go,' I said.

'Just go in the sea, for crying out loud,' said my father from behind his book.

'You are *not* going in the sea,' said my mother, as if it had been my idea. 'If all the little boys and girls started weeing in the sea, then what would happen?'

'I'm not a little boy. I'm nine!'

'I don't care how old you are. Come on, I'll take you up to the changing rooms.'

My brother struggled to free his arms from the mound of sand. 'I want to come!'

'You can't,' said Rachel. 'You're being *buried alive*.'

'You three stay here with Daddy,' said my mother, wrapping a towel around her waist. 'We won't be long. Come on, Matthew. Off we go.'

After using the toilet inside the clapboard changing room, I found my mother waiting for me on the walkway. The tarmac was hot under my bare feet and in the air was the mingled smell of sea salt and frying fat. Holidaymakers were eating candyfloss on sticks and chips from cones with wooden forks. A light aircraft buzzed overhead. My mother was smiling shyly, and when I reached her she bent down and whispered, 'Shall we have some ice cream?' She winked at me. 'Don't tell your father.'

I queued with her for a van advertising 99 flakes and Gob-stoppers, excited that we had a secret to share.

This was, I understood, my mother's way of making friends with me after the scene in the car. All the way to the ferry terminal my parents had fought. After the crossing, as my father got lost driving through unlit narrow lanes, my parents had the same argument again but this time in reverse, each of them attempting to retrace their dispute to the original sin and thereby prove the other was to blame. *You disrespected me. But you swore. But you wouldn't stop. But why didn't you. But you never. But you always.* When we finally found the small pebble-dashed home where we'd be staying, my mother slammed the passenger door, stormed up the driveway and let herself into the house. The next day it had rained. My mother stayed upstairs and out of sight, but her wrath seeped through every room of the house like an odourless poison gas. There was no TV, just shelves of dog-eared Christian books and board games, so my siblings and I played Connect 4, Twister and Cluedo until we were seething with boredom. My father sat morosely in the conservatory all day, occasionally turning a page in his book while rain drummed on the plastic roof. When my mother re-appeared again on Sunday morning to get everyone ready for church, she wouldn't meet my eye, and I wanted to throw my arms around her and beg forgiveness for ruining her holiday.

Now, once my mother had her blue Screwball and I had a cone of ice cream topped with a flake, we sat down on a bench. The walkway was lined with open-fronted shops selling fish bait, striped rock in plastic wrappers, glinting sunglasses and pinwheels rotating lazily in the slight breeze. There was an arcade, but I knew better than to ask my mother to take me into its shaded grotto of sinful machines.

Next to it was a shop stuffed to the ceiling with exotic treasures that were undreamt-of in my family: surfboards, stunt kites, wetsuits, snorkels, and dinghies hanging from hooks. Even the colours – reds and pinks and neon greens – seemed thrillingly at odds with everything my mother stood for, like the song in the car with the electric-voiced singer.

I pointed over at the shop. 'Mummy! Can we go in there?' I tried to arrange my face into an expression of desperate longing while simultaneously licking my ice cream.

'Matthew, *no*.' She was holding her Screwball at an angle to stop it dripping onto her hand; her mouth was stained bright blue. 'Do you think we're made of money?'

'But *Mummy*. I just want a rubber ring to go in the sea!' Staring at a black and white ring hanging from the shop's metal awning, I felt immensely forlorn. To my surprise, genuine tears prickled my eyes. I pointed at a sign in the shop window. 'Look! It's two-for-the-price-of-one! Rachel can have one too and we can go in the sea together!'

At this, I saw a flicker of hesitation in her eyes. I knew my mother only really loved two things: Jesus and special offers. In a way Jesus was the ultimate special offer, because all you had to do was believe in him to go to heaven for all eternity.

My mother looked nervously into her purse. 'Come on, then. But I don't want any more playing up from you on this whole holiday, do you hear me? And mind you don't go out too far. You'll have to stay close to Rachel. Remember what happened when you went into the deep end in the swimming pool in Pontypridd, and the nice lifeguard had to jump in and pull you out? I was mortified, absolutely mortified. You'll have to stay where I can keep an eye on you. *Are you listening to me?*'

We carried the rings to my father, who blew through their nozzles to inflate one and then the other. Leaving Jonathan and Abigail with my parents, I followed Rachel down to the water's edge. The sun was very warm now and its reflection on the sea was dazzling. I closed my eyes, and when I opened them a few moments later the world was bleached of colour, everything white and grey. I planted my feet in the muddy sand, sparkling foam rushing over them before sucking backwards again.

'Come on, Chilli,' said Rachel, using my name from the game we sometimes played, in which our parents had died and we were orphans fending for ourselves. In the game, which I found equally terrifying and exciting, Rachel always took charge, knew right from wrong, kept me safe. She ran ahead now, trouncing through the swash, slowing down as the water reached her knees, and then flopped forward into her ring. I followed, wading past the breakers, pausing when the water reached my crotch and the cold tingled down my legs, and then strode further out until I had to stand on tiptoe to keep my head above the surface.

A wave came and I half-swam-half-jumped over it, enjoying the weightless feeling in my body as it passed by. *Don't go out too far,* my mother had said. But how far was too far? The grown-up world was full of lines I was forbidden to cross, but most of them were invisible until I'd already strayed over them and my mother was furious with me. 'Come on, slowcoach!' called Rachel, floating inside her ring fifteen feet ahead, so I clambered into mine and suddenly the ground beneath my feet disappeared and I was floating on a blue-green sheet of ocean.

'Let's swim to America!' I said once I'd paddled over to my sister.

'We can't reach America from here,' she said with authority. 'We're in a completely different sea. This is the *English Channel*. You can almost see France if you look hard enough.'

I peered at the horizon, but all I could make out was a violet ribbon where sea met sky. 'Do you think there are sharks out here?'

'No, silly. There aren't any sharks in the English Channel.'

'But what if one got lost?'

Rachel clutched her ring with her legs, windmilling her arms backwards. 'Look! I can do a backstroke!'

'How long do you think it will take us to reach France?'

'Oh, a day or two, probably. But nobody will understand us there. They don't speak English or even Welsh. Just French.'

'We'll have to learn French then.'

'Yes, I expect they'll put us in a special school with other orphans who wash up on beaches. Until we're ready to join a normal school.'

'How long do you think that will be?'

'Oh, four or five months. At least.'

Another wave lifted us up and down, and now three things happened in quick succession. First, I noticed my rubber ring had begun to deflate. Second, I turned and saw that we must have been carried out by the breeze or tide, because suddenly the beach was a long way away and the people on it were small as figurines. Third, I remembered I could hardly swim.

I looked over at Rachel, her dark wet hair plastered across her forehead. She noticed the state of my ring, which was already becoming soft and crumpled, and then gazed back at the distant beach. Around us in three directions was nothing but water. For a moment she seemed to be considering our predicament with her usual pragmatic expression, as though she was about to explain, in her slightly bossy tone, the obvious solution. It wasn't until Rachel started screaming for help that I began to panic.

I kicked and flapped towards my sister, but the sea kept heaving us further away from each other. Out here it was strangely quiet; even Rachel's screams were swallowed up by the ocean's slow complicated noise of collapsing and pouring. There was no foam on the waves, just sunlight striating the water.

I began to recite the first prayer that came into my mind: *Our father who art in heaven hallowed be thy name thy kingdom come thy will be done on earth as it is in heaven—*

A wave reared up. Instead of passing underneath, this time it crashed through me. For a moment I was blinded. I was under the surface and I didn't know if I still had hold of my ring. When the air hit me again the place behind my eyes was stinging with pain, and my lungs were grappling air and choking out saltwater at the same time.

—forgive us our trespasses forgive us our trespasses forgive us our trespasses forgive us our trespasses forgive us our—

Everything went dark again. My limbs were struggling, but they seemed to belong to someone else. I felt unbelievably tired. I had a vision of myself from the seafloor: a tiny pair of dangling legs a hundred feet above, and all around me a permanent midnight, an infinity of airtight darkness.

—deliver us from evil deliver us from evil deliver us from evil deliver us from evil deliver us deliver us deliver us—

And then, suddenly, I was being hauled upward into the bright glaring world. My father had me under one arm and was swimming over towards Rachel. I grabbed hold of my sister's ring. As soon as my father started sidecrawling back towards the beach, the ocean seemed to shrink back to a normal scale. Up ahead I could already see people hopping over wavelets. My sister was wide-eyed, and we were both too breathless to speak as we were tugged back to safety.

The water was only two feet deep when my father let us go. Resting on one knee, his face alarmingly red, he was breathing in spasm-like movements. 'Please – don't – ever – do – that – again,' he said between lungfuls of air. And then he got up, staggered towards the beach, and collapsed onto his back beyond the strandline.

A man in swimming trunks approached. 'Hullo there. Is everything all right?'

'We almost drowned!' said Rachel excitedly.

'Yes, I saw you were a long way out. I almost called a lifeguard.'

'I prayed for God to save us,' I said proudly.

'And then our Dad swam all the way out and rescued us!' added Rachel.

The man smiled warmly. 'Come on, up you get,' he said, helping me and then my sister to our feet. 'No harm done. Look, I think that's your mother coming for you now.'

I could see my mother running towards us with Abigail in her arms and Jonathan following closely behind. Even from this distance I could tell that her face was wild with fury. She stopped when she reached my father lying on the sand, and called out: 'Matthew, Rachel! Get away from that man!'

The man looked over at my mother and back at me, his smile hardening. He retreated a few steps. 'All right then. You two run on back now. You'll have to be more careful next time, that's all.'

I could already feel the force of my mother's anger like a solar wind. She'd told me not to go too far out, I hadn't listened, and I'd nearly died. Under my breath, I promised on my word-as-a-Christian never to disobey her again. Was I too old now to be bent over my father's knee? There was something oddly comforting about the thought of his old leather belt and his wide, warm lap.

Rachel and I waded out of the shallows. Ahead, I could see my father sitting up. Next to him stood my mother, gripping Jonathan by the elbow and Abigail by the hand. Once I'd made my way out of the backrushing water, my limbs began to feel strong again. I picked up pace, followed by Rachel, until we were both sprinting over the wet sand – back to our family, back to everything we'd ever loved, back to the safety of our father's disappointment and our mother's rage.

Revelations

I was interrupted by the sound of the front door opening. From my bedroom I could hear the bustle and commotion of several pairs of feet, bags being set down, coats being removed.

'Come in, come in!' sang my father from the foot of the stairs. 'Go on through, the lounge is just to your left. Oops, if you wouldn't mind popping your shoes off. Otherwise Angela will have our guts for garters!'

'*Phil!*' protested my mother, straining to sound cheerful.

'Cats for gutters?' said a male voice in an accent I didn't recognise. 'Please, what does this mean, Brother Phil?'

My mood spoiled now, I buttoned up my jeans, pulled the duvet to my chest and, pointing the CD player remote, turned up the volume. 'Fake Plastic Trees' climaxed with zooming chords and sailing falsetto. I slid the Marks & Spencer catalogue under the duvet just in time for my mother to burst into the room.

'Matthew,' she said. 'How many times have I asked you to *please, please, please* not play that noise on a Sunday?'

'And how many times,' I replied, 'have I asked you to *please, please, please* knock before letting yourself into my room?'

She grimaced. 'I'd like you to come downstairs and meet the Sad Family.'

'The Sad Family?'

'That's what I said.'

'What are they so sad about?'

'Don't try and be clever. They've come all the way from Israel to see us, so I'd appreciate it if you could be charming and friendly for at least once in your life. I want you to make the Sad Girls feel welcome.'

Before heading downstairs, she paused. 'Why you feel the need to get back into bed like that in the middle of the day I will never know.'

'Thanks for the observation. Is there anything else I can help you with today?'

She stood watching me. 'What have you got under there?'

'Where?'

She eyed the duvet. '*There.*'

'Oh, that. That's just the machine gun for the massacre I'm planning at school tomorrow.'

'*Matthew.* What are you hiding there?'

With an exaggerated sigh, I pulled out the Marks & Spencer catalogue. 'I was thinking of buying some new jeans, ok? Is that illegal now or something?' I dropped it onto the floor, and it fell open to a gallery of dark-haired women in multi-layered white underwear fastened with straps and ribbons. My mother and I stared at the catalogue together for a painfully elongated moment.

'I want you downstairs in five minutes,' she said firmly, closing the door.

The Sad Family were, it turned out, the Saa'd family of Haifa Baptist Church in Israel. Pastor Boulos Saa'd had a thin moustache and expansive gestures that made me think of a minor Sicilian mafia boss. He introduced his daughters with proprietorial arms around their shoulders, as though congratulating himself for his ingenuity in creating them.

'This,' said Pastor Boulos, squeezing the shoulder of a steely, unsmiling girl a year or two older than me, 'is Rhoda, my future doctor!' Pinching her lips, she looked down at the floor.

'And this,' he said, beaming at the other girl, 'is Rana, my future high court judge!'

She glanced over at me. She was about my own age, perhaps a little younger. Her eyes were strikingly large and as dark as inkdrops.

'*Khallas Baba*, you're embarrassing us,' said Rana, not looking remotely embarrassed. She scowled affectionately and kissed him on the cheek.

My father cleared his throat. 'Well then, this is Matthew, our eldest son,' he said. He turned to my brother. 'And this is Jonathan, our – well, our other son. I'm afraid our daughters won't be joining us until later. Anyway, I'm sure you're hungry. Shall we go on through?'

Laid out on the dining room table were seven bone china plates with the best silver cutlery. Around them crowded Pastor Boulos, Rhoda, Rana, my father, my brother and me. My mother busied herself in the kitchen, from which wafted the thick smell of lamb gravy.

'Pastor Boulos was just telling me about the awful treatment the Arab Christians face in Israel,' said my father to my brother and me.

'That's right, Brother Phil.' He shook his head lamentingly and sighed. 'The Israelis, they persecute us because we are not Jews.'

'Terrible,' said my mother as she entered the room holding a plate of layered lamb cuts between chequered oven gloves.

'And the Palestinians, they persecute us because we are not Muslim.'

'Hamas and all the rest of it,' said my father knowledgeably.

My heart pounded. *'Blessed are ye, when men shall revile you, and persecute you and say all manner of evil against you,'* I managed to say.

Everyone, including Rana, turned to look at me.

Pastor Boulos held my eye. *'Rejoice and be exceeding glad, for so persecuted they the prophets which were before you.* Brother Phil, I can see you are raising a family that loves God's Word in this house.'

My father stiffened proudly. 'Matthew's always had a wonderful memory for scripture.'

'Matthew. Gift of God. An excellent name for a young Christian,' said Pastor Boulos.

I could sense Rana smiling across the table at me. My cheeks reddened.

'Matthew's doing his GCSEs soon,' said my mother, lifting lids from several tureens of steaming vegetables. 'And Jonathan's doing his Grade Eight flute next week. He's already got his Grade Eight distinction in piano, haven't you Jonathan? Mint sauce, girls?'

'We are commanded to *make a joyful noise unto the Lord,*' said Pastor Boulos, serving himself a slice of lamb.

My father nodded. 'Oh, absolutely. Will you pass the cauliflower cheese, dear?'

'And you'll have to tell us all about life in the Holy Land,' said my mother. 'It must be so *inspiring* to see all the places the Bible talks about every day. The Sea of Galilee, the Mount of Olives, the Battle of Jericho, you know.'

'It is our privilege,' said Pastor Boulos, 'to walk in the footsteps of the Lord. But our true home is not on this earth, but in heaven.'

'Amen, brother,' said my father.

'Anyone for Shloer?' said my mother.

Dishes were passed around, glasses were filled, grace was recited. While Pastor Boulos talked – about his small church in Haifa and his daughters' outstanding school grades – I experienced two overlapping agonies. The first was caused by my desperate attempt to catch Rana's eye, the second by my desperate attempt to avoid catching her eye. So it was with relief that, as soon as I'd finished my dessert of apple crumble and custard, I volunteered to wash up and excused myself to the kitchen. I was piling bowls and pans into the sink when I heard the door open.

'Hey,' said a voice from behind me. 'Want some help?'

Rana came over and stood at the sink, rolling up her sleeves. Looking at me with amusement, she said, 'Are you shy or something?'

Suddenly I became intensely aware of all the muscles in my face and what they were doing.

'It's just not every day we get a visit from a future high court judge.' I'd meant for this to sound jauntily satirical, but instead it just sounded hostile. I picked up a tea towel and stared at it despondently. Embroidered around its edges were the words: *As for me and my house, we will serve the Lord.*

'Ignore my father,' she said. 'That's how he inflates my price so he can get more camels from my husband.'

'What are you talking about?'

'It's just a joke.' She placed some glasses into the dishwasher. 'Where I come from, men used to buy women with camels. The better the woman, the higher the price.'

'I see. And how many camels would you cost?'

Rana shut the dishwasher door. She folded her arms, blew some hair out of her face and looked straight at me. 'A whole *flock* of camels.'

'Herd.'

'Excuse me?'

'I'm pretty sure camels come in herds, not flocks.'

She arched an eyebrow. 'Ok, thanks for the English lesson, mister.'

'Sorry. Your English is actually amazing, for a second language.'

'Third. Arabic, Hebrew, English.'

'Right. Ok, that's pretty impressive.'

'How many languages do you speak, anyways?'

'Just English. And Welsh, too, kind of. I used to speak it at school, but we moved to England when I was eleven. Here,' I said, throwing her the tea towel. 'You can help dry.'

I watched Rana as she concentrated on her task. Her clothes were scrupulously modest – high-waisted blue jeans, round-neck top, long sleeves – but they hugged her figure, and one of her black bra straps was visible where her top had slipped down her shoulder.

'So how about you?' she said. 'What are you going to be when you're older?'

'A man of God.' There was a brief silence, and I was immediately embarrassed by my sincerity. The dishwasher flushed and churned.

'Like your father?'

'Yeah. But – no, not exactly.' I thought of my father in his pulpit before a spellbound congregation. Then I pictured him at home, fretting over church politics and mortgage payments, exhausted by another argument with my mother. I tried to imagine my future, and the picture that came to me was of a long avenue of sycamore trees stretching away to the horizon with two figures walking between them, holding hands.

'Yoo-hoo,' said my mother, entering the room. 'How are you two getting along in here?'

I plunged a baking tray into the sink's murky water and began scrubbing it furiously. I felt like a ham actor overplaying the part of someone washing dishes.

My mother lingered in the doorway. 'Matthew, your father and I were wondering how you'd feel about taking a little trip with the Sad Family tomorrow. We could take the train down to London, show them Big Ben, the Houses of Parliament, that sort of thing. Would you like to come along?'

I looked over at Rana. 'Sure,' I shrugged. 'Might as well, I suppose.'

The girl with the inkdrop eyes seemed, that day, to promise a solution to a problem that had haunted me since I returned to school after the summer I turned twelve.

One morning earlier that year my mother and father had called a family meeting and made an announcement. God had spoken to them, they said, commanding them to leave Swansea and continue the work of spreading his gospel at a new church in England. Any sadness I may have felt at leaving behind the whole world of my childhood – the school with the white railings overlooking Mumbles Lighthouse, the church football team I'd helped turn into a powerhouse of the West Glamorgan five-a-side league – was tempered by the moving thought that, of all the families in the world, God had selected ours for this special mission. I pictured England as Egypt from the Book of Exodus, and my father as Moses, sent to lead the captives into the Promised Land.

A few weeks later a removals van pulled up outside 49 Sketty Avenue, our cramped terraced house on an arterial road into Swansea city centre, and packed up all our earthly possessions. When they were unloaded five hours later, it was not in a land of pharaohs and locusts but at 12 Carron Close, a semi-detached house in a neat cul-de-sac on the outskirts of a small market town an hour north of London.

The problem initially presented itself, on my very first day at my new school in Leighton Buzzard, in the shape of Emma Bosworth. In Wales, the fact of girls' existence had seemed as inconsequential as the sight of Swansea Bay, whose long curve was visible from my bedroom window. My sisters bored me, and the girls at school were an alien tribe with foreign customs. As long as they didn't stray onto the section of tarmac where we boys played football during lunch break, they aroused in me neither positive nor negative feelings. But when I glimpsed Emma's face across the bleach-scented classroom that September morning, I experienced an obscure longing. She had honey-blonde hair, skin white as candlewax, and blue eyes that for some reason made me think of distant galaxies. I'd never found a girl's face *interesting* before. For weeks I watched her, noting her adaptations of the school's uniform code – flared trousers one day, pleated skirt and knee socks the next – and wondered what she spoke about with her friends as they huddled around graffiti-scarred tables before registration.

One day Emma came over during morning break and said she wanted to speak in private. It was the first indication she knew who I was, and I stammered slightly as I agreed to follow her to a quiet corner of the schoolyard. We leaned together against the tennis courts' chain-link fence while she asked if I wanted to go out with Judith Fleming, a bow-legged, freckled girl I'd seen her talking to in class. I didn't know what to say, so I said yes. For three days I cringed with mortification whenever I sensed Judith glancing over at me. On the fourth day, Emma came over to tell me Judith had decided to break up with me. I nodded, she turned on her heels, and my first relationship with a girl was over.

All through Year 8, I kept my problem to myself. Although the other boys seemed to take more notice of the girls at school too, their attention was manifested in the form of sneering derision. I guarded my devotion to Emma like a holy flame, and dreamed up elaborate fantasies in which I'd rescue her from the persecution of my cruel-hearted schoolmates.

By Year 9, my problem no longer found sole expression in the bodily form of Emma Bosworth. It seemed to have spread alarmingly, encompassing most of the girls of Cedars Upper School. The feeling I had when I watched them removing their coats in the morning or hurrying to the toilets in their twos and threes – an untameable craving, but for what? – made me soul-sick and faintly mad. And I'd begun to notice it wasn't just me who felt this way. Whenever in Tuesday Period 2: Maths, Stacey Reid sashayed to the teacher's desk, leaning over it to ask a question, a mania would grip half the class that took the rest of the lesson to subside. When one wintry day in the changing room before P.E. Bruce Howley announced, his grin mixing awe and contempt, that Hannah Pantling had *gone all the way* with a boy from Year 11, the outpouring of hilarity among us masked a palpable mood of relief. At least now there were words to describe what was happening inside us.

By the following year we boys seemed capable of talking about only one thing. In whispered discussions between lessons and full-throated debates before and after school, the girls of Year 10 were assessed, graded and ranked. We carried out this task with an attention to detail previously reserved only for the collection of Merlin football stickers. The girls were sorted into the categories of Touchable and Untouchable. The former contained several subdivisions that defined precisely *how far* it was worth going with a given girl. The system was constantly refined, and was flexible enough to allow girls to move up and down with the vicissitudes of Year 10 popularity politics and the changes effected by puberty. Although limited personal taste was tolerated, for a boy to admit to fancying – let alone having actually got off with – one of the Untouchable girls signalled social death.

None of this new vocabulary had existed in the Welsh I'd spoken as a child, and it took some time for me to abandon the idea that sex and desire were exclusively English phenomena that stopped at the Severn Bridge toll booth. A second superstition was even harder to shake off: that, since I now spoke the same language with my parents and school friends, my mother was somehow able to overhear me saying what I'd like to do with the girls whose uniforms were growing smaller and tighter by the week.

And every day, when I raced home and locked myself in the bathroom to spend hour after hour mentally kissing and caressing the necks, arms, breasts and thighs of the Year 10 girls, I almost thought I could hear my mother's voice over the sound of the bath I was running as an alibi, begging me in its ringing Welsh accent to please, please, *please* leave those poor girls alone!

It was during one of those evenings that the problem took on a disconcerting new form. A process of trial-and-error had taught me that by moving my right hand with a certain rhythm and summoning certain images I could bring my pleasure to a point of almost painful elevation. I'd spent weeks visiting that precipice, each time with a different girl from Year 10. The images running through my mind grew more and more reckless. With horrified excitement I watched myself break into the school changing rooms while the girls were showering after hockey, finding Stacey Reid's white cotton knickers and burying my face in them, inhaling their sour, delicious odour. At this moment two things happened: my father began knocking on the door, shouting 'Matthew, there's a queue out here!' and my pleasure seemed to explode.

Once I could gather my thoughts, I stared in horror at the white, sticky substance congealing in my lap. For a few dazed moments I wondered if I'd injured myself. Only when I thought of a word I'd heard boys use at school – usually with a leer or a giggle – did I realise I hadn't invented the procedure that had just led to this astonishing result.

At school the next day, when I took my usual place next to Stacey for Period 2: Maths, last night's images came flooding back. Was there something sardonic in the way she looked at me, as though she knew exactly what I'd been doing yesterday evening? For an hour I sat while the teacher spoke about right angles and congruent triangles, and every time Stacey shifted in her seat, crossing one leg over another or leaning on an elbow to scribble on her graph paper, I convulsed silently with humiliation. I burned to be alone, feeling sure my shame was written on my face. When the bell finally sounded, I bolted from the classroom, ran down the corridor to the Year 10 common room, made my way into the bathroom and locked myself in a cubicle.

But since I was here, and there were fifteen minutes until the end of break . . . I unzipped my trousers and closed my eyes, trying to ignore the sound of people coming in and out, the taps running, the hum of the hand dryer. I imagined Stacey Reid astride me, her skirt riding up around her stomach, a gap-toothed smile spreading over her face. I flushed the toilet to drown out my gasps, and then I stood at the last moment to aim into the bowl.

Every evening that week I explored my diabolical new powers as steam clouded the bathroom window and the sky darkened outside. Once I'd worked my way through my favourite Year 10 girls – Stacey Reid with her dimples and gapped teeth, Hannah Pantling with her long lashes and ringlets, pouting Lucie Page, knock-kneed Nicki Rowe, tousle-haired Kate Hudgell, cherry-lipped Laura Povie – I decided to move on to the church youth group. I couldn't believe what I was doing any more than I could stop myself doing it. I imagined myself in the pew behind Livvy Hale-wood, her red curls falling down her back, her hips swaying to the worship music in black jeans. She looked over her shoulder at me, tossing her hair and biting her lip. Then she walked brazenly past the pulpit to the exit and turned, summoning me with her index finger and a look that could only mean one thing . . .

That Sunday I was late for church. I'd been up until almost dawn the night before, visualising myself locked in the supply cupboard at school with Mademoiselle Dubois, the twenty-five-year-old French teacher I now saw in an entirely new light. In the morning, my siblings had waited in the car while my mother thumped the door and shrieked *get out here, this instant!* I'd pleaded diarrhoea while flicking through a mental catalogue of my friends' mothers; Bruce Howley's, I now saw, wasn't at all bad. When at last I arrived at church with blood-shot eyes and a cramp in my wrist, my father was already reading the text for his sermon from the Gospel of Matthew:

> *And if thy right hand offend thee, cut if off, and cast it from thee: for it is profitable for thee that one of thy members should perish, and not that thy whole body should be cast into hell.*

My father stopped speaking and paused theatrically, three hundred faces turned towards him. Usually I enjoyed the sense of anticipation in the moments before my father began preaching, but today I felt a shrivelling dread in my stomach. My father explained that every day we were faced with a choice: between the narrow path of righteousness and the broad road of evil and destruction. Those who languished in sin, refusing to repent, were bound for eternal punishment in hell. Sexual immorality wasn't only a question of deed but of thought: Jesus said that anyone who looks at a woman with lust in his heart has, in God's eyes, already committed the imagined sin.

Did my father glance over at me when he spoke those words? Was it possible my mother had inspected my underwear while doing the weekend laundry, discovering my secret and tipping my father off as he prepared his sermon?

'*Mortify therefore your members which are upon the earth*,' said my father, quoting the Apostle Paul: '*fornication, uncleanness, inordinate affection, evil concupiscence, and covetousness, which is idolatry: For which things' sake the wrath of God cometh on the children of disobedience.*'

When my father finished speaking, my heart was thumping in my chest. He closed his eyes to pray, and it occurred to me that it wasn't my mother who'd told him what I'd been doing: it was *God*. I felt like Eve in the Garden after she'd eaten the fruit, her naked body exposed before the Lord. The congregation rose to its feet and began singing:

> *How sad our state by nature is!*
> *Our sin, how deep it stains!*
> *And Satan binds our captive minds*
> *Fast in his slavish chains*
> *But hark! A voice of sovereign grace*
> *Sounds from the sacred Word*
> *O, you despairing sinners come*
> *And trust upon the Lord*

I leaned over to my mother, told her I felt unwell, and asked to borrow her car keys. Her green Fiesta was in the little church car park next door. I sat in the passenger seat, the sound of singing from inside the hall mingling with the noise of Sunday morning traffic. *If thy right hand offend thee, cut it off . . .* For the first time in my life, the story of salvation struck me not as abstract truth but existential reality: sin entering the world through Adam and Eve, depravity passed down the human bloodline like a virus, God's wrath and love finding expression in Christ, who died in our place to save us from hell. I would plead for forgiveness, and then I'd be free. Never again would I allow my right hand to lead me into sin. I pulled down the sun visor and was suitably impressed by the look of chastened resolution on my face.

But since I'd resolved to stop, what could be the harm in one last transgression – provided I repented immediately after? The dashboard clock read 11.50: I had ten minutes until the service ended and people would begin streaming out to their cars. I undid my belt and reached inside my jeans. Instantly my anxiety was soothed, and I allowed my mind to drift – away from church with its air of divine judgement, away from my family, away from Leighton Buzzard altogether. I imagined myself lying on a bed in a tropical beach hut. To my surprise it was Emma Bosworth who came in, wearing a silk chemise over a bikini. Emma had receded from my consciousness over the last two years, but now I felt my old passion for her flare up again. Wordlessly holding my gaze, she undid one button of her shirt, then another, then another –

When I'd finished and opened my eyes, the car's dashboard clock read 12.18. Somehow I'd been lost in my vision for half an hour. Panicking, I mopped up what I could of the glutinous liquid splattered all over my lap and the gear stick, zipped up my jeans and looked around. I promised the Lord this would be the Very Last Time. My resolve was only strengthened when, with a horror that seeped into my marrow, I saw almost every other parking space around me empty. A number of families must have left church and, before driving off, seen the minister's son in the passenger seat of the minister's wife's car, eyes closed, head back, trousers open, fist flying.

*

After that it was always the Very Last Time. Sometimes I'd last a day, sometimes two. Once, in a particularly intense bout of religiosity sustained by morning Bible readings and evening prayer marathons, I lasted all the way from Sunday to the following Saturday. But each time, like a dog returning to its vomit, I found my way back to the four fingers and thumb of my hated right hand. No matter how hard I prayed, no matter how earnestly I pleaded with God for strength and forgiveness, the temptation was always there, at the end of my own arm and in the centre of my own crotch.

The problem only got worse when my father arranged for the computer in the study next to the kitchen to be connected, via a bulky modem, to the World Wide Web. By day my access to this gleaming new reality was restricted to keep the telephone line free, but after dark, with my parents and siblings in bed, I'd turn on the computer, click on the icon that set the router whirring, and after waiting an agonisingly long time for a dial-up connection, spend hours Asking Jeeves to serve up a smorgasbord of female bodies. I became an aficionado of bikini calendars and lingerie shoots. I was extremely interested in the Spice Girls. I yearned to be slayed by Buffy and tied up in knots by Ally McBeal's crack legal team. I was a spider, hunting the Web for female flesh to devour.

And, once I was done, I scoured biblegateway.com for passages that led me back to the foot of the cross, gnashing my teeth in repentance, pleading with the Holy Spirit to break the chains of evil desire and set me free.

Even when I wasn't wallowing in sin, all I could think about was the effort it cost to forswear it. In 1 Corinthians Paul promised God would never tempt us beyond endurance, but lust had a way of overcoming me like a bout of insanity. One moment my thoughts would be on the gospel, the next I'd be sprinting for the bathroom, slamming the door and applying myself wretchedly to the task at hand. Temptation, sin, despair, repentance: I cycled through the stages with ever-increasing speed. Each morning I woke up dreading the futile struggle the day would bring. Resisting temptation was so unbearable that often I simply gave in to get it over with. Sometimes I suspected myself of secretly craving the euphoria I knew would arrive after a bout of self-abasement and sorrowful prayer. I even wondered if my efforts to resist temptation were causing me to succumb more often by keeping the sin in the centre of my mind.

Of course, there was no way I could talk to either of my parents about what I was doing. But did they know? I couldn't be sure, but whenever I looked at them, I thought I saw my guilt in their eyes. Shame was the element in which I moved, the air I breathed. Just as Abel's blood cried out from the ground against his brother's crimes, so my encrusted boxer shorts cried out from the laundry basket, condemning me before God in heaven.

Even though my parents never showed they were aware of the abominations occurring daily under their own roof, I couldn't escape the feeling that my sin was weighing heavily on the whole family. Was this why the atmosphere at home was so thick with misery? My mother seemed to grow increasingly exasperated, ploughing her nervous energy into schemes to extract value from the Tesco Clubcard reward system. On Saturdays she went out under the alias QWERTY123 to meet other members of her online Clubcard forum, scouring Leighton Buzzard's 24-hour Tesco car park for receipts with unclaimed points to redeem instore. One day I came home from school to find the hallway stacked with plywood crates containing hundreds of bananas. My mother explained, with a wild look in her eyes, that bananas were currently worth more in Tesco points than they cost to buy, and that at this rate she'd soon be able to use her Clubcard to invest in a timeshare arrangement on a holiday chalet in Mallorca, God willing.

My father, meanwhile, had become increasingly with-
drawn, spending all his time in the study he'd built for himself
in the garage. One evening, when he was out visiting church
members, I let myself into the room, searching for some reading material to help me make it through the day without
backsliding. I sat in his office chair with its leather armrests,
inspecting the books lining the walls from floor to ceiling.
There were rows of calfskin-bound commentaries on the Old
and New Testaments; histories of the Baptists, Methodists,
Presbyterians and Pentecostalists; Calvin's *Institutes* and
Luther's *Table Talk*; sermons by Wesley, Edwards and Spur-
geon; *The Pilgrim's Progress* and Foxe's *Book of Martyrs*;
and a whole shelf of Bibles: the King James Version, the New
King James Version, the Good News Translation, Wycliffe's
Bible, the New International Version, the New Revised Stand-
ard Version. I opened one drawer of his knotted oak desk and
found, beneath a sheaf of sermon notes, a golden packet of
Benson & Hedges cigarettes, an air freshener spray, four
tubes of mints and a pile of half-empty packets of codeine
pills. I pocketed the cigarettes, took down a volume of George
Whitefield's journals from a shelf, and quickly let myself out.

Was the deadlock and resentment between my parents
new, or was I only now becoming conscious of it? I tried to
remember if I'd ever seen them kissing or holding hands, but
the idea was somehow embarrassing, indecent. Still, hadn't
the parental screaming matches of my childhood been punctuated by moments of warmth and tenderness? Didn't we
used to sit together as a family on Saturday evenings in Swansea, my parents on the sofa, my siblings and me on the floor
by their feet, eating Chinese takeaway and watching *Casualty*, *Gladiators* and *The National Lottery*? My mother
would relax her usual disapproval of secular entertainment
for this weekly occasion, finding a way of inserting a Christian moral into the evening. She insisted that everyone choose

six numbers before the balls were sucked from the swirling jar. When it turned out none of us had won the imaginary lottery, she'd declare triumphantly, 'Well, that's another pound saved!' Now, not only had my parents all but stopped speaking to each other except over fractious Sunday lunches, they hardly ever seemed to speak to my siblings or me. Could it be that the anguish in my own mind had leaked out and turned the air toxic? Sometimes, when my father arrived home from his pastoral visits only to head straight to his study to be alone with his books and cigarettes and painkillers, I longed to run to him and, like Jonah, beg to be thrown overboard so the storm would be stopped and the sea stilled.

On Sundays my father would emerge from his seclusion to mount the pulpit at church and preach sermons condemning the wickedness of the earth, pleading with his listeners to accept Jesus before judgement rained down from heaven like a purifying fire. His sermons grew darker and more withering. One Sunday he expounded on the hypocrisies of what he called the 'Sunday Christian' who spent all week piling sin on sin, before coming to church to enjoy an hour or two of spiritual entertainment, serving God with his lips but not his heart. It wasn't the unbeliever on whom the Last Judgement would fall most severely, said my father, but on the Sunday Christian who'd had every opportunity to repent but preferred to harden his heart against God.

Seeing myself all too clearly in these words, I left church that morning in despair. I'd repented so many times, I'd sworn over and over again that *this time* would be different, *this time* I'd change. But had I repented in my innermost heart? Was there some kernel of wickedness in me that stubbornly refused Jesus, defying him by desecrating the holy temple of my body? I'd tried to achieve total hatred for that foul, hidden part of me. But no matter how strenuously I directed my loathing inward, my soul remained a rank sewer.

Walking back home from church through the near-empty Sunday streets with their shuttered shops, I saw the week ahead unfolding with hopeless inevitability, and I pictured myself as the obscene and miserable figure I must be in God's eyes. I was exhausted. If every new bout of repentance led inexorably to the same result, what was the point in wasting so much energy resisting temptation? Why not accept damnation and, like the Prodigal Son, lie down in the swineyard of my own evil nature?

The next day – when, overcome by lust on the way to school, I'd slipped into a neighbour's unlocked garden and sprayed its flower bed with the seed of my loins – I alighted on a new solution. Inspired by my recent reading of Whitefield's account of the Great Awakening of 1763, it dawned on me that there was only one sure way to save my soul: to go out into the wilderness of Leighton Buzzard and save others.

An opportunity arose in Thursday Period 5: Biology. In a lesson on the circulatory system, the teacher grouped the class into pairs and asked us to take our partner's pulse. I found myself staring into Emma Bosworth's electric blue eyes while she placed two fingers on my outstretched wrist. I prayed God would put his words on my tongue just as he spoke through my father on Sundays, and help me to urge Emma into the arms of the Lord. But all I experienced was a dry mouth.

'Are you ok?' she said. 'Your pulse is, like, really fast.'

I could feel my new Adam's apple bobbing in my throat. 'You're probably counting wrong.'

'No, it's really racing. Are you sure you're not ill?'

As I walked home from school that balmy April afternoon, the drone of lawnmowers and leaf-blowers was in the air. At precisely the moment I was praying God would put a sinner in my path, I saw Emma walking ahead of me. She'd taken off her navy school jumper and tied it round her narrow waist, and her hair cascaded over her rucksack. Emma seemed oblivious to the fact that wearing a rucksack over two shoulders was considered seriously uncool. She also wore sheer tights rather than the usual black, which made her legs the colour of pear flesh. These minor but telling breaches of social etiquette determined that Emma, though undeniably beautiful, ranked only in the lower reaches of the Year 10 Touchable girls.

Absorbed in the music on her Discman, Emma walked under the bough of an elm tree, shadows rippling across her shoulders and down her pear-flesh legs. Suddenly I felt extremely concerned about her eternal destiny. The first time I asked what she was listening to, she didn't hear me. So I overtook her, cutting her off, and repeated my question.

'Oh, hi,' she said, removing her headphones. She was chewing gum and blinking at me. 'Pulp. *Different Class*. Are you feeling any better, by the way?'

For the rest of our walk home, we chatted about music. Emma contended that, although Blur were clearly superior to Oasis, they couldn't ultimately be considered a Great Band because they were too derivative. 'I mean, look at the Kinks. You've basically got the whole sound of Britpop right there. Know what I mean?'

I agreed, making a mental note to look up the Kinks and the word *derivative* when I got home.

We reached the lamp post on the little green midway between our houses. Before we went our separate ways, Emma tucked a lock of hair behind her ear and promised to lend me the new Longpigs CD, which I *absolutely had to listen to*. I'd become so caught up in our conversation that it wasn't until she turned the corner to her street that I realised I'd completely forgotten to explain God's plan of salvation to her.

Never mind, I told myself. This was groundwork. It was important to gain unbelievers' trust before attempting to win them for Christ. After all, didn't Jesus meet sinners in the midst of their ordinary lives – drawing water from a well, emptying their fishing nets by the shore – in order to spread his Father's Word? Borrowing Emma's Longpigs album would be the perfect pretext to begin the work of winning her soul.

Every time I saw Emma after that day, I'd set out with the gravest of evangelistic intentions. But no sooner would I look into her eyes than I'd be overtaken by a strange amnesia. In her company, the meaning of words like 'repentance' and 'sin' had a way of becoming cloudy. I reassured myself that I was simply forging a strong bond with her, the better to make my move and invite her to church when the time was right. Even after our walks home from school had become an established routine, even after I'd actually kissed her in a fog of cheap cologne at a house party, even after she'd agreed to be my girlfriend and I'd begun spending weekday evenings at her house, in some corner of my mind I held fast to the idea that my efforts were for a higher purpose.

And even the morning Emma and I met to bunk off school – equipped with the cigarettes from my father's desk and a bottle of vodka she'd stolen from her parents – I reminded myself that Jesus himself had turned water into wine at the wedding in Cana.

We sat down on a narrow strip of grass next to where Linslade Canal skirted the school's perimeter fence. Emma unscrewed the bottle with a cigarette in her mouth, and with a squall of anxiety I thought of my parents, the school, God. That was why it was crucial to remember why I was really here. Without knowing quite where I was going, I began telling Emma about Jesus's first miracle.

'So yeah, that one's not exactly my mum's favourite Bible story,' I concluded. I took a swig from the bottle, the liquid scorching down my gullet, before handing it back to her. 'She'd never admit it, but deep down she'd prefer Jesus to have shown up at weddings and turned all the *wine* into *water*.'

In the distance, an iron bell sounded for morning registration. Emma tipped her head back and drank. She shuddered, her eyes watering. She took a few deep breaths before speaking. 'So how does she explain it? Your mum, I mean.'

'Simple. She reckons he must've turned it into *nonalcoholic wine*.'

Even one of my favourite sounds – Emma's laughter – couldn't quite mute my disquiet. Was I just poking fun at my mother, or was I blaspheming God's Word? Around Emma I found myself saying things I'd never normally say, doing things I'd never normally do. But at the same time she made me feel more purely myself than I ever had before.

'And what does your dad think of your mum's theory?' she said.

'He doesn't have much time for it, put it that way. He points out the wedding guests said it was the best wine they'd had all night. Which suggests—'

'Which suggests Jesus was getting them good and pissed.'

I winced at hearing the Lord's name alongside even a mild swear word. Still, I said, 'Basically, yeah.'

So Jesus *had* turned water into wine – the real, alcoholic stuff. The notion that Emma and I were doing anything wrong here was downright *unscriptural*.

But had Jesus found himself, several hours later, emerging from a blackout with his feet in Linslade Canal, his girlfriend unconscious on the nearby grass and his headteacher looming above him, issuing a three-day suspension from school?

It wasn't until an afternoon a month later when my whole family was out, and I was struggling with a condom under a gaze palpably turning from impatience to boredom, that I finally accepted the truth: whatever it was that I was doing with Emma, it was not the Lord's work.

So when the preacher's daughter with the inkdrop eyes and olive skin showed up and I saw my future stretch out with her into a spiritual mist, I felt at last that here was the answer to the problem that had tormented me for so long. She was just as lovely as Emma, but her beauty had nothing to do with the world of shame I'd created for myself in Leighton Buzzard. Everything here I'd polluted with sin. With Rana, I could start again. She'd transform my carnal passion into godliness and purity, and she'd walk with me in paths of righteousness. Of course I wouldn't lay a finger on her until marriage – I wouldn't even look at her with lust in my heart until that day. How could I? She was my sister in Christ. All I had to do now was persuade her that she felt the same way.

Things progressed quickly. On Monday, as we toured London on an open-top bus, Rana and I sat together and talked all day while our parents sat dutifully listening to the audio guide through their headsets. The city's murals and monuments seemed absurd, irrelevant compared with the grandeur of what was happening between us.

On Tuesday, during a trip to Oxford, my father gave a solemn speech at the Martyrs' Memorial, where Latimer, Ridley and Cranmer heroically preferred to be burned alive than swear loyalty to Rome. Two apparently homeless men listened while sipping from brown tins of lager in the midday sun, and I threaded my fingers through Rana's, careful not to be seen by our parents. Later, on the upper deck of the park-and-ride out of the city, we confessed what we both suspected: that God had brought us together so we could share our lives, doing his bidding. We laughed about how shy I'd been when we first met, amazed it was just two days ago. The fact that we knew so little about each other only enhanced our exhilaration: there'd be so much to find out over so many years.

On Wednesday Rana was busy with her family, so I went along to the midweek meeting at church. An elder led prayers against the imminent removal of a ban on promoting homosexuality in schools, warning a tide of sin was in danger of sweeping the nation. Although I tried, I couldn't make myself feel much indignation over the issue. I closed my eyes, intending to submit a pro forma petition to the Lord, but when I did my thoughts were filled not with Section 28 but with Rana.

On Thursday, Rana and I spent the whole evening debating the doctrine of predestination, which she firmly opposed. This led to a dark night of the soul as I wrestled with the question of whether I could in good conscience marry a woman who held to the Arminian heresy. But by Friday morning I concluded that, if Jesus was willing to die for us despite our wickedness, then I could overlook this imperfection in one of his fallen creatures, while praying for her enlightenment in due course. That evening I took down my posters of ungodly musicians and placed them neatly in the bin downstairs, along with the other idolatrous things I owned: all my CDs except *Spring Harvest: Songs of Worship 1992*; my father's packet of cigarettes, with four left over from the day with Emma by the canal; and my collection of second-hand paperbacks by Huxley, Orwell, Kafka, Heller, Kerouac, Salinger and Plath.

On Saturday evening I stood in my best cream chinos and blue Kangol shirt, offering up a prayer of thanksgiving as I waited for Rana to ring the doorbell. Over the six days since she'd arrived in my life, I'd been shocked by the inexhaustibility of my happiness. Each time I found myself slipping back into my usual guilty despondency, all I had to do was think about Rana and the gloom would be banished. Peering into my bedroom mirror, I massaged Brylcreem into my hair until it had the dark gloss of fresh diesel. I popped one zit in the crevice between my left nostril and the bridge of my nose, and another above my right eyebrow, leaving a satisfying pulpy smear on the mirror. On the wall over my shoulder there were unfaded rectangles where my posters of Radiohead, Green Day and the Smashing Pumpkins used to hang. All that was over now. *Old things are passed away; behold, all things are become new.*

There was just one more task to complete before Rana and Rhoda came round for the evening: to call Emma and inform her our relationship was over. The fact that I had a girlfriend had barely registered in my mind all week. Emma was evidently nothing more than one of the temptations Satan had used to keep me apart from God. The Lord had so clearly put Rana in my path, it would have been sinful to defy him by letting Emma stand in our way. I dialled her number, hoping I wouldn't have to make small talk with her mother before getting her on the line.

'Hello?' she said.

'Hi, it's me.'

'Oh, hey. Where have you been all week? I tried calling but you were out.'

'Yeah, it's just, we've had this family visiting from Israel. You know, church stuff. I had to do my bit, show them around, that sort of thing.'

'Sounds boring.'

'Yeah, right.'

There was a pause.

'So what's up?' I could hear Emma chewing gum. 'You sound, I don't know, strange or something.'

Another pause.

'Look, I'm calling because I have to tell you something.'

'Ok. So tell me.'

I noticed I was drumming my fingers nervously. *If thy right hand offend thee, cut it off.*

'Matt, you're being weird. Stop being weird.'

'Sorry. It's just—'

'Christ, spit it out. The best years of my life are slipping away here.'

'I – I'm calling to invite you to my baptism tomorrow.'

'Oh, ok. You're getting baptised?' said Emma, as if I'd just told her I was thinking of buying some new trainers.

'Yeah. It's sort of to show your commitment to – well, to God, basically. There was going to be a baptism service anyway so I sort of asked Dad if they could add me to the list.'

'Cool. So you're getting all religious again? I love it when you get religious. You become so much fun.'

'It's nice you're taking this seriously,' I said, irritated. 'I really appreciate the support.'

'Hey, calm down. I was just kidding. I'd love to come to your pool party. When is it?'

The doorbell rang, so I told Emma what time to be at church in the morning and rushed downstairs.

Allowing Rana to come over for the evening without adult supervision marked a tacit but definite shift in policy on my mother and father's part. Once they'd become aware of my relationship with Emma after a call from school the day we bunked off, they'd acted swiftly and – in a show of unity with Emma's parents – banned any further contact between us. This only provoked our defiance, so every other day she'd been climbing in through my bedroom window as night fell and out again in the early hours. As a result, letting Rana in through the front door felt strangely illicit. Rhoda came too, but the older sister seemed uninterested in playing chaperone, and she barely seemed to notice when we left her watching TV in the living room and went upstairs.

Now I sat on the edge of my bed while Rana leaned back against my desk. The room was tiny; our knees were almost touching. When she leaned back, her top rode up, revealing two fingers' width of taut midriff.

'So,' she said. 'What are we going to talk about?'

With Rana standing squarely in front of me, looking anywhere other than her body was virtually impossible, so I was forced to crane my neck upwards. I realised that, although I'd spent all day longing for us to be alone, I had no idea what to do now we were. In a slight panic, I began summarising everything I'd learned about the Israeli–Palestinian conflict from two hours browsing *Encarta* the previous evening.

'I guess what I'm trying to say is that there's never going to be peace until both sides, you know, recognise that the other one even exists. As such.'

'You're boring,' said Rana, putting one leg between mine and knocking her thigh against my knee. 'And I don't need a lecture from you about my homeland, thanks.'

'Fine,' I said, ignoring the electricity jolting through me when her leg touched mine. 'What do you want to talk about then?'

Rana put her hands on my knees now, leaning into my face. 'Who said we have to talk?'

'Rana,' I said, closing my eyes. *The spirit indeed is willing,* I thought, *but the flesh is weak.*

'Mmm. Yes.' I felt her lips brush mine.

'We have to remain pure,' I said, gripping her by the wrists.

'Yes.' Now her tongue was inside my mouth. 'So pure.'

'I want to go further.'

'I know you do.'

'I want to.'

'Yes.'

'But God's watching.'

I was undoing the fourth button of her jeans when the door downstairs clattered open and a voice called out: 'Yoo-hoo!'

Rana calmly buttoned herself back up, sat on the desk, picked up my Bible, and was flipping through it when the door opened and my mother stepped into the room.

'Have you two been having a nice evening, then?' she said.

Before waiting for an answer she turned and made her way downstairs, pointedly leaving the door wide open.

Once Rana and Rhoda were gone and the house was quiet, I sat in my room in my boxer shorts with my Bible open on my lap. The next day I would stand before God's church and testify that I'd given my life to Jesus and been born again of the Holy Spirit. It was lucky things with Rana had gone no further, that my parents had come home when they did. Otherwise I would have defiled her body and destroyed the gift God had put in my hands. How could I have submitted to being baptised with that sin on my conscience?

But was it too late? Had I already looked at Rana with lust in my heart? My thoughts felt tangled up, like unspooled tape from a cassette. Lethargy descended on me. I turned the pages, looking for a passage that would help make sense of things. In the Book of Job I read:

> When I say, My bed shall comfort me,
> my couch shall ease my complaint;
> Then thou scarest me with dreams,
> and terrifiest me through visions:
> So that my soul chooseth strangling,
> and death rather than my life.

I looked down at my legs, hairier than they were a few months ago. I let the Bible rest on my thighs and looked at the palms of my hands, their sketched lines, the bottle-green veins showing through my wrists. I thought of those miserable people in medieval times who'd wander from town to town, mortifying the flesh by flagellating themselves half to death. I thought now I understood them: if the body was the enemy, wouldn't its destruction feel like freedom? I turned back to the pages, landing on the Song of Solomon:

> How fair is thy love, my sister, my spouse!
> . . . Thy lips, O my spouse, drop as the honeycomb:
> honey and milk are under thy tongue;
> and the smell of thy garments
> is like the smell of Lebanon.
> A garden enclosed is my sister, my spouse,
> a spring shut up, a fountain sealed.
> Thy plants are an orchard of pomegranates . . .

That orchard of pomegranates was what did it. As soon as I read the words, arousal possessed me like a demon. I pulled down the elastic of my boxers, closing my eyes. 'Oh Lord Jesus,' I prayed, 'I beg you: take this cup away from me.' But even as I was mouthing the words Rana appeared in my mind, not just her visual image but the feel of her skin on my fingertips and the smell of her hair in my mouth. I clenched my jaw, willing her away. I knew I must leave her untainted, so I summoned up a vision of Emma, a sacrificial lamb to take her place. I was so close now, a few hard strokes and I'd be there. But just as I was about to finish, I saw Rana and Emma together, limbs entwined, panting into each other's kissing mouths. Panicking, my mind sent a signal to my right hand to stop, but it was too late. I came in four thick spurts, soaking Song of Solomon chapters 4 and 5 where the Bible lay open in my lap.

In the morning I went downstairs intending to tell my parents I couldn't go through with the baptism. Outside there was a scribble of birdsong in the air. I could hear a kettle boiling and the chink of plates and spoons. In the kitchen, my mother offered to make me a cup of tea and my father told me, moist-eyed, how proud of me he was. Then he did something I couldn't remember seeing him do before: he actually put his hand on my mother's shoulder, and they both just smiled at me awkwardly as though posing for a photograph.

The candidates for baptism stood on the dais beneath the pulpit to declare they'd been born again, accepting Jesus as their Lord and Saviour. When it was my turn, I stared out at the congregation, hundreds of people packed in rows. High windows cast prisms of light onto their heads. The balcony was full on all three sides too, and on the upper left I saw Emma, smiling encouragingly when she caught my eye. Right at the front with her father and sister sat Rana, gazing up at me inscrutably. It felt dizzying to be looking down at the church from this perspective after fifteen years of watching my father from the pews.

Dressed in white, the men and women climbed one by one down a ladder into the baptismal pool, were gripped by my father and a church elder, and were tipped into the water, emerging to the sound of the organ and hundreds of singing voices. Dread distilled in me. I'd desecrated my sister in Christ, I'd desecrated God's Word, and now I was about to desecrate his holy sacrament in front of his gathered saints. *He which is filthy, let him be filthy still*, I said to myself when it was my turn to climb into the lukewarm water. I stood in the pool, my father holding me by the elbow. His shirt was soaked and I could see his nipples through it.

'Do you, Matthew Rowland Hill, accept Christ Jesus as your risen Lord and Saviour?' he called out.

There was a pause. Four hundred people waited for my answer.

'I do.'

'Then I baptise you in the name of the Father, the Son, and the Holy Spirit. Amen.'

Suddenly I was plunging backwards into the water. I shut my eyes against the sting of chlorine. My body felt heavy as I submitted to gravity, to the force of the water, to the arms around and beneath me. Up above, I heard the sound of the organ, gauzy and refracted. For a moment I allowed myself to hang suspended, exerting no effort at all, waiting for the arms to pull me back towards the light and the human voices. I didn't want to be lifted back up. I wanted to stay down in the water for a very long time.

Evolution

When I was a child I'd known only two categories of people: the saved and the unsaved. But when I was sixteen my mother and father decided I should sit an exam for an academic scholarship at a famous school that was the alma mater of prime ministers and poets, and I began to see that behind everything in life lay a hidden system called social class. My parents, I soon understood, had been born into the industrial working class in south Wales, and had struggled hard to gain a foothold in the provincial lower-middle class. Every few years God had commanded my father to go forth and take on a ministry that happened to pay him a higher salary, and my mother's careful management of the household finances meant that, of late, we'd been comfortable enough to go out for a biannual Chinese meal in a restaurant in the centre of Leighton Buzzard. The previous summer we'd even flown on an aeroplane for the first time, en route to a week's stay in Tenerife. Compared to the days in Swansea when it had seemed the height of decadence for our mother to send us to school with 10p in our pockets for pick n' mix at the local newsagent, the Hill family was now rich.

One May night a few years earlier we'd stayed up late to watch the results of the general election. My parents rarely smiled when they were together, so I only had to glance at them to know something historic was taking place. My father explained that Labour wanted to take money from the rich and give it to the poor, while the Conservatives wanted to take money from the poor and give it to the rich. He didn't need to tell me which side we were on.

But the opportunity to send me to a private all-boys' boarding school made my parents forget their mildly left-wing views in a heartbeat. It was partly that we had few other options: despite the fact that my GCSE grades were among the best in my year group, my headmaster informed us I wouldn't be welcome back at Cedars for sixth form. I'd been caught skiving with Emma and talking my way into fights too many times. I'd never heard of private schools, nor could I fathom why anyone would pay good money for education, which like air was available everywhere for free. But when I passed the entrance exam and was offered a full scholarship, the prospect of two years away from the miserable atmosphere at home, where the rows seemed to grow more bitter and sadistic by the day, inclined me to comply with my parents' wishes and go.

In the end my decision to accept a place at the Famous School had less to do with academia or even the mood at home than with another, unspoken, factor. I wanted to start over. I hoped this would be an opportunity to slough off my degenerate former self like a layer of dead skin. After my baptism I'd all but given up trying to resist evil. I got drunk and smoked weed regularly with my friends George Mentmore and Jack Romano. And I partook hungrily of the sins of the flesh, both alone and, since Rana had now returned to

Haifa, with Emma. I seemed incapable of moderation, either in spirituality or vice. Only perfect holiness was worth attaining, and since it seemed beyond me, I abandoned myself to sin. Posters of secular musicians began to reappear on my wall, except now they were of Jimi Hendrix and Janis Joplin. It was only rarely, during long nights of drinking and talking about music with George or Jack or Emma that – usually at around 2 or 3am – it would occur to me I hadn't thought about Hell in hours.

At the last minute it was also decided that Jonathan, who at fourteen was a prodigy on flute and piano, would apply for a music scholarship at the Famous School. He was quickly offered a place in the same boarding house, two years below me.

There would be no girls where we were headed. I hoped this would allow me, as Paul commanded, to set my affection on things above. The morning we were due to set off, I'd gone to the post office and bought a pile of light blue airmail envelopes, thin as tracing paper, on which I intended to write to Rana every day. As the car was idling in the drive, I locked myself in the bathroom and replayed my most recent meeting with Emma. As I finished off in the bidet whose real purpose I'd never figured out, I swore to myself – and this time I *absolutely meant it* – that this would be the Very Last Time.

'These years will be the absolute making of you,' said my father to Jonathan and me as we drove south. Drystone cottages and thatched-roofed farmhouses sped past, bathed in golden September light. I was sitting beside my father in the front seat and my brother was in the back beside boxes of clothes, books, records and CDs. 'I'm telling you now, they'll—'

'We know, Dad!' said Jonathan. 'They'll be the absolute making of us! Can we put some Debussy on please?'

'Yawn,' I said. 'How about some Dylan?'

'I don't think you do know. You're about to make lifelong friendships with the country's elite. People whose families control significant parts of the national and global economy. Your lives are about to change forever.'

'I thought money was the root of all evil,' I said.

'The *love* of money. Provided we don't make an idol of it, there's nothing wrong with money in and of itself.'

'But Jesus said it's easier for a camel to go through the eye of a needle,' said my brother, 'than for a rich man to enter into the kingdom of God.'

'That's a metaphor,' said my father. 'You can't take everything in the Bible literally.'

'I thought that's exactly what we were supposed to do,' I said. 'That's why we don't believe in Darwin, right? Because when Genesis talks about the apple and the snake, it means there really was an apple and a snake.'

My father smiled placidly. 'Very good, very good. I have a feeling you're bound for the ministry one day, Matthew. Once you've spent a couple of years soaking up secular knowledge, you'll be in a wonderful position to do the Lord's work. These years will be the absolute making of you, you know.'

Moments like this – when I found myself irritated by my father's unsatisfactory theological answers – were happening more and more often. Before my eyes he was shrinking from the infallible God-man of my childhood into someone of undeniably human dimensions, and I wished he'd stop.

Our father parked the Mondeo among the Jaguars, Aston Martins and Bentleys in which other boys were arriving with their families. After unloading our bags from the car he walked us to the door of the boarding house, a tall red-brick building that resembled a Victorian asylum, and hugged us goodbye.

Inside, I was hit immediately by the *smell*. I'd assumed Cedars Upper School's aroma of industrial disinfectant, Lynx deodorant and hairspray was the universal scent of education buildings. But as I lugged my possessions up a narrow stairway to my room, the harrowing reek of generations of male bodies almost made me gag.

In my room I unloaded my record player and crate of LPs, sellotaped my *Highway 61 Revisited* poster to the wall, and sat down at my desk to write to Rana.

4 September 2000

My love,

Well, here I am at my new school. I'm sitting in my room, looking out the window, which actually has a pretty cool view of the London skyline. I'm kind of nervous, but mostly I'm excited to discover what spiritual growth the next two years will bring. I pray the Lord Jesus will use me during my time here as an instrument of his will. I long for you every day, and I think of nothing but when we'll serve the Lord faithfully together, whether in England, Israel, or any place God in his wisdom may send us. It's not for us to imagine what trials and delights he has ordained. But one thing I do know is that, whatever life has in store for you, standing beside you will be

Your brother in Christ,

Matt

After I'd sealed the envelope to post later, I leaned back in my chair and closed my eyes. I could hear doors opening and closing in the corridors around me, but I suddenly realised I was completely alone. Nobody here knew me except my brother, whose room was on the other side of the boarding house. My father would already be making his way back up the M1. I felt a familiar stirring in my groin and had already reflexively undone the top two buttons of my jeans when I came to my senses. I opened my eyes, stood up, and with a slightly frantic energy busied myself with unpacking. I arranged my books in alphabetical order on the wall-mounted shelf, hung up my clothes in the wardrobe, and placed my Bible in the centre of my desk. When the room was tidy and all my things neatly arranged, I sank to my knees and begged God for strength.

It took some time for Jonathan and me to adjust to the new world in which we found ourselves. Homework was now called 'prep', registration was 'bill', our school blazers were 'bluers' and our trousers 'greyers'. Teachers were 'beaks', and when we passed them in the street we were required to tip our straw hats in salute. Poor people were 'skivs', and soon my brother and I decided to claim this term for ourselves, hoping our self-deprecation would defuse any awkwardness among the other boys about our unequal economic status.

On Sundays we were expected to dress in a ridiculous out-fit of striped trousers and tailcoats to attend chapel. From the outset we'd known this experience would be doctrinally challenging. Our parents barely considered the Church of England properly Christian, and doubted many Anglicans would join them beyond the pearly gates after Judgement Day. Still, we decided to begin with an open mind. We chose to overlook the Anglican error of infant baptism, and for a term and a half we sat listening fairmindedly to the priests' ten-minute 'sermons', breezy pep talks about nation and noblesse oblige whose contrast with our father's hour-long philippics could hardly have been more pronounced.

But as our first winter away was beginning to thaw, the time came for me to approach Jonathan with my case for revolt. 'I'm not sure these people even believe in the Virgin Birth,' I told him, 'let alone the Trinity or the deity of Christ. They might as well be atheists. Maybe they are. We can't put up with it any longer.'

My brother's cautious nature shrank from even the mildest disobedience, so it took some time for me to bring him around. But once I'd persuaded him it was our holy duty to mount a boycott, we went together for a meeting with our housemaster.

Mr Knight was a minute, bespectacled man who'd devoted his life to the unquestioning observance of every convention, no matter how pointless or trivial, and was therefore baffled by any display of principle. He removed his glasses, closed his eyes, pinched the bridge of his nose, and said, 'I think you'd better have a little chat with Father Pete.'

The next day Jonathan and I sat in a small, tenebrous office in the chapel crypt for an audience with the school's Head Priest. He must have been at least fifty, but under his immaculate grey hair he had the undiminished good looks of a matinee idol and a twinkling expression that seemed to betray a boundless and ineffable hilarity.

'Now, what's this about then?' he asked merrily. 'Don't tell me you boys have anything better to do than to sit through chapel every Sunday!'

On the wall was the kind of writhing, bloody statuette of Christ our parents had taught us to consider both idolatrous and tasteless.

'It's not about having anything better to do,' I answered firmly. 'It's just that your faith and our faith – they're not the same. Are they, Jon?'

'No,' said my brother, addressing the floor. 'They're not.'

Father Pete beamed. 'I *quite* understand. The school treats different faith traditions with the utmost respect. The *utmost* respect! Of course provisions are made for boys from Jewish families – or whatever it may be—'

I wasn't going to be disarmed by the priest's genial manner. This was a serious business. 'No, we're Christians. The question is, *Father*,' I said, loading the honorific with as much sarcasm as two syllables could contain, 'are *you*?'

Father Pete grinned widely, as though I'd said something extraordinarily clever. 'Goodness me, I should hope so! I've been wearing this bloody thing,' he said, tugging at his dog collar, 'for nearly twenty-five years, after all!'

I'd expected our mutiny to be met with rebuke, threats and punishment. So nothing could have been more infuriating than Father Pete's mirth. Nevertheless I pressed on, listing all my objections to the chapel's theology.

'And in a recent sermon,' I concluded, 'you condemned, at some length, the bullying of homosexuals. Which is all very well, of course. But not once did you mention the Bible's unequivocal condemnation of such – well, such actions. And if you ask me—'

Father Pete's smile hardened and the light faded from his eyes. 'Yes,' he interrupted, running his hand through his hair. 'Well, I didn't.'

A pained silence descended on the room.

Father Pete laboured to arrange his expression back into one of cheerfulness. 'Now then—'

I turned to my brother. 'Jon, how about backing me up here?'

Jonathan's arms and legs were tightly crossed, as though he was trying to recede into himself. At fifteen a recent growth spurt had left him six feet tall, long-limbed and unwieldy. He stared out the office window and said, almost morosely, 'As evangelicals, we – um, we find chapel too liberal for our liking and we don't want to go any more.'

'Well, it's not about what's to our *liking*, exactly,' I said. 'It's about what the Bible teaches. If you read Romans, Paul clearly explains—'

'Oh *Paul*.' Father Pete gave a strained chuckle, as though naming a troublesome neighbour. 'Yes, I'm afraid he could be an awful bigot at times.'

I was stunned. I'd never heard scripture spoken of so blithely. Stammering, I said, 'That – that's the kind of liberal dogma that—'

'Well, when it comes to dogma, better the liberal than the illiberal kind, if you ask me,' said Father Pete. 'But look, we're not going to see eye-to-eye today, are we? I'm not about to sit here and try and dissuade you from the faith you were taught at home.'

Did that remark contain a slight sting, as though only parental brainwashing could explain our peculiar notions?

'There's a lot to be said for the nonconformist tradition, even if frankly I can't go along with – well, quite a lot of it.' He began scribbling on some paper. 'Why don't you boys find a local church that suits your, ahem, tastes – and pop along there instead of chapel?'

He signed two slips, handing one each to my brother and me. I found myself holding written permission to be absent from school from 9am to 9pm every Sunday.

'Well, look – thanks for understanding,' I said, with a sense of anticlimax.

Father Pete winked at me and smiled warmly. 'Mind you two make the most of it.'

There was a sharp chill in the February air as my brother and I made our way back to the boarding house. We crossed the narrow high street along which the school's main buildings were gathered. I could tell Jonathan was in a sulk.

'What's up with you?' I said.

He looked vexed. 'I don't see why you had to be like that with Father Pete.'

'Like what?'

'Like, rude. He was being nice, and you were trying to provoke him.'

Still spoiling for a spiritual fight, I said, 'Jon, some things are more important than politeness. Was Jesus worried about offending the moneylenders when he threw them out of the temple?'

'Guess what, Matt?' said Jon, punching in the security code and letting us both in. 'You're not actually Jesus.'

I had nothing better to do, so I followed my brother down a musty corridor to the piano room. He adjusted the stool, lifted the instrument's lid, and began stroking the keys with his long fingers.

'Look,' I said, speaking over the jazz-inflected ballad Jon was improvising. 'I'm sorry if I made you uncomfortable back there. I just think – well, if God's Word upsets people, that's their problem.'

'But he wasn't especially upset,' said my brother, turning his melody into a twelve-bar blues. 'You tried to upset him, and it didn't work.'

'All I was doing was standing up for what I believe. What I thought we both believed. Unless there's something you want to tell me?'

'Matt, you can be a believer without being a prick. That's all I'm saying.' For a moment, Jonathan looked a little unnerved by his insubordination. On the piano he continued running his theme through new variations. 'Anyway, if you love God's Word so much, how come you're always being caught smoking and you've got a bottle of bourbon under your bed?'

'*All things are lawful unto me*,' I said with a shrug.

'*But all things are not expedient*,' Jonathan shot back, turning his tune into a waltz.

Jonathan's words smarted because he was right. A week at our new school had been enough to make a casualty of the optimism I'd arrived with. Though there were no female bodies here to incite my lust, sin seemed to stalk me like a shadow, and I quickly saw that my imagination alone was perfectly capable of leading me away from God's path into noxious back alleys of fantasy. The other boys' rooms were, almost without exception, covered with semi-pornographic photos of the World's Sexiest Women from *FHM* and *Loaded*. I was appalled by such vulgarity; the only female figure on my wall was Patti Smith's androgynous image above my desk. But lately I'd fallen into the habit of excusing myself from lessons on the pretext of fetching something from the boarding house, stealing into any bedroom I found unlocked, and relieving myself with the aid of its obscene wallpaper.

The door swung open, and my brother stopped playing.

'Oh, Hill. I thought I'd find you here.' A boy my own age, Felix Dashwood, was leaning against the doorframe with his hands in his pockets. Even from across the room it was impossible to ignore his skin, which was flagrantly stippled by acne scars. 'Do me a favour, will you? Go to my room, get my hat and my history books, and bring them down. And hurry up, please. You know how much I hate being late.'

For an incredulous moment, I thought Dashwood was speaking to *me*. I'd assumed Jonathan was somehow exempt from the system known as 'fagging' – generations-old and officially tolerated – whereby sixth formers delegated menial tasks to younger boys. My brother simply stared at the piano keys. I could see he was humiliated: not because he was being fagged, but because I'd witnessed it.

'What are you playing at, Hill?' said Dashwood in a tone of lazy menace. 'Planning on sitting there until you're old enough for your own fag or something? Come on, I haven't got all day.'

'How long has this been happening?' I said to my brother.

He refused to meet my eye. 'It's just the way things work here.'

'You mean it's been going on the whole time? And you never told me?'

Dashwood groaned. 'Spare me the family drama, will you? Come on, Hill. Chop chop.'

Suddenly I was ablaze with fury. All the anger I'd kept stowed away – over Father Pete's heresy and my own failure to live a holy life – burst out of me. Without knowing what I intended to do, I sprinted across the room to Dashwood, lunged at him and grabbed his throat. I pinned him against an oak panel where the names of alumni were embossed in gold leaf.

'Don't . . .' he rasped.

'If you ever, *ever* speak to my brother like that again—'

'Matt, stop!' pleaded Jonathan.

I tightened my grip. I could feel his muscles quivering like a hooked fish. He was utterly under my power. I was unbelievably excited. 'If you ever speak a *single fucking word* to him—'

Dashwood just croaked.

'Matt! Stop! You're going to kill him!' Jonathan was almost screaming now.

'If you even so much as *look at him*, I'll rip you into a thousand pieces. They won't even be able to identify your body. Do you understand me, you posh little rat-faced prick?'

Dashwood, wide-eyed, jerked his head in an attempted nod.

I let go of his throat. He collapsed in a heap on the floor, gasping for air.

I turned to my brother, his face a mask of tears. I said, 'Why the fuck didn't you tell me they do this to you?'

'Because I knew you'd react like this!'

Dashwood, still heaving, rose unsteadily to his feet and swayed out of the room, making a strange burping noise. A few moments later my brother followed, slamming the door behind him.

For the rest of the day I felt triumphant. I sat through my classes, but the Ninety-Five Theses and Iago's motives in *Othello* made as much impression on me as pink noise. I felt intoxicated, transfigured. All my life I'd watched impotently while my parents screamed at each other. Their rage had somehow wormed its way into my being, and had been eating away at me for longer than I'd cared to admit. I'd tried fighting at Cedars and mostly been beaten up. But among my well-bred schoolmates here, I was, I saw now, intimidating. No longer would my fury be directed inward. I was sixteen, almost a man. Now that I had my anger to protect me, I'd never allow anyone to hurt me again.

For my first few months at the Famous School I'd fulfilled my promise to Rana, writing to her after my morning prayer and Bible study, and for a while we swapped earnest missives in which our religious and romantic fervour bled together. But the vagaries of airmail made it impossible to maintain a sense of conversation. Her letters would be delivered out of sequence, or three would arrive on the same day. It wasn't long before I found myself struggling to think what to write. It was beyond me to describe this strange new world; I could hardly make sense of it myself. In Leighton Buzzard, where everyone I knew lived in identical new-build houses on the town's sprawling estates, I'd had no idea who was rich and who was poor. Everyone at the Famous School bar the dozen or so scholarship boys was rich, but among the rich there were distinctions I could barely grasp. Many of my schoolmates were the sons of fabulously wealthy capitalists, but for some reason to have earned one's own money was considered vulgar. The worst insult here was to call someone *nouveau riche*. Whenever money came up, which was often, I'd make a joke about my family's lack of it. After one such occasion another boy, Rollo Ponsonby, took me aside for a friendly word.

'Look, Hill,' he said. 'If you want my advice, you'd better shut up about being poor.'

'Why? Compared to you I *am* poor.'

'Yah, well, it's making the other boys feel hideously uncomfortable, that's all. And it's not winning you any friends. All right?'

I didn't feel I could explain any of this to Rana, and eventually I had to admit to myself I was growing bored by our correspondence. It was increasingly clear to me that, having spent only a week or so together during her visit, we hardly knew each other, and therefore had little to say beyond our avowals of eternal devotion.

One day towards the end of spring term I took a seat in the red telephone box that looked like it belonged on a London pavement but which was nestled below the boarding house stairs next to the piano room. I dialled the number I knew off by heart, and Emma answered on the fourth ring.

'I recognise that voice,' she said. 'It's nice to know you're still alive.'

I gave a sheepish chuckle. I hadn't spoken to Emma since Christmas. 'Yeah, sorry. School's been so busy, you wouldn't believe.'

'Right.'

'So what's up?'

'Nothing's *up*, Matt. I live in the world's shittest town, remember? The headline news in last week's local paper was *Man woken by barking dog*. I'm not even joking.'

'Ha, that's funny.' I realised it had been some time since another human being had made me smile.

'So when are you going to invite me down to visit your new posh friends?'

'Since you mention it, I was wondering if you'd like to come this weekend?'

'That could work. Just one question.'

'Shoot.'

'How religious are you feeling right now? On a scale of one to ten.'

'Shut up, Emma.'

'No, seriously. Any more than five and I'm not coming.'

Emma showed up on Saturday lunchtime in a camel coat and grey jeans with rips above both knees. She was wearing flamenco red lipstick and her blonde hair was tied back in a ponytail.

I took her on a circuitous tour of the school grounds, aiming to cross paths with as many of the other boys as possible to show her off. She smiled to herself when she noticed them gawping. It was against the rules to bring girls into the boarding house, but I ushered her through a back entrance up to my room. I opened a bottle of Jack Daniels, poured it into plastic cups and added a chaser of warm coke. We spent the afternoon drinking and listening to mixtapes Emma had made of songs by the Pixies, Talking Heads and Iggy Pop. After two drinks I wondered why it had taken me so long to invite Emma to visit. After four I realised it was not Rana I loved after all. After six I walked over to the window out of which Emma was smoking a cigarette and hooked my thumb through her belt loop, pulling her close.

My letters to Rana became more and more irregular as Emma began to visit frequently. We no longer bothered discussing what to call our relationship: my spiritual vacillations had led to so many break-ups and reunions that by now we'd both forgotten whether she was officially my girlfriend or not. She was my best friend, that was certain. For a while she even began attending church at my urging. But the next time we slept together her eyes wore a guilty ambivalence I knew all too well, and which I'd always been grateful Emma lacked. I saw that my efforts to convert her were in danger of becoming too successful, so I cooled my evangelism and began inviting her to visit on Sundays so that she'd miss church.

I lived for my weekends with Emma. In truth, I was miserable at the Famous School. Our family's habit of moving house every time my father was offered a new ministry meant that my childhood had been a series of interruptions. It had taken several years at Cedars to gather a small group of friends around me, people like George and Jack, and it began to look as though my time at boarding school would be over before I could do the same here. My friendless condition wasn't helped by the fact that I received regular visits from an actual girl. Nor had I endeared myself to my peers by protecting Jonathan from fagging and pointedly refusing to fag the younger students. The fact I was a scholarship boy with the wrong accent and vocabulary confirmed my reputation as an outsider with a chip on his shoulder.

I returned my contemporaries' hostility, and spent all my time when Emma wasn't around with Jonathan or alone in my room. But gradually it became clear to me that I'd turned the school and the other boys into lightning rods for a fury whose source lay elsewhere. It wasn't really Father Pete and chapel that I blamed for corrupting God's Word, nor was it the bullies among the older boys who I regarded as the main threat to my family's wellbeing.

It was me.

For years I'd been tormented by my belief in God's teachings, but lately an even greater torment had begun to afflict me: doubt. At first, the symptoms had been trivial enough. During my customary morning Bible reading I'd noticed a minor inconsistency in the gospels. In Matthew, Mark and Luke Jesus was crucified after Passover, but in John it happened *on* Passover. I checked and double-checked, but however much I did so the discrepancy stared back at me in black-and-white. Like someone who fears their misplaced car keys are the first sign of dementia, I struggled to banish a sense of disquiet from my mind. According my confusion any significance, I saw at once, might presage an irreversible psychic collapse.

I'd almost managed to forget this disturbing experience when, in a Philosophy & Ethics A level class, I was required to write an essay on the 'design argument'. I'd heard the idea from my father in the pulpit many times: that the only logical explanation for the earth's astonishing order and beauty was the existence of a transcendent Designer. This struck me as the purest common sense, and I'd never thought to question it. But as I worked, I found myself in a quandary. It was clear from the textbook and my teacher's notes that, in order to score a high grade, I was expected to argue that Darwin's theory of natural selection had dealt a major blow to the design argument. I hesitated. My desire to make a stand for the truth battled with my craving for academic success. I could hardly forget I was here on a scholarship; my whole identity was bound up with coming top in class. But in the end I decided to do the right thing. Pulling out the bottle of Jack Daniels from under my bed and taking a swig for courage, I wrote a diatribe not just against Darwin but the Enlightenment, the 'cult of Reason' and the whole of modern science. My essay concluded:

> *In summary, despite centuries of slanderous attacks on God's mighty word, the truth is unassailable. The Designer sits enthroned in heaven, and all his enemies – from Charles Darwin to today's so-called 'intellectuals'*

*who busy themselves sowing doubt and scepticism – will
one day bow down and worship him as Lord.*

Later that week the teacher returned my paper. On the bottom he'd simply written: *You might profit from reading* The Blind Watchmaker. *C-minus.*

The next day, in a mood of defiance, I went to the school library and borrowed the book. It was a five-by-eight-inch paperback with a plain white cover, so compact it fitted neatly into the pocket of my blue felt blazer. I thought of my father's bookshelves in the garage at home, hundreds of thick, imposing volumes comprising millennia of wisdom. *The Blind Watchmaker* seemed trifling by comparison. I calculated that three evenings would be enough for me to stub out the challenge of Darwinism like a cigarette butt.

I began reading in my room after dinner, only putting the book down when sunlight broke through the curtains. I'd expected to encounter a shrill, mean-spirited voice flailing hopelessly at God's indomitable word. Instead the author wrote in measured prose, certain of its authority and learning, warmly inviting the reader to follow its argument. By the time I turned the final page and collapsed into bed, all my certainty about the Bible's literal truth had been shredded like tissue paper. I made my way to my lessons after just an hour's sleep. Was that why I felt my world was blurring at the edges?

I recalled one Lord's Day a year or so earlier when a six-teen-year-old Rachel had, in the throes of some teenage pique, refused to attend church. My parents' faith was the DNA from which my life was made. So inviolable was our Sunday routine of church attendance at both morning and evening services that my sister's protest had at first seemed nonsensical to me, like announcing that she intended to go and live on the moon. A week later, having made her point, she took her usual seat beside my mother in the third row. Order was restored. But her act of defiance had revealed to me a truth I'd never previously articulated: that whether or not we chose to adopt our parents' faith was up to us. And for the first time, with a shudder of dread, I'd been able to imagine choosing not to.

Reading *The Blind Watchmaker* caused doubt to spread in my mind like a genetic mutation, but I was determined to contain it. If the Creation story wasn't literally true, it must be a divinely inspired allegory. I decided not to discuss this idea with my mother and father, fearing it might test their faith. When I visited home a few days later I hid the book in the bottom of my sports bag for their own good.

But discovering doubt was like learning a word that you then suddenly begin hearing everywhere.

I continued my habit of reading the Bible each morning, but now I found problems almost every time I opened it. I noticed one day that Matthew and Luke provided entirely contradictory genealogies for Jesus. The same week I found that Judas had died by hanging himself in Matthew, while in Acts he'd fallen and impaled himself on a branch. I even noticed a contradiction on the very first page of the Bible: in Genesis 1 man and woman were created together; in Genesis 2 the order was first man, then the animals and finally woman.

I reminded myself of another argument for God's existence from my A level textbook: Pascal's Wager. My own version went like this. If Christianity was true, unbelief would lead me straight to hell. But if it was *untrue*, it would lead me straight to hell-on-earth anyway, so guilty would I feel for the near-mortal wound my loss of faith would inflict on my parents.

So for some time I struggled to store my doubts away in a mental crawlspace that I walled off from my everyday thinking.

My behaviour became erratic. On Sunday mornings I was increasingly zealous and evangelical, knocking early on my brother's door to insist we attend local nonconformist churches. For a while we attended a Pentecostalist youth service, waving our arms in spiritual ecstasy while the band played Christian rock, the imp of unbelief dissolved in the heat of the swaying bodies. Then I'd run back to school, shower, spray some cologne, and wait for Emma to arrive, pulling her onto the bed the moment we closed my door. A morning of intense Christian worship was usually enough to work up a healthy sexual appetite. When, in a recent lesson, I'd learned a new concept – 'cognitive dissonance' – I thought of how my brain often felt like a broken radio, unable to tune into anything but snatches of disparate melodies, quickly swallowed by static.

On a Sunday afternoon in the summer term I was lying next to Emma, her head rising and falling on my chest as I caught my breath. Her skin was warm where it pressed against mine.

'There's something different about you,' she said.

'What do you mean?'

'You're – I dunno, more affectionate. More tactile.'

'Aren't I usually affectionate?'

Emma laughed. 'No, Matt, you're not. Usually you get really weird after sex. You close up like a kid who's been caught doing something bad.'

I could feel my cheeks burning. 'You never said anything about this before.'

'I'm used to it,' said Emma, settling back into the crook of my arm.

We lay still for a while, neither of us speaking.

'You never talk about God any more,' she said. 'You used to get really evangelistic after sex.'

I stayed silent.

'What's up with that?'

My whole body tensed. '*Nothing.*'

'Hey, don't get defensive. I'm just asking what's going on for you.'

I rose to my elbow, forcing Emma to sit up. I grabbed my T-shirt from the floor and began getting dressed.

Emma looked at me quizzically. 'I knew there was something. You can talk to me, you know.'

I pulled on my boxers and a pair of jogging bottoms. 'There's nothing to talk about.'

'Are you still a Christian?' said Emma bluntly.

Irritation crept over me. 'Of course I am, Emma. No thanks to you!'

'Hey!'

'Look, I don't think you should come any more.' I was sitting now with all my clothes on. 'You always end up persuading me to sleep with you. How many times have I made it clear—'

'Whoah! I *persuade* you?

'Have you been going to church?'

'No,' she said firmly.

'Why not?'

'Because I don't believe in it, Matt. I never really did. I gave it a try because it meant so much to you. But it just – it doesn't make sense to me.' She held my gaze. 'Do you believe in it?'

'What are you talking about?'

Emma's tone softened. 'Matt, I know it isn't easy for you.'

'What isn't?'

'Giving up your faith would hurt, wouldn't it? It'd feel like kicking your parents in the teeth.' Her eyes took on a faraway look. 'I know how painful it is to betray someone you love.'

'I'm not a Christian because of my parents.'

'Aren't you? So why *are* you a Christian?'

'Because – because Jesus lives in my heart.'

Even as the words came out of my mouth, they sounded lame, as though they were someone else's. Emma looked down with embarrassment. Then she too got out of bed and began getting dressed.

By my second year at school doubt was devouring my faith like an apex predator. Most non-Christians, I'd been taught, were merely ignorant of the gospel and deserved pity and prayer. But a few were downright evil: those who'd heard God's Word, understood it fully, and rejected it anyway. My image of such individuals was formed one day when I'd seen my father reading a thin book with the scandalous title *Why I Am Not a Christian*. Its author, a man called Bertrand Russell, was depicted on the front cover with what seemed to me a satanic sneer. Whenever I pictured that face a chill ran through me. It was impossible to think of myself as belonging among such people, but it was equally impossible to deny where my doubts were leading me. Thinking about such matters made me feel I was losing my mind, so increasingly I tried not to.

I was home one half-term when my parents began one of their customary rows. Listening to them fight always made me feel that I was alone in a world where happiness was illusory and love impossible. I threw my coat on, called Emma's new mobile and asked what she was doing. I'd only seen her once or twice since our falling out during the last school year, but I missed her now.

I could hear the din of music and conversation in the background. 'I'm with George and Jack, actually,' she said. 'We're at George's. Come over!'

'George Mentmore and Jack Romano?'

'Yeah. Why d'you sound so surprised?'

'I just thought they were kind of – I dunno, *my* friends.'

Emma laughed. 'Matt, you've been away for over a year. I see the guys every day at school. Do you think we don't talk when you're not around or something?'

'I'm not complaining, I just—'

'Are you going to keep being weird, or are you coming over?'

George's bedroom was my idea of paradise: it had a brown suede sofa, its red walls were decorated in bright kitsch wall art, and it housed a gigantic collection of CDs with everything from Billie Holiday to the White Stripes. Best of all, his father let us drink and smoke weed, provided we kept the windows open. Emma sat next to Jack, who had his shirt open and was moodily strumming his beaten-up Gibson.

'So how's it going up at the palace?' said George, carefully licking the edge of a cone-shaped joint. 'Hope you don't mind slumming it down here with us?'

'I dunno, man. Rich kids – they're weird. Know what I mean?'

'You sure it's them, not you?' said Emma. 'I wouldn't have called you exactly normal here either.'

I gave a hollow laugh. Emma's teasing somehow felt different in front of my friends. Or were they *her* friends now? It was strange I hadn't been invited this evening. But then again, it was hardly up to George and Jack to keep track of my movements back and forth from school. And by 3am, when the four of us were united in a chorus of 'Born to Run' as Jack played guitar, my misgivings had dissolved in a cloud of cannabis smoke and early-hours euphoria.

I went to church the next morning with a mouth that felt like sandpaper and a skull that felt like something was trying to punch its way out. As I sat in the pew listening to my father preaching on the doctrine of predestination, I wondered why, if my parents possessed all the answers to life, they were so unhappy. Why was it that joy seemed to belong to non-Christians like George and Jack and Emma?

After the service I was in a combative mood. Over lunch with my family I raised my voice above the clatter of cutlery. 'Dad, tell me something. If God's already decided who's going to heaven and who's going to hell, what's the point in praying for unbelievers to be saved?'

My father waved a forked potato like a conductor's baton. 'That's a very good question, Matthew. A *very* good question. Some of the finest theological minds in history have wrestled with it.'

'So what's the answer?'

'Scripture tells us that God determined our eternal destiny before time began. Take John 15: *Ye have not chosen me, but I have chosen you.* Meanwhile in James 5 we are commanded to *pray one for another, that ye may be healed.*' My father brought his potato to his mouth and chewed. 'Such teachings may seem irreconcilable to us. But trying to plumb God's wisdom with human reason is like looking at a tapestry from the back. We see no pattern, no meaning. But one day, when we're with the Lord, we'll see his plan in all its beauty. Will you pass the apple sauce, Jonathan?'

My father looked satisfied with this argument and went back to concentrating on his food. I didn't say another word, but inwardly I seethed. A few years ago such flimsy reasoning would have seemed to me the epitome of wisdom. But now I felt the scales falling from my eyes. I hadn't yet altogether lost my faith in God. But my faith in my father was shattered.

Back at school, keeping my doubts behind a locked door in my mind was increasingly consuming all my strength. As my final year wore on, I was more and more exhausted. Could it really be true that everything I'd ever believed – and the whole moral worldview that went with it – was a lie? If I couldn't trust a word my parents said, what could I be sure of?

The terms of Pascal's Wager no longer looked so appealing to me. Sure, if all your heavenly bananas lined up, you'd hit the eternal jackpot. But, if they didn't, and you spent all your days crossing your fingers, hoping to cash out at the exit by handing over the crumpled ticket of belief – well, in the loss column would go *everything*, including your single chance to create a life based on freedom, courage, dignity, intellectual honesty. After all, what would it profit you if, in attempting to win your soul, you lost the whole world?

As my A level exams approached I finally discontinued my morning Bible study. I realised that at some point I'd stopped performing this ritual for spiritual instruction and was instead seeking confirmation of my doubts. The first morning after making my decision, I just sat at my desk in an angry sulk, not knowing what to do with myself. I solved the problem by going to the library that afternoon and borrowing a small pile of paperbacks. For the rest of my time at school I began each day with a chapter or two from *On the Road* or *The Bell Jar*. I read these books with the same avidity, the same existential hunger, that I'd once brought to scripture. I'd been raised to believe the purpose of literature was to reveal the hidden truths of life, so now I simply transferred my reverence from St Mark to Kerouac, St Paul to Plath.

In June I finished my A levels and packed my bags the same day. I put on my headphones, played 'Like a Rolling Stone' at full volume, and walked out of the Famous School without a single goodbye.

That same evening I made my way around the house to my father's study in the garage. It was 9pm, a pale disc of moon suspended in the eerily light sky. When I knocked on the door I heard a scuffling sound and the spraying of air-freshener.

'Come in!' shouted my father after a long delay.

I let myself in, releasing a gust of cigarette-scented air. 'Don't worry, it's only me.'

'Young man,' said my father jocularly. 'How can I help you?'

'How about a cigarette?'

'You're too young.'

'Dad, I just turned eighteen.'

'Well, in any case, I don't smoke. You know that.'

I rolled my eyes. 'Ok, whatever. Look, I just wanted to ask you something. About a little theological puzzle.'

My father rubbed his hands together. 'Ah, excellent. There's nothing I like more than a good theological puzzle.'

'Right, that's what I thought. So here it is.' I explained to my father about the inconsistencies I'd found in the Bible, pointing out – though it was hardly necessary – that our entire faith was based on the infallibility of the text. If the Bible couldn't be trusted, how could we be sure anything we believed was true? There must be some simple explanation I'd overlooked, but for a while now I'd been going out of my mind with doubt, and—

My father cut me off. 'I know just the book for you!'

Standing on tip-toe, he reached for a volume on the top shelf behind his desk. He handed me a thick blue paperback with the title *Alleged Discrepancies in the Bible*. I blew a film of dust off the cover.

My father winked at me. 'That should clear up any difficulties you're getting yourself into.'

Back in my room, I flipped through the book. My own investigations had thrown up around twenty-five contradictions in the Bible. This book contained eight thousand. Far from reassuring me, its 'explanations' for the countless problems it listed were like petrol poured on the flames of my doubt. It was painful to witness the logical contortions the author was obliged to perform to discover what he evidently already believed: that there were no discrepancies of any kind in the Bible, even though there were.

I stood in front of the mirror and looked at my reflection with its three days' growth of stubble. A part of me understood there was no satisfactory answer my father could have made at this stage: it was too late, my God was already dead and buried. A brief scan of this pathetic book only confirmed what I knew. So why was the moment so unexpectedly painful?

Grinding my teeth, I strode downstairs and back to my father's study. For a moment I stood outside and collected myself, feeling like Luther at Wittenberg's church door. Then I barged in without knocking. I found him smoking with his feet on the desk, an ashtray in his lap and a hardback volume in his hand.

'Dad.'

My father almost fell off the chair as he swivelled around to face me. 'Good grief! Haven't I told you to knock?'

'Tell me something.'

He simply stared at me.

'If God's all loving and all powerful, why do children get cancer? Why did six million Jews die in the Holocaust?'

'The Lord works in mysterious—'

'No, sorry. That's not good enough.'

My father's eyes widened.

'If I was God, I'd never have let all those people die. Couldn't he even have saved a few? Couldn't it have been five million instead of six?'

'Well, the question of theodicy is certainly a challenging—'

'Do you know what *I* find challenging? It's not so much the stupidity, the evidence-free bullshit you've been filling my head with my whole life. No, the part I find *really* challenging is how offensive, how fucking evil it all is. The idea there's this maniac up there who's all-powerful and all-knowing and all-whatever, but at the same time so needy and thin-skinned he'll send me to hell forever unless I worship him. If, when I die, it turns out your God *does* exist, do you know what I'll do?'

My father was so shocked he'd forgotten to put out his cigarette, which was smouldering between his motionless fingers.

'I'd tell him to go fuck himself. I'd tell him I've got no respect for any being who lets millions die in genocides and famines, or who tells gay people their love's a sin, or who lets children grow up in broken homes, *fucking miserable homes where all anybody does is fight—*'

My father simply stared at me, his hands trembling. I'd dared to contradict him to his face for the very first time, and I was furious with him – for putting up so little resistance, for backing down so easily. Part of me wanted him to denounce my heresy with his thundering preacher's voice. My rage burst and sobs began pouring out of me. I turned and wailed into the cold brickwork. I waited to feel my father's arms around me for ten and then twenty seconds before I realised they weren't coming.

I ran indoors and up the stairs, hurled myself onto my bed, buried my face in the pillow and howled. Faced with even the tritest challenge, the most obvious question any sceptic might ask, my father had almost nothing to say. It was all a lie, the whole thing!

When my sobs subsided, I told myself to say it: *I am not a Christian.*

I stood before the mirror and watched myself speak the five unspeakable words.

'I am not a Christian.'

I said it once more. As I did so, I realised it had been true for a very long time.

When I woke up the next morning, I felt as refreshed as if I'd slept for days. I went into the back garden in my dressing gown to smoke a cigarette with my coffee, not caring whether my mother saw me. It had rained overnight but now the sun was angling through the pine trees that bordered the garden. Dew glittered on the lawn, and the hexagonal patio tiles shone. I couldn't remember feeling so buoyant in months, years maybe. The long struggle was over, and I was free. The guilt, the shame, the self-loathing: I could delete it all like an unsatisfactory draft of an essay and start over.

There was only one way to describe it: I felt born again.

I thought about Emma, who I hadn't seen since the night at George's. She was probably waking up now in her bedroom just a few minutes away on the street where she lived. I saw clearly that for years there'd been three of us in our relationship, and it was time to do away with the unwelcome party. She was my salvation, not the cartoon imago I'd been taught to worship. I ran inside, showered, brushed my teeth, styled my hair and put on the floral shirt I knew she liked.

At Emma's house I rang the bell, which sounded through the house with its tinny Big Ben melody.

'Matt,' said Emma's mother, who answered the door in her pink dressing gown. 'It's not even 8am.'

'I'm sorry. There's something important I need to tell Emma.'

She knitted her brow. 'Can I pass on a message?'

'No, that's ok. I'll just go up and see her myself.'

She put her hand across and gripped the doorframe. 'She's not awake yet. Why don't you come back later?'

'I can hear music playing in her bedroom.'

'Matt, I'm sorry. You'd better go.'

'Honestly, it's important.'

'Matt, please. She – she doesn't want to see you.'

Before I could think what to say, Emma appeared at the top of the stairs in a pair of grey joggers and a white tank top. 'Mum, I'll deal with it, ok? Hey, Matt. Shall we go for a walk?'

She led me to the patch of grass beneath the lamp post that was equidistant between our houses. It was where we'd parted ways the first time we'd walked home together from school.

'Cigarette?'

I took one and said, 'What was that all about?'

She didn't meet my eye. 'Let's sit.'

The grass was still damp where we sat with crossed legs. Emma had her eyes fixed on a spot in front of her, and her unbrushed hair fell around her shoulders.

'Listen,' I said a little breathlessly. 'I have something important to tell you.'

'I have something I need to say, too.'

I ignored her. I had the sense that if I kept talking I could override the foreboding I felt in my gut and restore the gorgeous mood I'd been enjoying just a few minutes ago.

'Look, Emma. For a long time there's been three of us in this relationship.'

'I know. That's what—'

'And it's time to cut the bullshit. It's just you and me now. I'm not a Christian any more.'

She looked up. 'You're not a Christian? Did you just say that?'

'I haven't been for – I don't know how long. I just couldn't admit it to myself. It's like you told me. It was my whole world. It was my bond with my parents. But it's over now.'

'Ok, wow.'

'What I'm saying is, it was really hard to accept that none of it's true. That it's all a load of crap, actually. But now I can see clearly. Jesus isn't my salvation. *You* are.'

She stared at me with her large blue eyes. She put a cigarette to her mouth and exhaled a cloud of smoke. 'I'll give you this. As a chat-up line, telling a girl she's a stand-in for Jesus is definitely – original. But that's not a role I want to play. It sounds like a lot of pressure. I don't want to be worshipped. I want to be *loved*.'

'But that's what I'm saying. I've loved you all along. We've been in love since we were kids. We made each other into who we are.'

'We did,' she conceded.

'So let's make it official. You and me. Nobody else.'

Emma stood up. I could see she was full of nervous tension. 'Actually, can we walk?'

I followed her down the path that cut through the estate, past picket fences and flower beds with lilacs and peonies in bloom.

'Matt, there's a reason why I can't be your girlfriend.'

A mind-altering wave of anxiety crashed over me. I struggled to catch my breath.

'Look,' I said, speaking rapidly. 'I know I've messed you around. I've changed my mind a thousand times. I never let you know where you stood. I was so ashamed all the time. I thought what we were doing was wrong. But I'm telling you, I've made up my mind—'

'I hear you. And look, I'm happy you've found some kind of – some resolution to the whole God question. I could see how much it was weighing you down.'

'Like I was saying, I've *decided*—'

'But two people have to decide to be in a relationship. And I'm telling you. I can't be your girlfriend.'

'Look, I know I've treated you badly. But that's all—'

She stopped, turned to face me. 'You're not hearing me! I can't be with you because – because I already have a boyfriend.'

For a moment I wasn't sure I'd heard her correctly. 'Sorry?'

'I said I already have a boyfriend. I've had one for over a year, actually.'

'But – that's – we've slept together more than once in the last year.'

'I know. And I feel terrible, I do. But it's like you said. There's been three of us in this relationship for too long. I need to grow up and choose. So that's what I've done. I've chosen Jack.'

'*Jack*?'

'Why are you so surprised?' she said, looking off to one side. 'We've grown really close while you've been away. We're – we're like soulmates.'

'*Jack Romano*?'

'I'm sorry, Matt. I've always loved you, you know that. But I was never enough for you. Never exotic enough, never exciting enough. I was just the girl from across the estate.'

There was a long, brutal silence.

'What does he have that I don't?' I said.

Emma couldn't quite suppress a smile as she thought about Jack. Anyone could see she was in love with him. 'Jack's just a beautiful person.' She paused. 'Sorry – I didn't mean—'

I saw that Emma had rendered the final judgement on my life: that I didn't belong among the whole, the lovable. She'd seen me clearly and discerned my true nature. On some level I'd always known I was destined to be a scavenger when it came to love, eating the crumbs that fell from the tables of the beautiful.

I could feel tears filling my eyes. What I said next surprised me. 'I'm not a bad person, Emma.'

She reached for my hand. 'Oh, Matt. I never said you were. I know you. You're a good person.'

'But I'm not beautiful.'

'Of course you are. But everyone's beautiful in different ways. Look, let's not keep going over this. It'll only be more painful. Jack's my boyfriend. I'm sorry. We should have told you much sooner.'

That *we* hit me like a blow to the ribs.

Without another word, I turned and hurried down the walkway leading out of the estate. I was struggling for breath. There was no way I could survive this moment. I'd lost my God and with him my parents. Now I'd lost the only girl I'd ever loved. I'd never felt so alone.

My God, you bastard! Why have you forsaken me?

The day was warming up now, clouds dispersing. Next to the community centre in the middle of the estate there was a little supermarket. I walked through the automatic doors into the conditioned air. At the counter I asked for a bottle of whisky.

'I'll need to see some ID first, sweetheart,' said the woman behind the till.

I searched frantically in my pockets, finally pulling out my provisional driver's licence.

As she rang my purchase through the checkout and handed over my change she said: 'Having a party tonight, are you?'

'Something like that,' I muttered, grabbing the whisky and heading out into the warmth and the pollen and the birdsong.

I ripped the plastic sheath from the neck of the bottle and unscrewed the lid. Tipping my head back, I poured as much of the liquid down my throat as I could bear. It burned my oesophagus like a Pentecostal flame. In one draught I managed to drink almost a quarter of the large bottle. Already I could feel my pulse slowing and my thoughts making sense again. A warmth bloomed in my chest like opening petals. Thank God for this stuff, I thought, taking another large mouthful. It was amazing grace. It was the power and the glory. Everything was going to be ok.

Law of Return

'And what,' said the woman behind the plexiglass at passport control, 'is the purpose of your visit to Israel?'

Still lightheaded from cabin pressure, I was tempted to try a joke: *Well, things have been tough at home lately, so I thought I'd try a place where there's less conflict going on.* For weeks Hezbollah's katyusha rockets had been raining down on Haifa and the Galilee. The woman's fierce expression and black epaulettes gave her a quasi-military air. On second thoughts perhaps this wasn't the time or the place for irony.

What was more, under a pile of books on the Israeli–Palestinian conflict in my suitcase, there was a mouthwash bottle three-quarters full of street methadone. Attracting undue attention while smuggling a banned substance through the world's strictest airport security was maybe not the smartest move. So I straightened my face, looked her in the eye, and said, 'Christian tourism.'

She inspected my passport and tapped her keyboard with varnished nails. 'What kind of church do you belong to?' Her

English was flawless, a marriage of mid-Atlantic vowels and Middle-Eastern consonants.

'Baptist. Evangelical,' I said, trying to strike a tone of serene fanaticism that would assure her my concerns were those of the world to come rather than anything troublesomely political. 'I'm here,' I added, laying it on thick, 'to walk in the footsteps of the Lord.'

Did I see the woman's left eyebrow rise slightly in amusement at this twenty-two-year-old man with his wheelie carry-on case and expression of half-baked religious zeal? I held her gaze.

Then she stamped my passport, handed it back to me and, without apparent sarcasm, said:

'Welcome to the Holy Land. Have a great trip.'

I rode an escalator between sand-coloured walls presumably meant to resemble ancient stonework, as though the airport had been dug out of the desert by archaeologists. The woman had posed a good question: what *was* the purpose of my trip? It was the summer vacation before my final year at university, and I'd ostensibly come to meet my parents in Bethlehem at the annual Assembly of Israeli Baptist Churches. But that was just a pretext. The real draw was Rana, with whom I'd resumed contact after several years of silence when she'd accepted my online friend request last summer. My life in the grey, damp university town I now called home was spinning out of control. The more it did so the more I found myself browsing Rana's photo galleries on the desktop computer in my college room, seeing in them a vision of all the qualities I lacked: beauty, goodness, authentic purpose. I'd even begun reading up on Israeli–Palestinian history with a diligence sorely lacking from my official study of English Literature. Increasingly I felt that my own life was abstract, fictive, and that reality was unfolding in Rana's physical ambit, halfway around the world.

I knew such thinking was ludicrous. My brief infatuation with Rana belonged to the Christian past I'd turned my back on at eighteen and ever since laboured to forget. So why did she, or her curated online presence, continue to exert such power over me? Why, when my parents had offered to pay for my travel to Bethlehem this summer – a transparent bribe to attend a religious event in the hope God would roll away the stone of my unbelief – did I immediately say yes?

As for my parents – what were they doing here? Officially they were forging links between Britain's Baptist churches and their two dozen or so Arab–Israeli counterparts. But they, too, had another motive: they were exploring the possibility of relocating to the Holy Land full time. In recent years, my parents' feud had been refreshed by a new point of dispute: which of them was to blame for their four children's defection from the faith? Rachel had simply stopped attending church one day shortly before she'd gone to study dentistry at Bristol. Abigail could rarely be located on Sunday mornings: at thirteen she'd dropped out of school and begun spending weekends joyriding our parents' car with a group of older boys from the estate. As for Jonathan, the same day he'd announced to my mother and father he was no longer a Christian he'd come out to them as gay. Arriving just a year after my own declaration of unbelief, this was the final blow as far as our parents were concerned. A silence descended on our family that was more painful than any shouting match.

So when my father was offered a job as a lecturer at Nazareth Bible Institute, a college for trainee preachers near the Sea of Galilee, they saw an opportunity to begin a new life. Now they wanted nothing more than to start again in the land where Jesus had raised the dead, next to the body of water on which he'd walked and stilled the storm – and which, my mother pointed out, boasted a Chinese restaurant with a lakeside view and an all-you-can-eat buffet.

As I stepped out of Tel Aviv airport, I was struck by the heat of July in the Middle East. It was its own palpable substance, different not just in degree but in kind from England's summer warmth, and like nothing I'd experienced on my handful of previous trips abroad. Already I could feel sweat trickling between my shoulder blades and down my back. Leaning against a guardrail, I lit a cigarette. White cabs with blocky Hebrew script on their sides were picking up and expelling passengers. Two men seemed to be arguing over an empty taxi while simultaneously conducting separate arguments into their mobile phones. Eyeing them were three teenagers in shorts and vests whose languid manner and dishevelled appearance might have marked them as gap-year travellers were it not for the machine guns slung over their shoulders.

As I smoked, I couldn't help forming an association between the temperature and the idea of this country I'd formed via my autodidactic efforts. Heavy, insistent and slightly berserk, the heat struck me as the atmospheric manifestation of all the feverish dogma and blazing monomania I believed Israel–Palestine epitomised. From my case I removed my calfskin notebook, rested it on a raised thigh, and scribbled down some first impressions:

> *No visitor to Israel-Palestine can fail to be struck by the fact that everyone here is a religious zealot. Even, in their own way, the nonreligious.*

That had a good ring to it; I'd figure out what it meant later. I went on:

> *Everyone here is a militant on behalf of some vision or grievance. Everyone staking their God-given claim to some patch of land. Everyone trying to turn the clock back to the beginning, or forward to the end. Everyone*

*prepared to blow themselves up – or to blow you up – for
the sake of their truth. Everybody yearning to return
home – even if that home is now unrecognisable, even if
somebody else claims it as their own. Return: that is the
name of the deity who reigns out here. The Law of
Return versus the Right of Return. And nobody giving
an inch, from the river to the sea.*

I glanced back over my words, not without satisfaction. As a
first attempt at on-the-ground political analysis, that wasn't
bad at all. Particularly from someone who hadn't even left
the airport.

Stubbing out my cigarette, I hailed a cab. The driver, in a
yarmulke and polo-shirt, took my luggage and asked me
something in Hebrew.

'Sorry, no Hebrew,' I said. 'English?'

'Of course,' said the man, tossing my suitcase into the
boot. 'Where you go?'

'Jerusalem. The Damascus Gate.'

My relief at the car's air-con was soon outstripped by
alarm at the way the driver accelerated and swerved into the
highway traffic. Seatbeltless, he held the wheel with one hand
and, with the other, dialled a number on his phone. Was everyone here constantly arguing, or was that just how the
language struck my ear? The road entered a landscape of
scrub plain dotted with biblical-looking foliage. The driver
was still talking or arguing into his hands-free thirty minutes
later when we climbed a pine-bordered valley and, at the
crest, glimpsed the distant prospect of Jerusalem, its huddled
domes and minarets shimmering in the heat.

Ending his call at last, the driver addressed me. '*Yerusha-
layim.* You see?'

I murmured in appreciation.

'You are English, yes?'

'British,' I corrected him mildly.

'You are Jew?'

'No, I'm nothing. Atheist.'

The man scrutinised me through his rearview mirror. He rubbed his chin. 'And why you come to Israel?'

That question again. I imagined the Israelites seeking their land of milk and honey; crusaders, pilgrims and pioneers with their earthly or heavenly dreams; my parents, worn out by Leighton Buzzard, pursuing a final adventure or refuge. Lingeringly, I pictured Rana. *Well, why does anyone come here?* I wanted to say. *To escape bondage and find the Promised Land.*

Or, failing that, to hasten the Apocalypse.

But instead I just said, 'Oh, you know. To have a look around. See the sights. The usual.'

The car dropped me off at the Palestinian bus station by the Damascus Gate of Jerusalem's Old City. Although Bethlehem was just a few miles from here, it would take the best part of two hours to reach it. First I took a bus to a military checkpoint between the two cities. There I passed through clanging turnstiles in a hangar-like building before being questioned by an IDF soldier. My heart pounded when I remembered my mouthwash bottle, but soon my passport was stamped and I was waved through into the West Bank. I sat by the roadside next to a few women in headscarves, waiting for a cab into Bethlehem while the sun cast shadows against the sentry towers behind us.

It wasn't long until a car pulled up, a brawny arm appearing from its open window. 'My friend!' called the driver, ignoring the women, who tutted loudly. He stepped out of the car, a thickset man in his thirties with designer Italian sunglasses tucked into the V-neck of his T-shirt. He smiled boyishly as he grabbed my luggage, revealing a gold molar.

I shrugged in apology at the women who'd been waiting in the afternoon heat. The man grinned while holding open the passenger door, as though I was precisely the person he'd been waiting to meet all day.

'Where from?' he said, pulling away from the kerb.

'The UK.'

The man seemed pleased by this information. 'Ah, English!'

'Not English. Welsh. You know Wales?'

'Yes, yes, Wales,' he said, apparently even more delighted. 'Ryan Giggs!'

'That's right. And you? You're from around here?'

The man shifted gear. 'Of course, of course. Me, Palestinian.'

'Yes,' I said solemnly, as though to convey a rich understanding of the significance of that word.

'Here, it is Occupation. Everything, Occupation. Very bad,' he said cheerfully. 'Many years Occupation, but now very bad. Fighting, fighting. Also now Hezbollah, fighting.' He mimed a falling bomb with his fist, whistling and then making an exploding noise. 'You are smoking?'

Keeping one hand on the wheel, he held towards me a soft-pack of Marlboro Reds. 'I am Jamal,' he said proudly.

'Matt,' I said, cordially accepting a cigarette and allowing Jamal to light it for me.

A few minutes later we pulled up at the Jacir Palace hotel, an Ottoman-style building surrounded by purple-blossomed jacaranda trees and covered in eucalyptus vines. Jamal rushed to open the boot for my case. Handing me his business card, he beamed, flashing his gold tooth again. 'We are friend!' he declared, pumping my hand.

'Yoo-hoo!' called out a familiar voice from the hotel entrance behind me.

'That's my mother,' I told Jamal, and for a moment he looked so unable to contain his joy that I wondered if I'd have to introduce them. But then he shook my hand one last time, climbed back into the car and, before driving off, said:

'Anything you need, you call me. Any time, you call. We are meet again, *inshallah*.'

My mother grabbed my arm as if to give me a hug, but then paused. 'Matthew! *What* is that on your arm? Is that a – a *tattoo*?' My mother uttered this final word as if it belonged to a foreign language and this was her very first attempt to pronounce it.

'Hello, Mum,' I said, giving her the most sincere hug I could muster.

'I want to have a look at that *thing*, please.' I allowed my mother to hold my left wrist so that she could inspect my forearm.

'It's lovely to see you too, Mum.'

'I've never seen anything so horrible in all my life.'

'Oh, that's very sweet of you. I've missed you too.'

'It's just so . . . tacky.' She shook her head ruefully. 'I gave birth to this body. And *now* look at it!'

My mother's disapproval was doubly infuriating. First, because it displayed her usual refusal to accept that other people's feelings and ideas might differ from hers. But also because she was right. I too had come to dislike the anchor on my left arm. I'd originally conceived it as a subversive commentary on the idea of a tattoo but, the very day after I had it done in a parlour on Camden High Street, I recognised it as pretentious, clichéd, and – my mother's was *le mot juste* – tacky.

'Oh well,' she said, as though the mutilation of the skin of her firstborn son was just one of the many burdens it was her lot to bear. 'I expect your father will be pleased to see you, anyway.'

Sometimes I had to admire my mother's talent for finding the most subtly hurtful thing to say at any given moment.

Her face brightened. 'Tell you what, though. You won't *believe* the food they have in the buffet here. Bacon, salmon, stuffed aubergine, pitta. Eggs cooked three different ways. And that's just the *breakfast!* Please don't tell me you forgot to book your room with the all-inclusive coupon I emailed you. I'll be *furious* if you forgot. You didn't, did you?'

Whenever I saw my mother after some time apart, I was amazed to find she was a short, middle-aged Welsh woman who existed on an entirely human scale. In my imagination she was impossible to look at directly, like a collapsing star of frustration and distress that sucked every nearby object into its life-extinguishing core. My abandonment of the Christian faith had laid bare a disapproval I'd come to believe my mother had harboured for me all my life. Even her chatter about food and special offers carried a payload of bitter criticism that was all the more enraging for being undetectable to anyone else. It seemed to me she'd been telling me since I was a child that I was too expensive, that I'd cost her things she'd never been able to afford.

'Well, here he is!' said my father, making his way from the hotel's glass doors towards me.

'Hi Dad,' I said, accepting his comradely thump on the back in lieu of a hug. 'How are you?'

'Oh, very good, very good. Did your mother tell you about the food here?'

'Yes. Salmon and bacon and three types of eggs, and that's just the breakfast.'

My mother gestured to my father's thin hair and pink scalp. 'Phil, mind you don't burn! It's still hot out here.'

'Angela, please don't start. Matthew's come all the way to see us. Haven't you, Matthew?'

I scanned the area for Rana and smiled blandly.

'Well,' said my father, turning to me. 'Here we are, in the town of our Saviour's birth. What a *thrill*, eh?'

My mother had always treated my loss of faith as an act of adolescent obstinacy which could surely be overcome with enough resistance. But my father's strategy was simply to ignore it had ever happened, as if his obliviousness could reconstitute me as the faithful Christian I'd been on the day of my baptism seven years ago. My first urge was to point out to him that few modern scholars accepted Bethlehem as the true birthplace of Jesus. It annoyed me that he wasn't aware of this well-known fact, even though I'd only learned it myself that morning in the departure lounge at Luton Airport while speed-reading a book called *Jesus: Myth and History*. My second urge was to point out that Bethlehem, as well as being a destination for hare-brained evangelical tourists, was a town under military occupation as a result of a political conflict in which literal-minded religion played a toxic and exacerbating role. But instead I clenched my jaw and managed to say:

'Well, it's good to see you both looking so well. Shall we get out of this heat before we all melt?'

'Here, let me take your suitcase,' said my father, grabbing the handle.

'*Phil*, he's not a child any more. He can manage by himself.'

'Angela, what did I tell you just a minute ago? Don't. Start.'

'I'm not starting. I'm just saying he's twenty-two years old. You're – well, look at you. Do you want to give yourself a stroke carrying that suitcase all the way up to his room like he's a child?'

'Look, it's fine,' I said, trying to wrestle the suitcase away from my father. 'I can take it.'

My father tightened his grip. Keeping his voice low, he stared at my mother and hissed: 'What difference does it make to you if I want to carry his suitcase?'

'*Phil! Keep your voice down!*'

'If I want to carry the suitcase, I'll *bloody well carry it*.'

'So you're swearing at me now, are you? In the middle of Bethlehem. *In the town of Jesus's birth*! All because I'm concerned about your health. All because I'm saying—'

'Has it ever occurred to you that you don't have to say every single word that comes into your head? Has that ever, ever occurred to you?'

'Can we *please* not argue, Phil.'

'Well don't argue then!'

'I'm not arguing! I'm just—'

'Excuse me, sir,' said a brisk man in a porter's uniform who'd emerged from the hotel. 'May I help you with your bags?'

My father let go of the suitcase, the vein in his forehead pulsing. He stormed into the building. My mother shrugged at me as if to say: *now do you see what I have to put up with*?

My mother and I stood in the hotel lobby with its mosaic floor and spiral staircase, waiting for somebody to show me to my room. Leaning close to me, she whispered: 'It's not a satanic tattoo, is it?'

'Mum, what on earth are you talking about? And why are you whispering?'

'I just want a simple answer. That tattoo of yours – please just tell me if it's a satanic tattoo.'

'I don't even know what you mean.'

She lowered her voice even further. 'Well, I was reading an article about Satanists. You know, devil-worshippers.'

'Right . . .'

'And most of them are *covered* in tattoos.'

I sighed. 'Yes, I can imagine that's probably true.'

'So I just want you to tell me if there's anything satanic about your tattoo.'

'Mum, it's an anchor. It's basically the archetype of a tattoo. I'm pretty sure it's got nothing to do with Satan.'

'But did you ask the man who did it?'

'Did I ask the *woman* who did my tattoo if it had a satanic meaning?'

'Yes. Or if she was a Satanist. Because if she was, she might have given you a secret satanic tattoo without telling you.'

'No, Mum. I didn't ask the artist whether she worshipped Satan before getting my tattoo, for a number of reasons. The main one being that I'm not completely insane.' Conversations with my mother had a way of making me regress into a surly, resentful teenager – a fact for which I naturally resented her.

'So you're basically telling me that, as far as you know, you could be walking round with a secret satanic symbol on your arm?'

'Well, even if, for the sake of argument, the tattoo artist *was* a Satanist, all she did was give me the tattoo I asked for. So I don't see how she could've given it some secret meaning I didn't know about.'

'Satanists are *very* crafty, Matthew.'

'I'm sure they are. But then if she was determined to give me a satanic tattoo, whatever that is, she could have just lied, couldn't she? So what would have been the point in asking her?'

My mother looked triumphant. 'All the more reason to stay away from tattoo shops, then!'

I could hear the squeaking noise my teeth made when I was grinding them extremely hard. 'Look Mum, I know you find this difficult to understand. But I don't really believe there's such a thing as a satanic tattoo, just like I don't believe in Satan.'

'Well, Satan will be absolutely delighted to hear that, let me tell you.'

'I know that's what you think. It's just not what I think. We've got something called a *difference of opinion*. You're a fundamentalist Christian, and I'm an atheist. But since you're my mother and I'm your son, we have to try and find a way of getting along while respecting each other's views.'

'Matthew, I wish you would stop speaking in that ridiculous way.'

I groaned. 'Mum, do you know what's ridiculous? This childish, paranoid world of Gods and devils and heaven and hell and angels and demons and satanic tattoos! Can't you see how mad it all is? Can't you see what a ridiculous conversation we're having? It's all just complete *insanity*.'

My mother looked anguished. 'You think you're so clever, don't you? With your books and your fancy education, you think you're too clever for your Creator. But let me tell you something. *The wisdom of this world*—'

'—*is foolishness with God.* 1 Corinthians 3, verse 19. I've heard it a thousand times, Mum.'

'And it's just as true now as the first time you heard it.'

'Ok, look. I need to go upstairs and unpack, so can we wrap this up?'

'There's a Day of Judgement coming, my son. And on that day, it will be too late. Nothing I say then will stop you being thrown into the fiery pit.'

'That's lovely. Well, at least you'll have won this argument. Hopefully they'll give you a chance to remind me you were right before they chuck me into hell forever.'

My mother gave me a sombre look, shaking her head. Then she walked away and began climbing the stairs.

Immediately I felt sorry. My mother's fantasies of hell and judgement were so bizarre to me by now that I sometimes forgot she truly believed them. Her obsession with sin had always been the true core of her faith. She prided herself on being a biblical literalist, but in reality it was just the nasty and mad parts of the Bible – the talking snake, the fiery pit, the demonology – that my mother took literally.

All the nice parts about love and compassion and forgiveness she seemed to view as a kind of abstract and impenetrable symbolism.

Everything went dark. 'Guess who!' said the owner of the hands that covered my eyes as she stood behind me.

Rana came round to face me and, in a single movement, wrapped me in a hug.

She drew back and smiled. 'It's *so* good to see you. I can't believe you're actually here!'

'Well, here I am,' I said, a little bashfully.

'Can you believe it? We're, like, *grown-ups* now. Oh my gosh, you *have* to meet Todd. Todd, *yalla*,' she said, turning to a man I hadn't noticed. He had a shaved head and was perhaps six or seven years my senior. 'Come and meet Matt.'

'Matt, it's *awesome* to meet you,' said Todd in an American accent.

'Right, hi,' I said, shaking his outstretched hand.

'I'm glad I won't be the only pale and out-of-shape westerner around here,' he said. Todd was not at all pale. He was, in fact, lightly bronzed and undeniably in excellent shape.

'Ha ha,' I said.

'So, how long's it been?' said Rana. 'Five, six years? I told Todd *all about* our little romance when we were kids. He's so jealous, aren't you, Todd?'

'Excuse me, sir,' said the porter from earlier. 'Are you ready to go to your room?'

'Look, it's great to see you guys,' I said. My teeth sounded like a chorus of demented mice. 'Shall we catch up properly over a drink in a little while?'

A few hours later I was lying on the bed in my room, flicking through the channels on the hotel TV. I'd hoped that seeing my parents away from England – the scene of my loss of faith, a trauma for them no less than for me – would help set our relationship on a new footing. We simply held different beliefs; that was no reason for conflict. But five minutes had been enough to derail my peacemaking mission, and my optimism had given way to the delirium of hurt and outrage that unfailingly overtook me in their presence. Determined now to soak in a soothing bath of resentment, I inwardly rehearsed my case against them. They'd raised me in a land of make-believe from which I'd liberated myself only after a long and miserable effort that consumed my adolescence. Their notions of right and wrong had led me into a morass of self-loathing. Not only had they taught me to despise myself, they'd taught me to despise tolerance itself and every social symptom it had spawned, from homosexuality – or indeed any sex outside Christian marriage – to abortion. They'd taught me I belonged to a small class of the 'elect' who possessed a truth that was unknown to the ignorant masses. Officially I'd been instructed to love 'sinners', but in reality I'd learned to view what my parents called the 'world' and its hell-bound inhabitants with a fear of contamination laced with contempt. What better way was there of warping a person's sense of reality than persuading him that the 'world' was a synonym for everything frightening and depraved before sending him to live in it?

What was more, insofar as there was anything positive in what they preached, my parents had failed to practise it. Every Sunday morning until I was sixteen I'd watched my father expound on love, repentance and forgiveness; then every Sunday lunchtime I'd watched my parents forsake those qualities and resume their never-ending argument, their eternal blame-game.

I was angry about all this, and I was angry that it had taken me so long to see it, that I'd lived for years in a purgatory of confusion, terrified by the knowledge that my mother and father were fanatically wrong about every important question. And on some level, I was angry that they'd been unable to prevent my backsliding, that they hadn't protected me from the collapse of my Christian world where everything had been as simple as a children's book.

Or was I merely angry about Rana's suave, handsome American boyfriend? There was no pornography among the hundreds of channels on the wall-mounted TV. I didn't particularly want to watch porn; I just felt it would nicely round off the tableau of seedy isolation and self-pity I'd created with my overflowing ashtray and half-empty bottle of room-service bourbon. The nearest thing I could find was an Arabic pop music channel where women in thick makeup sang in quivering glissando. This was nowhere near close enough, so I clicked the screen off.

What I needed, of course, wasn't porn – it was heroin. Or rather, it was the plush, elegiac oblivion only heroin could provide. Unscrewing my mouthwash bottle, I fixed a methadone-and-whisky cocktail so foul that tears pricked my eyes when I gagged it down. Methadone: heroin's distant and ugly molecular cousin. It was a pitiful substitute for the real thing, but at least it was an opiate, and the large dose I'd just taken would deliver a hazy, lethargic buzz that was the closest thing to smack I could hope to find this evening.

Then again – might there be any way of scoring out here, in the Holy Land, under the omniscient gaze of a hi-tech military occupation? I took Jamal's business card out of my pocket and considered it for a moment. Picking up the hotel telephone, I dialled the first few digits. No, this was madness. As usual, seeing my parents had opened a sinkhole inside me, a cavity that devoured everything good: hope, purpose, the idea of love. And then, as if to confirm what the disappointment in their eyes told me, the sucker punch: Rana and her smug, seal-skulled boyfriend. But I was a grown-up now, as she'd said. I didn't require my parents' permission to create a meaningful life. I had no idea what that might mean, but avoiding unhinged decisions would surely be a good first step. I put Jamal's card back in my wallet and replaced the handset. Then, congratulating myself on my abstemiousness, I called room service and ordered another bottle of whisky.

It had been a long time since alcohol had acted on me like the elixir it was when I was eighteen. The autumn after my final breach with Emma, drink filled the shape of her absence. Back then, booze made me think of Jonathan and his flute: it was like an instrument on which I was discovering I possessed a virtuosic gift. A gin and tonic at lunchtime could enchant the dullest shift in the Milton Keynes call centre where I was working to fund a summer trip around southeast Asia with my best friend George. A bourbon and coke at 5pm bevelled the edges off the day's stress. Later in the evening I'd usually meet George at the Starlight Snooker Club to play pool, drink lager and insert 50p coins into the jukebox with its selection of tracks by the Rolling Stones and Led Zeppelin. The pints of golden liquid had a way of gilding even midweek evenings with a savage beauty. Four or five drinks were enough to ease the constriction in my chest I associated with Emma's departure.

And in this way I got through the year. The summer finally came and, shortly after my nineteenth birthday, George and I took the twelve-hour flight to Thailand. We rode tuk tuks through humid, cicada-filled Bangkok evenings, making our way from one drink to another. Geckos climbed the walls of heaving bars, and in the streets outside grasshoppers and crickets were roasted on barbecues. Sometimes there were afterparties with men who tried to kiss us and women who may once have been boys and lines and lines of cocaine. I didn't like the coke any more than I liked the feeling of a man's tongue inside my mouth. But, according to the binary logic by which I lived, liberation took the form of whatever my parents opposed. Besides, provided everything was softened by a cottony blanket of alcohol, it couldn't hurt.

In the autumn George left for his first undergrad year in London. I'd originally applied to do Theology at university, hoping disciplined study would lead me out of my spiritual confusion, but since then my faith had entirely vanished and with it any desire to spend three years analysing fairy tales. I decided to swap to English Literature, which meant waiting a further year while a place became available. The prospect of another twelve months at home filled me with dread, particularly as everyone I knew had left town and I was locked in a standoff with my parents, who insisted that while I lived under their roof I show up to church. Before heading off to London George came up with a solution: why didn't I borrow his room at his father's place? I needed about four seconds to think before accepting the offer. My parents' house was only ten minutes away, but I spent the next year avoiding it like the site of a radioactive disaster.

I moved into George's, resumed my daily commute to the Milton Keynes call centre, and tried to remember that twelve months and eternity were not, in fact, the same thing. In Leighton Buzzard there was nothing for me to do, and nobody to do it with. Increasingly, even the sight of the town's slightly absurd name on the station platform filled me with a sense of futility.

Part of the problem, I reflected, was that purpose and hope had once been, for me, religious feelings. And I no longer had those, not if I could help it – although there were some, like shame, that felt both intensely religious and as omnipresent as God. One evening I found myself turning the pages of the

Bible – or, rather, scrolling through it on my laptop, since I hadn't bothered to bring one to George's – to remind myself what purpose had once meant: *If any man come to me,* said Jesus, *and hate not his father, and mother . . . and brethren, and sisters, yea, and his own life also, he cannot be my disciple.* Here was, in black and white, Christianity's fetish for unlimited sacrifice and self-immolation, which even now remained bound up with my idea of a meaningful life. No wonder that, after losing my faith in God, I'd immediately sought someone else at whose feet I could hurl my entire self – and that, when Emma told me she had a boyfriend, it had felt less like a breakup than a cosmic disintegration.

As for Jesus's words, I was doing a reasonable job of hating my parents, to whom I spoke only occasionally in strained telephone catch-ups. And I saw less and less of Rachel and Abigail too, since the thing that united us – the family – was the source of pain from which each of us was in flight. I'd turned my back on my family, but I had nothing to replace them with except my nine-to-five job, the two or three novels I read each week and the bourbon with which I washed them down while sitting alone on George's sofa.

My brother was the only one to whom I stayed close. Whenever he came home for a break from school we'd meet and drink together, sharing our latest cultural enthusiasms. I'd lend him books by Camus and Beckett, and he'd burn me CDs of Bach's cello suites and piano works by Ravel. We formed a united front against our parents' religion, laughing about the 'reconversion camp' they'd tried to persuade him to attend by handing him a leaflet headed *GAY?! PRAY!!!* Jon called it 'camp camp' and wondered whether it might be a good place to meet other boys.

Since he'd come out I'd felt protective of him in the same way I had when he'd been bullied at school. My parents had assured him, with a tragic air, that though they 'hated the sin' they 'loved the sinner'. I was enraged by their failure to see that such distinctions meant nothing when the so-called sin was the place where the so-called sinner sought love. But it was Jon who insisted I see the matter through their eyes. The commitment they'd made to an inflexible theology had left them so entrenched in their positions that, by now, acknowledging the possibility the Bible may be mistaken would mean the collapse of their entire world.

Jon, too, was preoccupied by how to find meaning without religion, and we'd spend long evenings drinking at George's and debating the question. By the end of his final year of school, Jon had worked his way through much of Sartre and Camus and begun calling himself an existentialist. I was less intellectually rigorous, but I felt my consumption of as many cigarettes as was practicable each day, and my penchant for withering tirades against anything that smacked of 'bourgeois convention', entitled me to follow his lead. Existence, we agreed, was capital-A Absurd. Our task was to find some kind of cause or calling to which we could hand over our lives. Otherwise, we'd have done nothing but exchange faith for bad faith. Camus and Beckett had joined the anti-Nazi resistance, but the only war available to us was the bloody fiasco unfolding in Iraq, against which we'd both marched. Whatever we were looking for, we both hoped we'd find it when we moved on to university.

But when in October I finally arrived for my first term in the town of colleges, quads and spires, it didn't take me long to see how misplaced such hopes were. I soon understood what I should already have known. I'd arrived at the institutional embodiment of every principle I regarded as the enemy of freedom. My peers showed little interest in dismantling the bourgeoisie, and few of them seemed to share my view of life as a Sisyphean trial. Far from liberating me from such conventions as hierarchy, elitism and tradition, my time here would only leave me inextricably implicated in them. Though I felt a chasm separating the other students and me that all the alcohol in the world couldn't fill, I followed them to venues that played the same chart music every night, taking advantage of the two-for-one deals. One December night in a cavernous club I was queuing for the bar next to Jo Sidhu, a pretty dark-haired law student from college, when I heard the first sultry chords of "Son of a Preacher Man". Leaning over, I tried a joke: 'Not a lot of people know this, but this song was actually written about me.' She smiled politely and continued trying to attract the barman's attention. The next thing I knew I was being woken up from where I lay slumped on a corner sofa by a bomber-jacketed bouncer, who then marched me out into the cold night.

This can't be all there is, I thought to myself in the softly falling rain. Groups of laughing students traipsed home in scarves that flapped in the wind. As I passed the Martyr's Memorial I kicked a can, watching it skid through the leaf-plastered gutter. It hit a man who was sitting with his back against a limestone wall.

'Shit, sorry,' I said.

'I'll forgive you if you've got a spare smoke,' said the man, who had a filthy sleeping bag pulled up to his chest.

I shook a cigarette from my pack and handed it to him. He had deep, skeletal eye-sockets and a grin that revealed ruined brownish teeth.

'You're a gent,' he said as I passed him a lighter.

'It's soaking. Haven't you got anywhere to go?'

'I'll be out of here the minute I've got enough cash, don't you worry.'

'You're raising money for somewhere to stay?'

'If I told you that's what it was for, would you give me a fiver?'

'If you told me the truth I might.'

The man fixed me with a stare. 'You ain't Old Bill are ya?'

'Fuck off.'

He looked me up and down. 'Nah, you're a stone-cold fucking student, clear as day. I'm raising money to score, as it goes.'

'To score what?'

'You ask a lot of questions, don't ya?'

I folded my arms.

'Gear. Brown. Am I getting my fiver or what?'

I thought of William Burroughs, Lou Reed and tragic glamour. I pulled out my wallet and found a twenty-pound note. Then I heard myself saying, 'Is that enough for me too?'

He stood up with a surprisingly spry movement, stepping out of his sleeping bag. 'All right, Student. Let's go.'

Half an hour later Alfie – as he'd eventually introduced himself – gently pulled a needle out of my arm as we sat side by side on the single bed in my college room. I felt immediately and violently sick. On four occasions that night I had to crawl to the communal toilet to vomit. Each time the mirror revealed a disturbingly pale young man in a sweat-soaked T-shirt. I was showing all the outward signs of being extremely ill. And yet, inwardly, I noticed a strange phenomenon. I understood that an alarm bell had been screaming inside me every second of every day for some unknown period, years certainly. Its ringing had been long and persistent enough that, like tinnitus, it had become intrinsic to my consciousness. Now, I was engulfed by a gorgeous, amniotic silence. And it was only this silence that alerted me to the alarm's former sound and how desperate I'd been to silence it.

For twelve hours I lay on my bed – motionless except when I needed to puke – experiencing the sensation of painlessness for the first time I could recall. When, after a night of exquisite insomnia, I was finally strong enough to stand and leave my room, I wandered out in search of Alfie and more of what he'd given me. I found him after a few hours, instantly agreeing to pay the fee he named, even though it had doubled since yesterday. This time Alfie – perhaps disconcerted by my appearance last night and eager to avoid the storm that would blow his way if I wound up dead by OD – showed me how to smoke the stuff.

'You do know what this is, don't you, Student?' he said, placing the brown powder in a creased piece of kitchen foil.

'Of course I do,' I said. He held a lighter underneath the sheet to melt the powder into dark rivulets, whose smoke I inhaled through a foil tube.

I wondered a little anxiously if the second time could possibly repeat the experience of the first. But again there was the transcendent silence, the annihilation of all unhappy thoughts. The only difference was the absence of nausea.

I knew that for my contemporaries taking heroin would have meant crossing a frightening boundary, but I'd long ago crossed virtually every boundary I'd been taught to fear. Since according to my parents anything that wasn't strictly Christian was impermissible, I'd been living in a universe of taboo since I was fourteen. Indeed, acting out my resistance to everything my mother and father stood for felt like constructing a self. And smack was one of the few original sins left for me to try.

I was only a little more successful making friends at university than I'd been at school, so keeping my new extra-curricular hobby a secret was possible for a while. But Alfie was conspicuous whenever he visited the sixteenth-century college where I lived, and people talked. A couple of concerned acquaintances asked me what the hell I was playing at, but I batted them away. To the high achievers here, with their networking and corporate internships, my behaviour was scandalous. But that didn't bother me at all. Not only did my peers' disapproval provide an easy alibi for my relative social failure, it also cast me in the familiar role of the nonconformist. After all, I'd been raised to see myself as set apart, an outsider possessing the secret of salvation. What was more, spending time taking Class A drugs with Alfie felt like an apt expression of hostility towards this place and everything it stood for.

And smack – well, it was just heartbreakingly lovely. Other substances I'd tried – alcohol, weed, cocaine – palpably altered my mind's function and impaired my sense of reality. In contrast heroin seemed to gently pull back the veil that had been obscuring all the beauty and joy that already existed in life. When I was high, I didn't feel my consciousness was being modified so much as refined into its purest essence.

It was only with the elimination of my distress that I saw how poisoned was the air I habitually breathed. I'd tended to see myself as manageably disenchanted or, I sometimes liked to think, Byronically moody. All my favourite films were about suicidal Scandinavians, the books that most spoke to me had titles like *The Outsider* and *Invisible Man*, and the songs I loved were all in a minor key. But the immense well-being I experienced on heroin made me wonder whether this was how most people felt most of the time. Was I pathologically unhappy? Was that why I felt so misunderstood, and why other people often baffled me?

For some time after my discovery of heroin, I was – somewhat to my own surprise – able to use it with a moderation notably lacking from the rest of my life. Cigarettes tasted like air to me: I smoked from the moment I woke up to the moment I slept. I continued to drink copiously, but now it felt more like a chore than a conduit to the realms of grace. Booze barely muffled the alarm that heroin silenced, and its vaguely tranquilising effects only made me hunger for the real thing.

On some level I could feel dependency's gravitational pull from the first time I used heroin. But for a while I told myself 'addiction' was one of those lies – like God, the nuclear family and Weapons of Mass Destruction – that the powerful used to control people. And hadn't I been extremely moderate – hadn't I been downright responsible – since first trying smack? Once again, I decided, what I'd been taught was wrong. I'd have to make up my own mind about this drug, just as I'd long made up my own mind about everything else. The most important thing was never, ever, to listen to the appointed authorities with their fear-mongering and bullshit.

It didn't take me long to find out that, in this instance, received wisdom might have proved a better guide than my own instincts. But for a few months at least I was able to keep my heroin use under control. Why? Because my moderation was the true measure of my love. I feared that if there was any truth at all in the usual warnings, once I'd crossed the Rubicon into physical dependency there may be no way back. During my first undergraduate year it was an occasional treat. Strictly no more than once a month I'd call Alfie or, if he wasn't available, venture up the Cowley Road, attempting to pick out the tell-tale darting eyes of a junkie avid to score. Meanwhile I went through the motions of my degree, despite its increasing unreality in my mind. I continued to show up to tutorials when absolutely necessary. I handed in the occasional piece of work. And when summoned to the principal's office to explain my delinquency I lied craftily, pretending I was struggling with 'mental health issues' and promising, absurdly, to discuss them with the college chaplain.

As my first year wore on, I made only a couple more friends. I was lonely, but I told myself I didn't care. Simply knowing that heroin existed – that it was an option *in extremis* – slightly quelled the alarm inside me.

And yet, careful as I was to rein in my consumption of the drug, its infamous habit-forming properties gradually began to assert themselves. At the beginning of my second year my monthly ritual became fortnightly. I kept to this routine all the way through to summer term, but then the prospect of several months in Leighton Buzzard caused my self-control to crumble. Twice a month turned into every weekend, which soon became all weekend every weekend. Then the weekend would begin on Thursday and end on Tuesday. Eventually one Wednesday, after a couple of weeks when I'd forgotten to take a day off, I woke up with a host of novel and unpleasant symptoms: cold sweats, diarrhoea, vomiting, a simultaneous restlessness and exhaustion.

I called Alfie, who agreed to visit in exchange for a 'loan' of forty quid. On arriving, he performed an apparent miracle: by injecting a small amount of heroin into my arm, he caused my symptoms to disappear immediately. With an almost paternal pride, he said:

'You've only gone and got yourself a fucking habit, ain't ya, Student?'

He went on to explain my predicament as though laying out the facts of life. A 'habit' meant I was physically dependent on opiates. Now I'd need to tend my addiction like a newborn child, feeding it several times a day to avoid the 'cluck' – the illness I'd woken to this morning. The more I fed it, of course, the more voracious it would become. Fortunately, there was good news. Provided I renounced two things, I should be able to raise enough money each day to outrun the cluck.

'Which two things?' I asked warily.

'Dignity and principles. Look, Student, I know you think you're cut from a different cloth than the likes of me.'

'Alfie,' I protested. 'When have I ever—'

'It don't matter and I don't give a fuck, to be honest with ya. Point is, we all started out with self-respect. Lines we wouldn't cross, all the rest of it. Me and all, believe it or not. But a habit's a habit, mate. It don't care about your morals. It don't care about your posh education.'

'Ok, Alfie, I get your point.'

'Fact is, Student, the life of a junkie ain't no seminar on' – he picked up a book randomly from the pile on my desk and flipped to a marked page – '*Ode to a fucking Nightingale* by John fucking Keats.'

'Right,' I sighed, elbows on my knees, cheeks resting in my hands. 'So what do I do?'

'Well, first thing you got to do, you got to get used to ham and egging.'

'What?'

'Begging. That's gonna be your mainstay.'

I pictured myself sitting on the floor next to the cash machine my contemporaries used outside college, and decided this was not the kind of nonconformism I'd been aiming for. 'But what if I don't want to spend every waking hour feeding my habit like it's a newborn child?'

'You can't just neglect a newborn child, you fucking monster!'

'Alfie, I'm not really in the mood for humour.'

It took some time for me to understand that, as far as Alfie was concerned, a habit was a fate to be accepted stoically and without negotiation. Similarly it took some time for him to see that I had no intention of organising my life around a dependency on heroin.

'What I want,' I said at last, 'is to go back to the way I used before. Once or twice a month, you know.'

Alfie gave me a withering look. 'Otherwise known as having your cake and fucking eating it.'

'Not long ago that's exactly what I was doing.'

'That was then. But once you've got a habit, you ain't going back to using the way you was before. Trust me, Student. Them days are gone. The switch in your brain's been flicked. It's all or nothing now, mate.'

I felt like someone who, thirsting to death, had been informed the precious water source he'd discovered was poisoned.

Alfie explained that if I indeed intended to overcome my habit and live without opiates, I'd need to let the cluck run its course. This would mean enduring a grisly fortnight of withdrawal. 'Except it'll get worse, much worse,' he said with what seemed like relish. 'Oh, and you can forget about sleeping till it's all over too.'

When Alfie left, I felt profoundly alone. I longed to throw myself on someone – my parents, Rana, Emma, anyone – and beg for their protection and care. But of course this wasn't something I could discuss with my mother or father. It had been some time since I'd spoken to Emma, who was studying in Leeds and for all I knew still happily in love with Jack. And with Rana I'd exchanged only a few online messages. I considered calling one of my uni friends and confessing everything, but pride stopped me. How could I admit I'd been foolish enough to believe I was immune to the well-known effects of a notoriously dangerous drug – and that the all but inevitable had happened?

So I had a further motive to accept my mother's offer to fly me out to the Middle East that summer. By physically removing myself from temptation, I'd break my habit before it broke me. I paid Alfie £50 for a large bottle of methadone with which I planned to wean myself off heroin in the Holy Land. When, shortly before my visit, war broke out between Israel and Hezbollah, I barely gave a second thought to the Foreign Office no-fly warning. I had too much riding on this trip: everything had to change, and in Israel-Palestine I would change no less than everything. The sense of boundless potential I felt as I set off for Luton Airport the morning of my flight was tempered only by the anxious thought of the 200ml of unprescribed methadone in my suitcase. Perhaps my elation had been bolstered by the enormous hit of smack I'd taken before setting off. But what was the harm in that – since after all it would be the Very Last Time?

All my hotel room lights were on as, outside, dusk fell over Palestine. A porter knocked on the door, and after tipping him I unscrewed the cap of the second bottle of whisky and took a swig, no longer bothering with coke. I placed my notebook on the desk, which overlooked a walled garden of snapdragon and almond trees. Perhaps it had boosted my morale to resist calling Jamal, or maybe there was some alchemy in the seemingly unpromising combination of methadone and booze. Either way, I felt galvanised. I had an overpowering urge to write – but about what?

I looked out the window, beyond the garden, over the West Bank's settlements, towards the distant hills beyond Jericho. Out there was an apparently intractable conflict pitting reason against dogma, moderation against zealotry. And I thought I saw a familiar logic in the way each side obsessively traced the sequence of outrage backwards to prove the other was to blame. *You razed our olive groves. But you fired a rocket. But you took our land. But you tried to destroy us. But you tried to destroy us.* A surge of powerful lucidity ran through me. My parents and Rana had the Word, but I had words; they had their Book, but I had books – to read and perhaps even to write. Now, with a burst of energy, I wrote:

With Enemies Like These: Conflict in Israel and Palestine

It was, undeniably, a good title. I felt sure it pointed to a profound truth. I simply had to discover what it was. Letting my cigarette hang from my lower lip in a way that seemed to me tremendously literary, I wrote:

The trouble with the Israeli–Palestinian conflict is that both sides

It was a shame I didn't have a hat – a beaten-up old fedora, for instance. The room tilted like a storm-lashed ship. I crossed out my first sentence and started again:

Those who wish to understand why peace between Israelis and Palestinians has proven so elusive must first of all understand that neither side

Then there was a banging at the door and a charring smell. Feeling seasick, I realised someone was shouting my name. The room righted itself and I saw my cigarette had fallen and burned across several inches of carpet. On my notebook's page was written:

The trouble with the Israeli–Palestinian conflict is that both sides

Those who wish to understand why peace between Israelis and Palestinians has proven so elusive must first of all understand that neither side

Those who wish to understand why peace in the Middle East has proven so elusive could do worse than to heed the words of the great Israeli author Amos Oz, who

Those who wish to understand why peace in the Middle East has proven so elusive could do worse than to heed the words of the great Palestinian author Edward Said, who

Those who wish

The trouble with the

I answered the door to Rana. Stepping inside, she wrinkled her nose and made a show of waving air from her face. 'Wow, so I guess you started smoking.'

I shrugged.

'So look,' she said. 'Me and Todd were thinking of heading into Jerusalem for the evening. Want to come?'

'*Todd*!' I said, almost expectorating his name. I stared at her as if I'd posed a searching question. Then I felt my eyes closing and when I opened them again the floor was rushing towards me. It slammed into my face.

'Matt! Are you ok?'

I opened my mouth to say yes, but the sound that emerged was somewhere between a whine and a sob.

'Can you stand up?' She helped me to my feet before leading me to the bed, where we both sat down.

'Matt, *habibi*. We're old friends. You know you can talk to me, right? What's going on?'

'I'm doing just fine, Rana, honestly. Or if you want that in American, I'm, like, *awesome*!'

'Have you been drinking?'

My first instinct was to deny it, but there were two empty bottles of whisky on my desk. I respected Rana far too much to lie to her so ineptly. I resolved that if I ever succeeded in detaching her from Todd, I'd honour her by telling only the most watertight lies.

'Look, Rana, I've had a few drinks, sure. But that's not fell over why now I just.'

For a moment, she looked perplexed. 'So why did you fall over?'

'Jetlag?' I said, like a gambler making wild bets while his chips rapidly disappeared.

'But the flight's only five hours, Matt.'

'Look, my body's actually very sensitive to time zone changes.' I was pleased to hear myself utter a sentence whose words were in the correct order, but Rana looked embarrassed for us both.

'No, I totally get that. I'm sorry,' she said, placing an assuaging hand on my arm. 'I was just worried about you for a minute back there.'

'I understand.' I drew her into a forgiving hug. 'So where are we going?'

'Huh?'

'In Jerusalem. Me, you and Todd.'

'Matt, do you think that's a good idea? You don't want to take a rest, get some sleep? Jerusalem will still be there tomorrow.'

'Rana, I've come halfway around the world to see you. We've started on the wrong foot this evening. Let's just go out for a few drinks, and—'

'I thought you came for the convention?'

'Yeah, I mean, obviously that's the main reason. But would I have come if I didn't think you'd be here too? To be honest, probably not. I've missed you.'

She smiled. 'You're sweet, even if you're slurring your words and you smell like an ashtray.'

'I'll jump in the shower, freshen up a bit. Then I'll meet you guys down in the lobby in, like, thirty minutes?'

'Ok, you convinced me,' she said, with a tone of ironic reproach. 'But I want you to behave yourself this evening, ok mister? And please be nice to Todd. He's a great guy and he's very special to me.'

'Of course. I can't wait to get to know him properly.'

In the American Colony Hotel bar, the ceiling light shimmered like tinsel on Todd's scalp. He was explaining that he worked at a joint US–Israeli firm in the finance sector, just outside Tel Aviv. As often as he could, he travelled up to Haifa Baptist Church to worship the Lord.

I glanced at Rana, rolling my eyes in derision. She stared back blankly.

'And what about you?' Rana said to me. 'Do you still go to church?'

'Oh, sure. Religiously. Ha!' I said. 'Does anyone want another drink?'

Rana's large, dark eyes expressed several layers of concern. 'Matt. Don't tell me you lost your faith?'

I was flummoxed. For some reason it had never occurred to me that smart, spirited Rana would still be subject to the filial brainwashing I knew all too well. 'Don't tell me you kept yours?'

The heartbroken look on her face answered my question. 'Oh, Matt. That's so sad, I'm sorry.' She clasped my hand tightly in hers. 'I remember you getting baptised like it was yesterday. You were so passionate about doing the Lord's work.'

'Well, that was a long time ago.'

She was staring disconsolately across the room. 'I just never thought—'

'I'm going to get a drink. Anyone else for one?'

At the bar I downed two fortifying shots of vodka, adding another to my Guinness, before returning with three glasses.

Evidently not yet ready to change the subject, Rana said, 'So now you're, like, what? An actual – unbeliever?'

'An actual unbeliever, the real thing,' I said, attempting to inject some energy into the conversation, even if merely in the form of sarcastic merriment. 'A backslider, an infidel. Whatever people like you call people like me. The Prodigal Son. Hell-fodder.'

Todd, who'd been listening in silence, shifted uncomfortably in his seat.

'*Khallas*, Matt,' said Rana. 'Some things you don't joke about.' She took a sip of her new drink, leaving her previous one half-finished. 'Can you help me understand something? So one day you just wake up and walk away from everything your mother and father have taught you to believe since, like, forever? How does that happen?'

It was a sincere question, so I tried to answer it sincerely. I began telling her about the slow hollowing out of my faith, about my terror of accepting I no longer believed. I wanted to give an articulate description of my adolescent turmoil. But as Rana listened I saw myself through the lens of her certainty as the embodiment of everything she'd been taught to pity about unbelievers: a confused man slurring confusedly into his pint about his spiritual confusion.

I finished my drink in one long draught and stood up to make my way back to the bar. But then time buckled and bent, and I found myself sitting down again as Todd told me:

'Essentially, it's an equity crowdfunding technology that links up accredited financiers and pre-vetted startups alongside the usual venture capitalists and angel investors.' He shrugged, running a finger gently along his abdominal muscles and sipping his drink with his other hand. I understood he was telling me that such worldly matters were ultimately no big deal, but also that in a strictly worldly sense he was as humbled as I must be by his self-evident talent and success.

'We're just getting started really, but we've already channelled over 800 million into everything from biotech to security to AI.'

'Anyone for another drink?' *Maybe a pint of battery acid?*

Ignoring me, Rana said, 'Tell Matt about the political side of it.' On the table were three glasses of Guinness. Todd's was half full, Rana's was three quarters full. Mine was empty, streaked with rusty brown foam.

Todd beamed. 'That's the *best thing*. Because it's not just Israeli firms we're working with. We're moving into the Palestinian sector too. Until now, Israeli venture capital has seen the conflict as a threat to their investment portfolios. If there's a new Intifada, the economy takes a hit and their stocks tank, right? But we want to show them that the Palestinians aren't a threat – they're an emerging market, an untapped labour pool and potentially a high-return investment opportunity.'

I decided it was time to put an end to this inane nonsense with a fusillade of eloquence and insight. 'The trouble with the Israeli–Palestinian conflict,' I said, and then the room seemed to swing upward and time stumbled and blurred, and everything was colour and light and noise.

Then I was outside, smoking a cigarette while Rana waited with folded arms. 'No, no, no,' she was saying. 'It's not like that! Todd's practically my *brother*. Oh my gosh, I couldn't even *imagine—*'

Then, though I couldn't recall deciding to do so, I became aware that I'd shut my eyes and was leaning towards Rana's face. I kept listing until I stumbled forward. When I opened my eyes again, she was standing several feet away with a look of benign amusement. 'Listen Matt. It's just – look, I had no idea – and I'm flattered, honestly – but what you need isn't my love—'

'Ok, I get it.'

'What you need—'

'Honestly, Rana, I understand.'

'What you need is *God's* love, Matt! There's nothing I can do for you that God won't gladly give you.'

Instead of replying, I reminded myself there are some things you don't joke about.

'You know, the Prodigal Son made it home in the end. Jesus said that whoever knocks on the door—'

'*It shall be opened unto him.* Matthew 7 verse 7. I know.'

'Have you ever tried just, you know, knocking? We could do that right now. Do you want to pray with me, Matt?'

I browned out again and, when lucidity returned, Rana was staring into the middle distance. '*He died*,' she said under her breath.

'Sorry, what?'

'That's what *Matt* means in Arabic: *he died*.'

More time passed and we were in a cab on our way back to Bethlehem. I could feel the alcohol coursing through my blood and I was singing an old Welsh hymn.

'BREAD OF HEAVEN, BREAD OF HEAVEN, FEED ME NOW AND EVERMOOOOORE!'

We stopped, the driver opened his window, and I continued singing while a red-haired IDF soldier several years my junior inspected our car. When he stood up to speak into a walkie-talkie, Rana whispered, 'Matt, are you crazy? Do you want to get us all shot?'

The soldier asked me something in Hebrew. 'WHEN I TREAD THE VERGE OF JORDAN, BID MY ANXIOUS FEARS SUBSIDE!' I sang by way of response. Rana elbowed me in the ribs and spoke mollifyingly to him. Then I looked down and saw I was holding my passport.

'BE THOU STILL MY STRENGTH AND SHIELD!' I sang, handing it to him.

Then Rana and Todd were helping me into bed . . . I was pissing in the bathroom sink . . . I was shouting into the hotel telephone handset . . . 'No more room service, no more room service,' the voice on the line was saying.

Then I was outside the hotel, powerfully conscious in the eucalyptus-scented air. Crickets were singing and my feet were cold. I looked down and noticed my left shoe was missing. I tried to replay the evening in my mind, tried to understand why I was standing here, but all I could summon was a jumble of broken images, like spilled jigsaw pieces. My head was pounding and I was thirstier than I'd ever been in my life. When a car turned the corner up the street, the glare of its headlights made my eyeballs ache.

The yellow taxi cab stopped before me. The driver's window was lowered and a brawny arm appeared.

A slightly hoarse voice called out: 'In, in.' Recognising Jamal, the driver from this afternoon, I climbed through the passenger door. As I took my seat I recalled why I was here, and was filled with a sense of giddy purpose.

'My friend,' said Jamal seriously. 'Why you call me? Is late, very late.' He pointed to his dashboard clock, which read 01.37.

'Jamal,' I said, in an equally earnest voice. 'I need you to help me. Will you help me?'

He nodded wearily. 'I help, I help.'

'Look, I'm writing an article. An article, yes? About the Israeli–Palestinian conflict. And I've decided to look at the drugs angle.'

He stared at me blankly.

'Do you understand? I'm a writer, a journalist, investigating the flow of illegal drugs – drugs, yes? – into the Palestinian territories. Into Palestine.'

'Palestine,' said Jamal, uncertainly.

'Do you understand what I'm saying?'

'You want to buy drug?'

'Yes, drugs, drugs. For research. For writing. You know *writing*?'

He nodded decisively, miming the word with a scribbling motion. 'You want to buy drug for to help writing?'

'Well, no, not really. But in a way. Whatever. Yeah, sure. So I need you to help me buy heroin. *Heroin*, right?'

'*Heroin*.' His look of distaste indicated he knew exactly what the word meant.

'Yes, heroin. If you help me, I help you,' I said, opening my wallet to reveal a thick wedge of Israeli shekels.

Jamal gave me a thoughtful look. Then he patted my knee reassuringly. 'We are friend. I help you.'

As Jamal eased into first gear, I sank back in my seat. We trundled quietly into a deserted central Bethlehem, past the Church of the Nativity. The ghostly eyes of a cat, one of the countless strays that wandered the streets out here, flashed in the car's headlights before it leapt out of our path.

Now that the prospect of getting high was in view, I couldn't fathom why I'd been so depressed earlier. Who cared if my parents preferred to waste their lives on their deranged beliefs and interminable fighting? And Rana – well, if losing my faith meant that to her I might as well have died, then she was right: I didn't need her love. When I made it back to the hotel with the smack, I'd get straight to work on 'With Enemies Like These'. Every word I needed already existed out there somewhere. All I had to do was capture each one in turn, like impaling butterflies on pins.

We now seemed to be heading down a wide, cypress-lined avenue in a well-off suburb of Bethlehem. There were large stone houses with wrought iron balconies and well-tended gardens. Even under the Occupation there were, evidently, winners and losers. But looking over at Jamal with a rush of gratitude that bordered on passion, I felt our implicit affinity meant it was *we* who'd won. What we shared transcended differences of wealth, power, nation, even language.

Feeling talkative, I offered him a cigarette and held my lighter under it as he steered. 'So, Jamal, tell me. Is your family from around here? From Bethlehem?'

'My family is refugee family,' he said. 'From Yaffa. In Yaffa, before Nakba, my family has many lands. Many, many lands. Now, all gone.'

I felt genuinely moved. I patted him reassuringly on the knee. 'One day, Jamal, this terrible conflict will be over and the Palestinian people will be free. I really believe that.'

'Yes,' he said. 'Palestine, free. *Inshallah.*'

'The trouble with the Israeli–Palestinian conflict,' I began, but then the car thudded over a large pothole, banked and lurched, causing me to lose my thread. Now I noticed we'd entered a different kind of urban landscape. Here the buildings were arranged haphazardly along the street, which was little more than a dirt path spouting clumps of grass. Instead of central Bethlehem's graffiti of stylised English peace slogans there were spray-painted Arabic words in green, red and black. Electricity poles spewed tangled arteries of multicoloured wires. As our headlights raked the sides of buildings I saw peeling posters of keffiyeh-clad *shuhuda*, national martyrs.

'Where are we?' I said, aiming to sound curious rather than nervous.

'This, Deisheh. Is refugee camp.' The car slowed to a crawl, the tyres churning over gravel. 'You are religion?'

Was there some special significance to this question, I wondered with a spasm of anxiety, or was Jamal simply making small talk? All of a sudden it seemed crucial to retain his sympathy. But would that aim be best served by professing devout belief, even in a God other than his own? I gambled on honesty. 'Me? I don't have a religion.'

'You are not religion?'

'I'm not religious, no. I'm an atheist.'

'A-theist,' he said, rolling the word around his mouth like the pit of an olive. 'Me? I am Muslim, thanks God.' He brought the car to a halt before a two-storey breeze-block building with an outside ladder leading to a flat roof. A washing line ran from the house to a pole mounted in a yard where thistles grew from cracks in the asphalt. He shut off the engine and climbed out of the car.

'Jamal, where—'

'*Shh*,' he said, putting his finger to his lips and motioning for me to follow him.

He opened the door with a key and held it open for me with a ceremony that seemed to satirise our mission.

We entered a lounge lit by a bare bulb, the air heavy with lavender musk. Into the small room were crammed an armchair, a PVC couch and a varnished wooden coffee table. On the wall hung a gilt-framed black-and-white photo of a wire-moustached man, the family patriarch perhaps. His outfit, the evening wear of an Edwardian Englishman, recalled the tailcoat I'd worn for chapel at boarding school. Everything was extremely neat and clean – the short row of books on the shelf above the fireplace, the chintzy coasters stacked on the table – except for the wall plaster, which was cracked and crumbling.

'Now,' said Jamal in a half-whisper. 'Money. Please.'

'How much?'

He clenched his jaw. 'Five hundred shekel.'

It was a shamelessly unfair price, but I knew there was no point haggling. With a bitter sense that the true nature of our relationship had been laid bare, I counted the notes and handed them over.

'Now, wait,' he said. 'Sit, sit.'

I did as I was told. Already he seemed to have dropped the *my-friend* schtick. With a manic air he strode out of the room.

Alone now, and increasingly sober, I began to question the wisdom of coming to a refugee camp at 2am to find hard drugs with a man who was, in truth, a perfect stranger to me. My earlier euphoria had burned itself out and been replaced by its opposite: dread. A westerner who'd come here with the sole aim of stimulating the local drugs trade would, I suspected, be far from popular with many of the locals. I wondered for a moment whether the fact that I'd read a number of Edward Said's books would help my case, and decided this was unlikely. Hearing Jamal speaking upstairs, I presumed on the phone, I wondered what on earth had led me to believe that his true loyalty lay with me. Exactly as with Hebrew, conversations in Arabic sounded to me like bitter quarrels. I tried to amuse myself with the thought of my mother negotiating a ransom with a group of hostage takers: *Now I'm just about at my wit's end with you! Either you give me a half-price deal or I'm walking away!*

But my reserves of levity were beginning to run dry.

Jamal seemed to be shouting down the phone now. Yes, there was no denying it: coming here had been an idiotic move. The Jacir Palace, where my parents and Rana were all surely fast asleep on duck-feather pillows, now seemed almost exotically safe, a fortress of luxury and contentment. In England, trying to score had led me into a number of risky situations – they came with the territory and were a part of the excitement – but this was undoubtedly the most stupid and dangerous thing I'd ever done. I considered walking out and making a run for it, but I had little sense of where I was, and no idea of how to find my way back to my hotel. I was beginning to think that the appearance of a squad of IDF soldiers, breaking down the door to arrest me for conspiring to buy illegal narcotics, wouldn't be such a terrible outcome at this stage – even if my hosts could be forgiven for feeling differently.

I felt an urge – both utterly alien and as familiar as my own pulse – to pray.

Now I became aware of a second, quieter voice upstairs. I heard two sets of footsteps before Jamal reentered the room, followed by a short woman swathed in blue from her headscarf to her ankles. She was rubbing her eyes and wearing a thin smile.

'This, my mother,' said Jamal.

'Your *mother?* Jamal, what the—'

The woman, looking at the floor, clasped her hands together and bowed. She said something to Jamal and soon – I was sure – they were arguing. It was only after some time that the blizzard of words raging between them began to subside. Now the woman stood silently with folded arms while her son kept saying, '*Walla ishi, ya mama. Walla ishi, ya mama.*'

Turning to me eventually, he said, 'I come back. You, wait.'

Then he left the house and slammed the door.

Jamal's mother stood awkwardly, pursing her lips. She spread her arms wide in a gesture I didn't understand but which may have meant *welcome to my home*. Then again, perhaps a more accurate translation would be: *what the hell are you doing in my home at 2am, you one-shoed maniac?* She limped heavily into the next room, turned on a light, pulled the door closed after her and began opening cupboards and rattling drawers.

There was nothing to do but sit and look back on one of the strangest days of my life. It had begun almost twenty-four hours ago with a flight from Luton airport and would end who knew when or how. Several times today I'd been cross-examined on my religious affiliation and beliefs. Few things could be more absurd, of course, than to travel to the world's epicentre of fanatical religion, to visit my religious parents at a religious event, only to be bothered by all the religion I'd come across. And yet I couldn't help being rankled by Rana's response to my profession of unbelief, or what I could recall of it. I'd thought I was immune to feeling hurt by judgement from Christians. After all, the child-like desire to please my mother and father was just one part of myself I'd been forced to amputate in order to survive my loss of faith (*if thy right hand offend thee, cut it off*). Rana had asked how I'd woken up one day and simply walked away from everything I'd ever been taught – as though led by whimsy or vanity. If only it had been so easy! Why hadn't I told her that I still sometimes had nightmares about burning in hell, waking up terrified it was all true?

The door to the kitchen opened and the woman emerged with a tray bearing a number of small bowls: hummus with chickpeas and oil-drenched zatar, sumac-spiced onions, glistening black olives. I watched, bewildered, as she set them down and gestured for me to eat. I stared at the food, my stomach shrivelled by anxiety. I'd never felt less hungry in my life. What could this early-hours ritual of Middle-Eastern hospitality mean for my predicament? Would Jamal have drummed his mother out of bed to fix me a snack if he'd been planning on turning me over to Hamas? Was there some obscure Arabic tradition by which one was obliged to feed a man before executing him? Bowing in a gesture of thanks, I forked some hummus into my mouth.

I'd barely made a dent in the first course when, with horror, I watched her arrive with another tray. This one was filled with plates containing babaganoush, stuffed courgettes and grilled squash sprinkled with pine nuts. Then she limped back to the kitchen, I feared to continue cooking. I choked down as much food as I could, wondering whether Jamal's protracted absence – he'd been gone well over half an hour now – was a good or bad sign.

The woman piled up the half-full bowls and carried them out to the kitchen, waving away my offer of help. Then she returned and I watched desperately as she laid out dessert: sesame cakes and sticky baklava plus cardamom-spiced coffee. I thought she saw my look of despair, and could almost swear I noticed her grin sadistically. But every time I tried to catch a further glimpse of her face she was wearing a fixed expression of humble duty. I placed some glazed pastry in my mouth.

As I chewed miserably, my thoughts returned to Rana. The trouble with religious fundamentalists was that they didn't understand unbelievers could be every bit as sincere as they were. If only we'd take the question of faith seriously, they thought, we'd surely see the self-evident truth of their claims. *Have you ever tried just, you know, knocking?* she'd said. Why hadn't I told her that my whole adolescence had been one long plea for God to rescue me from doubt? The question wasn't whether I'd ever knocked, but whether I'd ever stopped knocking for a moment during those years. I'd knocked until my knuckles were raw, until my fist was bloody. I'd knocked and knocked and knocked—

Then the door opened and Jamal barged in. He was alone, which was an excellent sign, and I was additionally encouraged by the fact that he looked as nervous as I felt.

'*Yalla*,' he said. 'We go.'

I jumped to my feet. Bowing to his mother, I bolted for the door before she could torture me with any further hospitality.

Back in the car, Jamal showed me an open palm. 'Five hundred shekel.'

'Are you serious?' I said. 'I just paid you five hundred.'

He stared levelly at me. 'Is more.'

I sighed, opened my wallet, handed him the notes. When he'd counted the money, he reached into his pocket, passed me a plastic parcel, and started the engine.

With the drugs in my hand a wave of exhilaration passed over me, immediately drowning my resentment over the money and Jamal's long absence. The dashboard clock read 03.57. It had taken several hours, but I'd succeeded in scoring in this most unpromising of places. I looked over at Jamal as he concentrated on driving, resisting the urge to lean over and hug him.

'Jamal, my friend,' I said. 'I really think one day Palestine will be free. Maybe one day soon. I really do think that.'

'*Inshallah, inshallah.*'

My eyes were slightly wet. 'We just need to pull together. Ordinary Palestinians like you will be a key part of the movement. I'm talking protests, strikes, nonviolent resistance of all kinds. There'll have to be sacrifices. We're all going to have to make sacrifices.'

He just kept on driving.

'But with the backing of people like me – you know, the global intelligentsia, for want of a better word – we can do incredible things. Historic things, Jamal. We can put an end to this terrible conflict once and for all.'

He nodded wearily. I wondered if I saw a flicker of impatience in his eyes, but decided he was probably just tired.

We passed slowly down a street that ran between two low walls topped with barbed wire. I realised I should have asked Jamal's mother for some cooking foil in order to smoke the heroin. I'd have no choice but to find some pretext for waking the Jacir Palace kitchen staff. This thought sent a jolt of anticipation through me, and although I knew it was bad etiquette to inspect the drugs before leaving one's dealer, my excitement got the better of me. Without removing the parcel from my pocket, I peeled it open slightly, careful to catch any of the contents as they shook loose. A few grains spilled onto my fingers. I lifted my hand to my nose and inhaled a familiar smell.

Livid, I turned to Jamal. 'What the fuck is this? Is this weed? *Hashish*? Jamal, are you fucking with me?' I opened the parcel in my lap, revealing about an eighth of brownish marijuana leaves.

He looked at me and smiled scornfully. 'My friend.'

'Don't give me that *my friend* shit. I paid you a thousand fucking shekels. *A thousand shekels*. And this is what you bring me? An eighth of *weed*? I don't even *like* weed! Heroin, Jamal! Heroin! You understand, yes?'

He stared straight ahead.

'Turn the car around, please. I want to go back and get what I paid for. This is pure exploitation, Jamal! Do you understand? You're exploiting me!'

He took a deep breath, let out a long sigh, and brought the car to a halt. Keeping his hands on the wheel, he rested his head against his forearms for a moment, muttering under his breath in Arabic. Then he got out of the vehicle, marched around the bonnet, and opened my door.

'Out. Now,' he said.

I looked up at him. He wasn't tall, but his forearms were thick and cabled. 'Jamal,' I said. 'Look, don't be like that. All I'm saying—'

He leant down, grabbed my T-shirt in two hands and, with his face inches from mine, stared at me with fury in his eyes. 'OUT! OUT! OUT! OUT! OUT!' he roared. Spittle flecked my face.

Wretchedly, I obeyed. Jamal slammed the door shut, marched around the car, got in, reversed down the road and drove away. Shivering, I lit my penultimate cigarette. Over the distant hills, dawn was beginning to break in saffron streaks. Suddenly, the call to prayer blasted out over a loudspeaker, followed moments later by several other amplified muezzins, the air cacophonous with droning voices. Then there was a fizz of static followed by silence except for the barking of dogs.

There were rooftops and minarets in the near distance; I thought I could see the Church of the Nativity a mile or so away. Among these buildings somewhere was the Jacir Palace. The thought of my parents sent a howl of loneliness through me. Feeling desolately sober now, I saw that my mother and father hadn't been my pretext for coming to see Rana, as I'd thought. It was the other way around: Rana was how I'd concealed from myself the desire to reconcile with my parents. I'd pretended they mattered so little to me because they mattered so much. I'd hacked away the part of me that craved their approval – I knew I had, I could remember doing it – and yet here it was, regrown: ghastly, animate and irrepressible.

I was in a kind of layby. There were a few parked cars on this stretch of road but no buildings. The gently sloped street was strewn with mule dung and there were kerosene cans leaning against a wall. In the sky there was the kind of blood-dimmed moon that inescapably made me think of the Book of Revelations. The barking of dogs was being replaced by the first chirruping of bulbul birds. I lit my final cigarette and, with one bare foot, began trudging my way up the hill towards Bethlehem.

Rapture

It felt like the first morning of summer. Maria was sitting at the kitchen table, finishing her tea while I washed our breakfast things. Sunlight spliced through the window blinds and water rattled in the sink. When I looked out into the garden the world seemed to contain more space and colour than it had yesterday.

'You can't just do nothing.' said Maria. 'Why don't we at least get a few of your friends round for the evening?'

It was sweet of Maria to remember the date of my birthday, even though I was pretty sure I'd only mentioned it once in the six weeks we'd been living together. She had a way of remembering things. She knew I preferred milk in my cup before tea, teasing me for claiming this was a relic of my 'lower-middle-class' roots. She recalled the names of the unfamous towns in which I'd grown up. She remembered details about my family, even though it was only Jonathan I ever really saw these days, since my mother and father had moved to Nazareth and I was as good as estranged from my sisters.

Maria's memory, and the attentiveness it showed, stung me with a little arrow of guilt. I knew she'd been born in Gloucestershire in the same year as me, but I had no idea, come to think of it, when her birthday was. Some time in October, maybe?

'I just hate all that kind of shit,' I said, turning off the tap and making my way over to where she was sitting. 'You know, *occasions*. Birthdays, weddings, Christmas.'

'Wait. What have you got against *Christmas*?'

'Put it this way, I've noticed people tend to enjoy Christmas about as much as they enjoy spending time with their family. And parties just aren't the same these days – you know, now I'm clean.' I began telling Maria about the last birthday party I'd been to. I'd been getting high with Adam and Rose all day . . .

'These were your dealer friends?' said Maria, who wasn't fazed by my stories about drugs.

'They aren't really dealers. They're just other addicts. Their house is kind of what you'd call a crack den, in a way. They can help you get whatever you need, day or night. For a price, obviously.'

My stomach growled and a film of sweat prickled my skin. I needed to be alone soon. 'But hang on, don't you need to get to work?'

Maria glanced at her watch. 'It's fine, I've got ten minutes. I'm the only one at the office this morning, so I can be a bit late. When did you say this was?'

'Oh, I don't know. Around Easter, I guess.'

Maria looked thoughtful. 'Really? Easter?'

There was no need to panic. As long as she was gone in ten minutes, I'd be fine. I'd become expert at reading my body's distress signals. Things would start getting serious in about a quarter of an hour. I'd better tell her the story in a way that didn't arouse suspicion I was trying to hurry her out the door.

'So anyway, I'm getting high with Adam and Rose, and then I remember I'm supposed to be at this party for a girl I know from university. Private members' club. Full of media types and actors and lawyers. You can imagine.'

'Not really. Private members clubs aren't really my scene. Nor crack dens, for that matter.'

'Well anyway, I know this is going to be sort of a posh thing, basically. And Adam's a smackhead who's spent most of his adult life behind the door.'

'Behind the door?'

'In prison. So as I'm leaving, he says, *Wouldn't it be a laugh if I came too?*'

Maria began sweeping her things – phone, laptop, keys – into her rucksack. 'You've got five minutes to wrap this up.'

I know.

'So I run home and grab a pair of suit jackets. And we show up, both of us in a state, obviously. Somehow I manage to get us past the door staff. People are staring at Adam as soon as we're inside. But then he actually starts *mingling*. At one point I find him, this grizzled forty-year-old junkie, chatting up a pretty girl I remember from college. He's asking her what she does for a living, and she says, with a straight face, terribly polite, *I'm a senior speechwriter at the Foreign Office. And what do you do?* And he goes: *Well, I used to do burglaries, but these days I mostly just steal bikes and fiddle the Social, to be honest.*'

Maria pursed her lips. 'It sounds like you were taking the piss, if you ask me.'

I sipped my tea. 'Why? He was my plus-one. He had as much right to be there as anyone else.'

'I meant taking the piss out of Adam. You didn't really bring him as your friend, did you? You just wanted to have a laugh against your old uni crowd.'

'Oh, he was fine,' I said, a little irritated by the failure of my anecdote. 'There was a free bar, and I kept him supplied with drugs all night. He could've bought a membership for the club with all the money I've given him over the years anyway.'

'What I don't get's how you remember so much, considering you were high all the time.'

I had a few minutes before I started feeling extremely ill, but I was determined to act natural. The thing about heroin and crack, I explained, was that they didn't destroy your memory the way booze does. Sometimes I wished they did: there were whole years of my life I'd prefer not to remember. It was more that they scrambled the emotional signals memory depends on. Everything felt roughly the same. You could forget the most important things and have perfect recall for the smallest details.

Maria stood up, brushed some crumbs down her dungarees. 'Well, I'd better go.'

'Sorry. I keep holding you up.' *Please leave. Please leave.*

'Can I just ask you something? You said you went to this party at Easter.'

'Right.'

'It's May now. Which means I was living here then. So why were you hanging out with Adam?'

Aiming for a tone of light-hearted exasperation, I said, 'Look, I can't remember the exact date of every party I've been to. Not everyone has a perfect memory like you.'

'No, I guess not.' She chewed the inside of her mouth and looked down. 'But you've been clean three months now, right? Since that day in the pub?'

I swallowed. 'Um, right.'

She sighed. 'Ok, I'd better get to work. Good luck with the job hunt today.'

As soon as the front door clicked shut I sprinted up the stairs, removed the lid of the toilet cistern and grabbed the screwdriver I kept duct-taped to its underside. I unscrewed the bath panel behind which I kept my works. Withdrawal was already kicking in – my hands were shaking – so I had to move fast. When at last I pressed the plunger and the soul-stilling liquid was draining into my arm, I heard the front door open. I took a few deep breaths, letting the hit subside. The world was the right side up again. I composed myself and walked out of the bathroom.

Maria was at the foot of the stairs, staring up at me.

'Are you ok?' I said.

She screwed her eyes. 'I just left my purse on the kitchen table. Are *you* ok?'

'Me? I'm totally fine!'

Maria stared at me very intently for five, ten seconds.

'Ok, see you later,' she said eventually, turning around and shutting the door firmly behind her.

When I returned to the bathroom to clear up the mess, I saw in the mirror that my left arm was bleeding from the wound I'd just made with the needle. A dark bead of blood was running down my wrist onto the floor. In the reflection over my shoulder, I could see a thin red trickle leading back to the spot where moments ago I'd been standing at the top of the stairs.

Twenty minutes later I arrived at the cash machine on Kingsland Road. It was blustery and the pavement was sun-glittered. I entered my PIN, holding my breath as always.

YOU HAVE INSUFFICIENT FUNDS
TO CARRY OUT THIS TRANSACTION

So here it is, I thought to myself: the end. Amazing, really, that I'd managed to defer this moment for so long. The relief uncoiling in me was, I supposed, like that of a long-time fugitive who, seeing the blue lights closing in, accepts at last that the game is up.

Or almost – very almost – up. I decided I might as well call Armani and try scoring for the Very Last Very Last Time. I dimly recalled all the occasions I'd recited similar words to myself. But I was out of money. At last, thank God, abstinence would be forced on me by brute financial reality.

Armani answered after two rings. 'What you sayin', bruv?'

I'd never met Armani's current incarnation, though I spoke to him virtually every day. His gear was delivered by a revolving cast of teenage 'runners', few of whom I'd met more than once or twice.

'Armani, look,' I said. 'Can you do me a favour?'

I aimed to sound as relaxed as possible when I asked him to tick me one-fifty, as though I barely cared whether he agreed or not. I knew that, like all dealers, Armani had an official policy of no-tick-under-any-circumstances. But I also knew that, like all dealers, he granted unofficial exceptions on a case-by-case basis. I was a valued customer. He undoubtedly spent much of his time flogging one-and-one to beggars with handfuls of shrapnel. He'd be reluctant, I knew, to lose my fifty-to-a-hundred-a-day habit to a rival dealer.

'One-fifty? Bruh, why you even askin' me that? That ain't a ting.'

I explained I meant a hundred and fifty pounds, not one pound fifty.

He grew quiet. 'That's bare *p*s, fam.'

'You know I'm good for it. It's just a cash flow thing. I'll pay you by noon tomorrow.'

In the ensuing pause I could hear my heart beating like a snare drum.

'Twelve tomorrow, yeah? Swear down?'

'I swear.'

'Corner of the park,' he said at last. 'Fifteen minutes.'

Relief percolated through me. I figured that, of all the deceptions I'd perpetrated lately, depriving Armani of a fraction of the cash I'd given him over the years would be among the less grave.

*

The strange thing was that I'd asked Maria to come and live with me in part because, from our first meeting, I'd felt unable to lie to her. Not long after graduating and moving to London, I was at a house party in Clapton, queuing for the toilet next to a waifish young woman of about my own age. She had an asymmetrical smile and black, self-cut hair. Bad music pounded from a speaker in the next room, and we cradled plastic cups of blue-green liquid from a giant bowl in the kitchen. In response to her comment about the drink's 'sinister' taste, I blurted out how attractive I found her. Then I admitted I had a girlfriend, immediately regretting this attack of honesty. She seemed to view my gaucheness with a kind of ironic charity, but made it clear she had no interest in getting involved with someone who was in a relationship. Still, over the next thirty minutes, while the queue shuffled around us, our conversation – about the tedium of adolescence in small English towns – flowed easily, and she seemed to have a rare sincerity that was especially concentrated in her warm laugh. When she left, she gave me her number, and told me to maybe call her some time for what she pointedly called a 'friendly catchup'.

From then on we met for a drink once or twice a year, and each time I found myself disclosing things I'd told nobody else. Around other people I tried to impersonate someone who had an answer for all the important questions. But Maria's natural manner helped me drop the act. We'd sit together in an alcoved beer garden, or by a fireplace in a

Victorian saloon with frescoed ceilings, and confessions would tumble out of us: about our anxieties over work and career, our issues with this girlfriend or that boyfriend, our complex families and growing distance from them. We'd have two drinks, maybe three – enough, I felt, to bathe our time together in a faint agony of wistfulness – and then she'd say it was time to go.

'You know, I hardly ever drink except with you,' she said one time. 'Our catch-ups are the closest thing I ever get to debauchery.'

I laughed. 'These chats are the closest thing I ever get to *therapy*.'

I'd never tried the real thing, despite the urgings of my brother. Jonathan claimed his work with a 'psychodynamic counsellor' was helping him come to terms with his loss of faith, his identity as an ex-Christian gay man, his imposter syndrome in his work as a TV and film composer. He pressed on me books with names like *Inside Lives*, *The Examined Life* and *Lives Transformed*.

'Why can't the people who write this navel-gazing crap at least come up with a new title?' I said one time when he came to visit me at home. Not long after graduating, George Mentmore and I had moved together into 29 Belgrade Road, a two-bed flat in Dalston we filled with second-hand furniture and the bric-a-brac George specialised in sourcing from charity shops. Jon was sitting on my battered green Chesterfield sofa, and I was leaning against the bookshelves I'd made out of bricks and painted floorboards, which covered most of one wall of my room. 'You'd learn more from reading *Crime and Punishment* or *Jekyll and Hyde* than this stuff. You know, proper books. Anyway, maybe it's your idea of fun to sit around moaning about how Mummy and Daddy argued too much and didn't have time for your needs. But it's not mine.'

My brother rehearsed his usual argument: that all I'd done was replace one faith, one canon, for another. 'Words in a book are just words, Matt. You're not supposed to revere them, you're supposed to relate them to your life. Have you ever noticed you're only comfortable discussing the inner worlds of fictional people? Do you realise you never talk about your feelings?'

'*Please*. I talk about my feelings all the time.'

'I don't mean that thing you do when you come out with obnoxious comments just to provoke people. Emotional honesty isn't the same as being tactless, you know.'

'Look, here's some emotional honesty for you. I want to move on from Christianity, God, all that bullshit – not spend years wallowing in it. Ok?'

What I didn't tell Jonathan was that I could hardly afford to follow his advice. After graduating I'd worked for a while as a hotel night porter, a minimum wage job that came with minimum responsibilities: all I had to do was sit there from 11pm until 7am. I'd planned on using the time to write a novel about a man who finds love while brokering peace in the Middle East. But after nine months I hadn't completed a page, and my Vitamin D levels felt as depressingly low as my bank balance. More and more I found myself falling into old, dangerous habits. I needed a change. So I quit and, in a panic, applied for every position on the Jobs page of the *Hackney Gazette*. I turned up to the only interview I was offered, accepted the role a few days later, and became a careers advisor at Holloway & City Community College. Now I spent all day advising teenagers and adult learners on how to pursue their dreams, meanwhile wondering what mine were, or if I had any.

'So you're telling me you've become a careers advisor because you have no idea what to do for a career?' asked Maria archly the next time we met. We were in an Irish boozer, solo men tending pints along the bar, dog racing on overhead screens. In the background there was the thud of a dartboard and the noise of men calling out scores.

'The irony of the situation isn't lost on me. Anyway, in a way I think I'm a good example to the students. Of what *not* to do with your life.'

'What's so wrong with your life?' she said, wiping foam from her upper lip. 'I can think of worse things than being a careers advisor.'

And then it came out. That I was worried about how much time and money I'd been spending lately on – well, a certain drug.

'You're doing too much coke? Pills?'

'Actually, it's, uh, heroin.'

'Wow. Ok.'

I explained I wasn't a full-blown addict. At least I didn't think so, not yet. I'd run into a spot of trouble with my using at university, but since then I'd managed to restrict it to no more than, say, once a week.

Her eyes widened. 'Wait. You're taking heroin every week?'

'I mean, not *every* week. I go through periods where I quit, and I don't touch the stuff for months. But it has a way of pulling you back in. Famously, I guess.'

Curiosity and concern vied on her face. 'What's it like?'

I considered the pointlessness of trying to describe the effects of a drug like smack to someone who'd never taken it, so I settled on a cliché. 'It feels like *heaven*.'

She looked thoughtful. 'That's weird. Last time I saw you, you were complaining about your parents' obsession with heaven. I remember exactly what you told me. You said, *I don't want to live in some other world. I want to live in this one, right here.*'

The men around the dartboard broke out in cheers. I glanced over at them. 'Bullseye,' I said.

I saw Maria only twice more before she moved in with me. The first time, sheets of rain were falling outside the windows of the smart hipster bar we'd chosen. Taxidermy hung from the walls, moody hip hop played from speakers, and the staff were better looking than any of the customers. My news wasn't good. Over the last year my using had crossed an invisible boundary from *recreational* to *medical*. Now I needed heroin every day. My habit had proven incompatible with a nine-to-five job, but the Community College had been so keen to get rid of me they'd paid me off with a generous redundancy package. I was living on that as well as any scraps of casual work I could find.

Maria, meanwhile, was in an entirely different kind of mess. She was in a broken relationship with a man she'd agreed to marry. Virtually all her money was tied up in the house they'd bought together.

'Wait, you bought a house with this guy? How did that happen?'

'Well, sometimes things just start, and then they keep going, and then they cross a certain line. And you don't realise where you are until it's too late.'

I chuckled grimly. 'I hear you.'

There wasn't much we could do for each other, but as always I was overtaken with almost physical relief by the opportunity to tell Maria the unalloyed truth. In the street I hugged her goodbye before watching her walk off under a black umbrella.

The next time I saw her, our plan to save each other was hatched. She explained that the situation at home was untenable. She had to leave and figure out what to do with the house later. She only had a few thousand pounds in a joint account with her partner; she'd have to withdraw her share and find somewhere new to live. For the first time since I'd met her, Maria seemed genuinely distressed.

When the conversation turned to me, perhaps feeling licensed by her low mood, I held nothing back. My using had grown so bad that George had asked me to move out, I said. He was making plans to leave town himself, as though my presence had cursed not just our home but the whole of London with some dark narcotic spell.

It was no surprise, really. After that last time with Alfie, I'd spent years smoking heroin from tinfoil, but lately financial necessity had sent me back to what junkies called 'the pin'. Ronnie, an Italian guy who slept outside the local KFC, had taught me how to carry out the delicate procedure. Injecting felt like a neat, efficient surgical operation to excise my ever-present misery and self-loathing. And it was a remarkable economy. It made smack three times stronger, and my addiction three times cheaper – at first. But tolerance was infinitely elastic, and I could see mine growing rapidly. If I wasn't careful, soon I'd have swapped an expensive smoking habit for an equally expensive – but far more dangerous – needle habit. It didn't help that Ronnie had introduced me to crack too, which doubled the bliss and the turmoil and the expense.

'So George is sick of finding needles on the bathroom floor, he's sick of me bringing people back to the flat who steal things. Once or twice he's even had to call an ambulance when I've overdosed.'

'Matt, this is terrifying. I can't believe this is your life.'

Anyway, I'd left for now, I said. I was subletting my room, which provided me enough cash to maintain my addiction, especially since I was living rent-free with Sinead.

'Sinead?'

Sinead was, well, my girlfriend, in a way. She was a corporate lawyer who had a taste for partying. We'd met six months ago and, from that evening, when I'd pulled out my crack pipe and explained to her what it was, she'd made it her mission to help me get clean. She was convinced she could achieve this if I lived under her roof, so when George and I fell out I'd moved in with her. It wasn't long before I discovered she had a fairly serious drinking problem of her own. More often than not she'd come home late from work to find me using drugs – with *her* money. She'd lent me her card and told me I could use it in 'emergencies', a word whose definition I'd stretched to its limit.

'And she knows?' said Maria. 'About the card and the money?'

'She knows, sure. But at the same time, she doesn't. People see what they want to see, right? But basically she knows, yeah. She's pretty loaded. She puts up with it. Like I say, she thinks she's helping me.'

'What a nightmare.'

'But here's the worst part. After she gets home and finishes having a go at me, more and more often she joins in. So I came to her to try and get rid of my habit, but if I'm not careful soon there'll be two of us with one.'

She looked at me, startled. 'Jesus, Matt. You have to—'

'Get the fuck out of there, I know.' The conversation was leaving me in need of a morale-booster. I excused myself to the bathroom, wondering if Maria knew what I was going there to do. When I returned, there was no sign she had any idea. It only occurred to me later that this was the first time I'd hidden something from her.

'So it looks like we're both kind of stuck,' I said.

'You and Sinead?'

'No. Well, yeah, but – I meant me and you.'

The minutes after a hit of crack always filled me with a gorgeous lucidity. It felt as though the universe had rolled over and presented itself to me like a pet to be stroked. That was when I arrived at the plan I'd later come to see as absolute insanity, even by my standards.

George was no longer really speaking to me, but he'd agreed that when he moved out I could reoccupy my bedroom and find someone to fill his. That was in four weeks. So if Maria could survive another month with her partner, she could take the spare room in the flat. The rent wasn't much.

'That's sweet, Matt. But look – no judgement here at all – I don't think I can live with someone who's using.'

I'd have plenty of time to reflect on the gap between how easy my next words were to say and how hard they were to execute: 'I'll stop.'

'Just like that?'

'I'll get a methadone prescription, and I'll wean myself off. It'll be two weeks of hell, but it's nothing I haven't been through before. It's not like I've got a job to go to now, is it? By the time you arrive, I'll be good as new.'

'But what'll stop you from going back to it?'

'You'll ask me,' I said, leaning back in my chair. The crack still blanching through me, I felt I'd struck on a brilliant solution. The problem with Sinead, I said, was that she didn't *require* me to lie. She just asked me if I'd been using and I told her the truth. She got angry, but five minutes later she poured herself a drink and forgave me.

'You're different,' I said to Maria. 'I've never been able to keep anything from you. If I use drugs, I'll be putting you in an impossible position. I couldn't do that.'

I needed so badly for what I was saying to make sense that, in that moment, I allowed myself to believe it did.

'So I'll just have to stay clean. I'll do it for you. We'll be doing each other a favour.'

Perhaps Maria was infected with my crack-fuelled optimism. Perhaps she was even more desperate than I'd guessed. Perhaps, like mine, her feelings ran deeper than a mere desire to help. Anyway, to my surprise, I heard her saying yes.

'And I'll move in as your—'

'Friend, obviously. There are two rooms. George's has a nice double bed and everything else you need. And if things go well—'

I left my last sentence hanging, leaving Maria to interpret it however she liked. We both smiled. It wouldn't be long before I looked back on that moment as akin to the split second when someone who's falling imagines he's flying.

Waiting for Armani's runner on the green bench at the northeast corner of Hackney Downs, I applied the full force of my will to the effort of ignoring my watch. I'd read somewhere that time slows down as you approach an object of immense mass, and waiting for drugs I could believe it. Opposite was Open Doors Baptist Church, a sign outside reading TRESPASSERS WELCOME. Picnickers in sunglasses sat on blankets rolled out on the grass. People think drug addicts have no willpower, I thought to myself, but it's the opposite. I'd spent the last few years of my life resisting temptation a thousand times a day. *All I did* was resist temptation. If people knew how often I resisted temptation, they'd consider me a paragon of self-restraint.

It was just the five or six times a day I succumbed that were the problem.

Just once more. A part of me knew I was doing that thing drug addicts did, that I'd done myself a thousand times: making a trade in which I rewarded myself with real drugs now for hypothetical abstinence later. Unfortunately, every time was the last time. I'd probably have been happier if I'd spent the last five years like Adam and Rose, eschewing all the failed attempts at self-reform, accepting my life revolved around drugs and nothing else.

But now I was out of money. You can't buy drugs without money. Or not for long, anyway. Once I'd fleeced Armani today he'd stop answering my calls. That was the genius of my idea. That was exactly why I *needed* to take drugs once more. I'd turn running out of money, and alienating my dealer, into a means of escape from the straitjacket of addiction.

Yes, this was an excellent plan.

I allowed myself another glance at my watch. Just three minutes had passed. The second hand seemed to be moving into a violent headwind. Armani had said fifteen minutes, but in dealer-speak that meant more like half an hour. Addicts were always early – and dealers always, always late. Whenever I waited to score, time dilated and my bench or stairwell turned into a bitter purgatory, a dark night of the soul. I remembered reading a poem at university in which the narrator described time warping as he waited impatiently for his beloved, an hour becoming a day and a day becoming a year. Well, poets did have a way of exaggerating. Surely nobody, while waiting for a mere lover, had endured what I was going through now.

My phone vibrated in my pocket. I took it out and found a text:

Hi matt haven't heard from you I'll be in the uk for two more weeks if you want to meet up Mum

I deleted it and carried on waiting.

Maria, who had a hippyish belief in the redemptive power of nature, had taught me the names of the local flora, how to distinguish an ash from a fir from an oak by the texture of the bark, the shape of the leaves. I stared grimly at the tree in front of me, trying to practise the act of *quiet noticing* which, Maria said, was her way of meditating. But my mind broke loose. How the fuck was a *tree*, of all things, supposed to help anyone? I couldn't resist another desperate glance at my watch. Another sixty seconds had passed. Armani was thirteen minutes late.

The church across the road was quiet, but on Sundays gospel music could be heard echoing from inside, and later the congregation would spill out onto the pavement. The worshippers never glanced over at the addicts and dealers who frequented this place – the drugs economy didn't stop for the Sabbath – and we never looked over at them. This spot was like an intersection in the multiverse, a portal between two parallel worlds, one representing my past and the other my present. The worlds couldn't be further apart but here they lay side by side, almost kissing like snooker balls.

A teenager pulled up on a pushbike. ''Scuse me, mate,' he said.

Thank God. 'Where the fuck have you been?'

'What? I was going to ask you the way to London Fields.'

'Oh, sorry. It's just—'

'Forget it,' he said, pedalling off in a hurry.

Was this really the end of my using? I could try to borrow more money of course, but realistically I'd long ago run out of people willing to extend me credit. I owed my older sister Rachel several thousand pounds; the unpaid debt was one of the factors in the breakdown of our relationship. The only people I saw regularly were Adam and Rose, but our ambiguously transactional friendship was strictly one-way: I'd never turned up at their house without drugs or money, and if I did I wasn't sure I'd be let in. No, I couldn't ask a couple who lived on begging and petty crime for a loan.

I hadn't always been so friendless. The flat I used to rent with George, and now shared with Maria, had once had a reputation for epic parties. A crowd of arty types – would-be musicians and writers – would descend every Friday and spend all weekend talking excitedly about the radical work they'd begin just as soon as they overcame whatever was standing in their way. Over time the personnel thinned out, the drugs got harder, the mood became surlier, and the word 'party' seemed less and less apt. George began to find the whole scene distasteful, spending more and more time at his girlfriend's. Eventually a hardcore group of five or six regulars converged weekly to tell each other the same story. We'd begin our lives just as soon as we'd kicked the drugs. Every week we met, took our drugs, and became collectively inspired by the idea of quitting them.

A kid strolled over and sat down next to me. Sixteen or so, he was wearing a grey hoodie, black joggers and Nike Airs. 'You waitin' for somethin', fam?'

'You with Armani?'

'Safe.'

He spat my order into his hand from where he'd been hiding it. With his sleeve he gave the clear plastic baggie a perfunctory wipe before handing it over. When I stuffed it into my sock, it produced a satisfyingly large bulge.

Before leaving I explained he was on the territory of G, another local dealer, and that shotting here was risky. He and his boss might want to consider doing business a couple of streets over.

He hooked his arm around the back of the bench and leaned towards me. His hoodie made a grey halo around his face and his breath smelled of weed. 'Blud, do I tell you how to do *your* fuckin' job?'

Over the years I'd seen countless kids overplaying the gangster shtick in this way, their nervy aggression plainly a disguise for fear. 'I don't actually have a job. But if I did, and you knew a way I could do it that might stop me getting my head kicked in, I'd probably appreciate the advice.'

The kid stood up. 'Yeah, well. Guess what? Tell your brer G, or whatever his fuckin' name is, I *beg* he come down on man. Prick'll get fuckin' murked, I swear.'

'Whatever. It doesn't matter to me. I was just trying to be helpful.'

'Tell you what,' he said, stuffing his hands in his pockets and walking away. 'Go fuck yourself, you filthy fuckin' junkie.'

Under ten minutes later I could already feel withdrawal kicking in as I rapped Adam and Rose's letterbox.

'Come on, in you get,' said Rose.

'I need to use the bathroom, quick.'

Rose nodded. Unusually among hardcore addicts she wouldn't touch needles, and only permitted me to use them out of her sight. I began squeezing past her in the narrow hallway with its filthy, peeling wallpaper.

'Do you have anything for me?' she said.

'Sorry, of course.' I handed over the usual one dark and two light.

Adam and Rose's bathroom was sepulchral, odoriferous and coated in some kind of vile grease which turned everything – tiles, taps, shower curtain – a disturbing yellowish colour. Like the rest of this place, it couldn't have been cleaned for many years. Panting, I pulled the needle out of my arm. I was vibrating like a tuning fork as I grasped the edges of the sink.

When my thoughts settled I made a mental note that it was past noon. Maria would be back from work by six, so there were five hours before I had to get home and, as best I could, erase the signs of today's activities from my hair, teeth and clothes.

I took a seat in the living room, where Adam and Rose were sprawled on the bed. All three of us were holding frosted miniature glass bottles, the necks stuffed with gauze, from which we smoked our gear. The room was piled with broken TVs, radios, printers – anything Adam believed he could fix up and sell. And the walls were hung not with decorations but the tools of his trade: bolt cutters, hacksaws, angle grinders.

Now that Adam was high, he became ebullient, talking unstoppably, dispensing wisdom like an underworld guru. Though he was a self-confessed 'crim' who'd spent much of his adult life behind the door, he had a passionate, if selective, sense of justice. He was a 'standard-issue nutter', he insisted now, but he wasn't a 'shit-cunt'.

'That's an important distinction?' I said, breathing out a pearly, petrol-scented billow of smoke.

'It makes all the difference in the world,' he said.

'So who's a shit-cunt?'

'Here we go,' said Rose.

'Nonces, snitches and people who hurt animals.' Adam's face creased up in disgust. 'Oh, and slymongers.'

'Slymongers?'

'People who hit you from behind. You should always hit from the front. That shouldn't even need saying.'

'What about just not hitting anyone?'

'Look, I agree with you, in principle. In an ideal world, nobody gets beaten up. But you've got to be realistic, at the end of the day.'

'I see. Anyone else?'

'Child protection workers,' he said emphatically. Now he recounted once again the story of his childhood and its litany of traumas. He'd never met his father. His mother drank and was partial to the occasional pipe when things got stressful, but she was Adam's whole world. 'She was a fucking angel,' he said. One day when he was twelve two social workers arrived at his house and asked if he'd like to go to McDonald's. He followed them to the car, and instead they drove for hours until they reached a children's home in Carmarthen in Wales, not far from Swansea. His mother had been judged unfit to raise him, he was eventually told, and was banned from making contact. By the time he went looking for her as an adult, she'd died of liver failure.

'After that day with the child protection I made myself two promises. Never take drugs. And never trust nobody, ever again.' He pulled on the underside of his pipe. 'Well, one out of two ain't bad.'

I sometimes thought about Adam's trip down the M4 and wondered if it was possible my family had passed him coming the other way, en route to some doomed holiday. He'd progressed from children's home to juvy to adult prison. Meanwhile I'd gone from a famous school to a prestigious university. He'd enjoyed no privilege at all, whereas I'd ended up with privilege to burn – which I'd literally proceeded to do. And here we both were.

'Ok, so child protection workers go in with the snitches and nonces. What about the police?'

Adam looked aggrieved. 'I ain't anti-filth,' he insisted. 'A lot of people think I'm anti-filth, but I ain't. Far from it.'

'He's not anti-police,' chipped in Rose. 'He's just pro-criminal.'

'Look. There's good filth and bad filth. Believe me, I've dealt with the lot. Everyone's got to work to pay the bills.'

'Except you,' said Rose, scooping a mound of white powder into the neck of her bottle.

'All I'm saying is, when you get nicked, you better pray you get nicked by good filth. If you do, it's your lucky day.'

'Ok, the police are off the hook,' I said. 'Who else?'

'Anyone who don't pick up their dog shit. Junkie, crackhead, I don't care. You pick up your dog shit, end of story.'

Not for the first time, I marvelled at Adam's equanimous spirit. Life had dealt him the unluckiest hand, and yet he had no detectable self-pity. For a moment I doubted my decision to quit drugs today: were Adam and Rose the sane ones and were ordinary, 'respectable' people mad? Why waste your time chasing happiness via unreliable and circuitous routes like property, stock portfolios, interior design, fashion, food – or family, work, love, whatever – when the feeling could be bought in £10 wraps, or three for £20, and injected straight into the bloodstream?

But no, I thought to myself: I couldn't keep living like this. I couldn't take any more of the duplicity, the shame. Or the loneliness. Were Adam and Rose my friends? At first, years ago, our relationship had been a straightforward exchange of money for drugs. They knew how to get their hands on gear and I didn't. But for a long time now I'd had Armani, so why did I need them? Only sometimes did I admit to myself the truth: that I was essentially paying them for their company. I'd always been contemptuous of the kind of people who visited sex workers – there were some depths even I wouldn't sink to – but perhaps I wasn't unlike one of those pathetic men who paid other human beings to pretend for a few hours that they cared.

These thoughts bolstered my determination, for a moment, to make this the Very Last Very Last Time. And since this would be my final visit here, I decided to ask something I'd always wondered about. 'Adam. Tell me something.'

'Can I call my lawyer first?'

Ignoring this, I said, 'Do you ever wish things had turned out differently for you?'

'What do you mean?'

'Like, do you ever wonder what your life might've been like if things had been different? Or do you ever think about trying to live another way?'

'You've lost me.'

I thought about how to rephrase my question. 'For instance, do you ever wish you'd been born in another time and place?'

'Yeah, actually! Come to think of it, I wish I was born in the fifties.'

I was intrigued. 'Why the fifties?'

A look of happy reverie floated across his face. He didn't have his teeth in, so his smile revealed a gummy maw. 'No CCTV, no DNA. Fuck me, you could get away with anything! I was born too late, that was my problem.' He shook his head ruefully and took a consolatory hit on his pipe.

'*Bliss was it in that dawn to be alive*,' I said.

'You what?'

'It's a poem, you daft cunt,' said Rose. In contrast to Adam, who'd barely seen the inside of a classroom, Rose had finished school before dropping out of society. Her father had been a psychology professor – *and a fucking psychopath*, she never failed to add. While Adam would talk about anything, Rose was reticent about herself and her past. I didn't dare put to her the same question I'd asked Adam, fearing the answer would be unbearably sad.

The gauze in the neck of my bottle had dried out, so I stuffed more in. 'You two don't ever think about getting clean, going to rehab? Getting a job? Building a normal life?'

'Fuck, no,' said Adam.

'You don't care that your habit's going to kill you in the end, one way or another?'

'It don't bother me in the slightest,' said Adam.

'There's too many people in the world anyway,' said Rose.

'If you ask me,' he said, 'when they get to sixty everyone should be, what's it called, put down.'

'Euthanised,' she said.

Using a gas canister, I refilled my lighter. 'Why's that?'

'After you're sixty, you're no use to society. You're just a burden.'

'Hang on a minute,' said Rose. 'What use to society are you?'

'I keep the police busy. I keep lawyers in business. Judges. Parole officers. It's people like me that keep the world spinning round.'

It was difficult to know whether Adam was joking. He could have a dry sense of humour. But he did occasionally express some ludicrous opinions, like his firm belief that Australia didn't exist and that all 'visits' there were part of a government-sponsored hoax.

I checked my watch. 'Shit, Maria'll be home soon.'

'Your new lady?' said Rose.

'I guess you could call her that. I mean, it's complicated. She moved in as a friend, but, well—'

'And she don't know about your habit?' said Adam.

I sighed. I explained that I'd never meant for things to go this far. I'd believed I'd get clean before Maria moved in. And I'd tried. But of course I couldn't stop, and the day she was supposed to arrive kept getting closer, and suddenly she was at my front door with her suitcase. She had nowhere else to go; she was depending on me.

'How the fuck have you got away with it?' said Rose.

'I mean, I don't know. I'm careful to clean up after myself. I try my best to act straight. Maria's so . . . *good*. She doesn't do drugs, she hardly even drinks. She's not from a world where you'd come into contact with this stuff. You know what it's like – it takes another junkie to know the signs. She knows something weird's going on, I think. I keep my pyjamas on in bed so she doesn't see my track marks.'

'Kinky,' grinned Adam.

'But on some level, she knows.' I thought about a dream Maria had recounted recently where she'd reached into her pockets and pulled her hands out all bloody, full of syringes. Another day she told me she'd dreamt I was smuggling things into the flat behind my eyeballs.

'She knows but she don't know,' said Adam.

'Exactly. It reminds me of a time when I was younger. Even though I knew everything my parents had told me was bullshit, I couldn't—'

'It's a question of loyalty,' interrupted Adam. 'If you've got to choose between the gear and your missus, there's only going to be one winner.'

No man can serve two masters, I thought to myself. *For either he will hate the one, and love the other; or else he will hold to the one, and despise the other.*

'I mean, you've got to have trust in a relationship. Look at me and Rose. Most junkies'll sell their mother for a hit, but we ain't like that. We don't fib, we split every bag fifty-fifty. If you ain't got that kind of loyalty with your missus, you're fucked.'

I couldn't believe I was being lectured about relationships and honesty by Adam, a hardened addict and professional criminal. But he was right, both in principle and about his own practice. Adam and Rose sometimes seemed to me like seafloor creatures who survived with barely any light, sustenance or warmth. Despite their lives' desperate conditions, they clung on because they had each other. The truth was that Adam and Rose arguably had the most functional, loving relationship I'd ever seen up close.

'Anyway, I've got to stop. Now. Today. I'm out of money. I just ripped off Armani for £150.'

Adam gave an ominous whistle. 'He'll be after you.'

'Good. All the more reason to keep my head down, stay away from that world. So anyway, I guess what I'm saying's goodbye. I'll see you around. But I won't be coming here any more.'

Adam chuckled. 'Yeah, I've heard that one before and all.'

'No, this time it's different. I'm going to get a methadone script tomorrow, get a job, sort myself out.'

'You'll find some money sooner or later,' said Rose. 'Probably sooner.'

I took a final hit, held my breath for as long as possible to let the crack suffuse my lungs, and exhaled. 'I can't. I can't keep lying to Maria. And I hate myself for living like this. I'm done.'

Adam and Rose were both suppressing smiles as I made my speech, and seemed to be avoiding each other's eye.

'Right you are, then,' said Rose. 'Good luck and all the rest of it.'

'It's been nice knowing you guys,' I said, gathering up my remaining white and blue wraps. 'I've appreciated it. Honestly.'

I let myself out. As I shut the front door, I heard Adam call, 'See you tomorrow, mate!'

When I arrived home, I found Maria in the hallway.

'Hey!' I said. 'You're home early.'

Then I noticed her bags piled next to the banister.

'What's going on?'

A day's consumption of drugs had altered me so drastically that my vague memory from this morning – Maria staring up at me from the bottom of the stairs, blood streaming from my arm – felt like one from years ago.

She said nothing, refusing to meet my eye as she picked up her things.

'Maria – listen—'

She pushed past me. I looked up the stairs. Through the open bathroom door I saw the bath panel lying on its side.

The front door slammed shut and she was gone.

I found the bathroom scattered with used and unused needles, lighters, spoons, filters, broken glass bottles.

A text arrived from Maria:

I'll be back in a week to collect the rest of my stuff.
Don't call me.

Moments later, another:

By the way, you forgot to put the screwdriver away.

After Maria's gone I don't want to think. I go through the rest of Armani's gear with vicious abandon. She's left her silver metallic suitcase in our room and it watches me in judgement as I sit on my Chesterfield, cooking up one hit after another, becoming sloppy, not caring how much I'm taking. I know I don't have enough to last very long. But who cares? With any luck, among the blue and white wraps on the coffee table is the one that will end it all, like the single bullet in a spinning chamber. I keep going.

I aim the pin at the constellation of scabs and blotches on my inner left arm. I'm running out of usable veins, can't draw blood. *Ask, and it shall be given you; seek, and ye shall find.* Maybe I'm so fucked, or so anxious, or so angry at myself for what's happened, that I'm losing precision. Kicking off my shoe, I press the needle carefully into the vein in my left instep. If I miss I'll do serious damage. I watch the speedball draining into my foot.

Early hours. Blue lights flashing outside the window, muffled sound of walkie-talkies, police helicopter blades thrashing.

Don't panic. Just hallucinating. Happens all the time with crack psychosis. Another hit of smack to subdue the fear. I drop to the floor to avoid being seen, crawling on my hands and knees, pulling the curtains shut just in case.

Another hit crashes through my blood-brain barrier. The feeling, I'm sure, is like falling in love. But what would I know? I thought I was in love with Maria, but before long wasn't I just taking the money she paid me in 'rent' each week and spending it on my habit? Didn't I use her like I ended up using Sinead, like I've used everyone? Using, using, using. She removed the cash each week from a brown envelope she kept in the suitcase, and once she left for work I'd take it straight to Armani or Adam, sometimes stepping over eviction notices from the landlord, which I'd later hide.

Morning. The drugs are finished and a cold wind of desolation passes through me. As I do every time after a serious binge, I get on my hands and knees, scavenging the carpet for crumbs fallen from the table, crystals of crack I dropped earlier when supplies seemed endless.

I fill the neck of the bottle with a pile of what I'm sure is mostly crack, sucking hungrily, holding my breath until I'm woozy, desperate for a few more moments of ecstasy before everything goes dark.

I wake up a few hours later, unsure whether I've overdosed or just passed out from lack of sleep. It's gone 4pm and there are no drugs left. I have six missed calls on my phone from Armani. Withdrawal is already racing through me like a fever. I still have all my clothes on, so after a trip to the bathroom to vomit I use every ounce of remaining energy to walk to Adam and Rose's.

'Look, I'm sorry,' I say when Rose lets me in. 'I've got nothing. I'm clucking, bad. Please, just this once, can you spare me something?'

Rose looks at Adam.

He shrugs. 'Wish we could help—'

'Can I just scrape out your pipe?' I know I can recycle the residue of crack and heroin that's gathered on the inside of a bottle to produce a few decent hits.

Adam sighs. He hands over his pipe, filthy with fossilised brown-grey matter. I use a screwdriver and a piece of gauze, catching what I can in a little mound on a CD case. When I take a hit the storm in my nervous system subsides, the panic in my gut is quelled, and I feel sane again.

I know what I have will last an hour or two at most. But at least now I have some time to think.

As I'm leaving Adam says, 'By the way, there's a price on your head.'

'A price on my head? Who am I, Robin fucking Hood?'

'One-and-one for anyone who can tell Armani where you live. He rang me earlier.'

'You didn't—'

''Course I didn't,' he says. 'You think after all this time I'd sell you out for one-and-one, you dozy cunt?'

So how much would it take? Two-and-two? Five-and-five?

'Don't tell him anything. Please. I'll find some money. And I'll sort you out too.'

'Just a word to the wise,' says Rose. 'I wouldn't take too long if I were you. People like Armani, they don't play about.'

I walk home, thoughts skittering everywhere. The glinting towers of the City of London loom over Kingsland Road. The world is full of money. All I need is £150 to pay Armani, maybe another £100 for enough drugs to quiet my brain for twenty-four hours, to think straight, to find a way out of the

185

mess I'm in. There's a small queue of people at the cashpoint over the road. An old, white-haired woman stuffs a roll of notes into her handbag. No, I haven't sunk that low. *Think*.

My parents? But I haven't spoken to them properly in months, longer even. My father's stipend at Nazareth Baptist College isn't much, and I exhausted what little generosity he could afford some time ago. I can't ask my mother to help after what happened last year when, in a brief attempt at self-reform, I arranged an internship at a national newspaper and asked if she'd lend me enough to cover my living expenses. Although she couldn't help, she nervously admitted that my grandfather may be able to advance a small sum he'd saved for my inheritance. My mother's father had left school at twelve and spent most of his working life in the same railway signal box outside Pontypridd, putting away what little he could. He agreed to transfer a couple of thousand to his hyper-educated grandson, who quickly proceeded to get sacked from the newspaper for turning up high and incoherent. When my mother wouldn't stop peppering me with questions about the internship, I finally had to admit that all my grandfather's money – every penny – had been spent on heroin and crack. Now, on the rare occasions I speak to her, she's become just another person to whom I pretend everything is fine and all my troubles are in the past.

Back at home, the threat of withdrawal rumbles through my organs like a distant thunderstorm. *Maria*? Would she want me to be maimed for the sake of £150? I've seen her take hundreds from the envelope in the suitcase over the last six weeks. It probably contains thousands. Surely if I called and explained—

I sit down on the sofa in the bedroom. Maria's suitcase is next to the bed.

The money probably isn't even there. She'd have taken it with her, wouldn't she? Anyway, it's locked with a three-digit security code.

It'd be an interesting experiment, though, wouldn't it? How long would it take to try a thousand different combinations?

My phone rings. Armani again. I ignore it. He'll be trying Adam and Rose again soon. Can you trust a hardcore drug addict not to fuck you over, even when on some level he cares for you?

Can he trust himself?

Looking over at Maria's suitcase again, I laugh out loud at the naivety of my question.

001

On the floor, suitcase between my knees, hands busy at the dials. The important thing to remember is that this is only an experiment. If and when I find the right code, I'll decide what to do.

012

Who the fuck are you kidding, you piece of shit? If anyone could see you now—

055

But that's the point. Nobody can see me. There's no-one watching. I gave up that idea a long time ago.

I need to slow down because the worst thing would be to reach 999 and discover I missed the correct code. For each combination I wrangle the lid to check if the lock springs open.

My hands are getting tired. Each number takes longer to try. And I keep blacking out and worrying I've missed one, forcing me to go back. At this rate I'll be here all day.

Don't worry. Once withdrawal kicks in, you'll sit here all week if you need to.

Armani could be at the front door any minute. *Deliver me not over unto the will of mine enemies.*

Look. Any addict who found himself alone in a room with a suitcase full of cash, hounded by withdrawal and an angry dealer, would do exactly the same thing.

Anyway, who said I'm planning to take the money? I'll cross that bridge when I—

203

Still telling yourself that lie, are you? Aren't you ashamed of yourself?

222

Yes. Yes. Yes.

236

And here's the other thing. Even if you find the cash, you'll never get away with it.

247

I wake up, cheek pressed to the floor. Go back a couple of digits, just in case. Another call from Armani. I let it ring out, but my hands are trembling now.

271

Here's what I'll do. I'll stop at 450. That way there's a one-in-two chance. If I find the envelope, I'll help myself to £250, pay off Armani and buy enough gear to clear my head so I can figure out a way of replacing the money before Maria comes back.

276

But what if the code's 451?

I want to do the right thing. But sometimes you just find yourself over the line, and—

For to will is present with me; but how to perform that which is good I find not. For the good that I would I do not: but the evil which I would not, that I do.

This is getting absolutely fucking—

My patience snaps. I'm heading to the kitchen, grabbing a bread knife, perforating the case and sawing it open. It's hard work, but easier than the fucking lock. Eventually there's a six-by-six inch gash, big enough to push my hand through.

I have my arm in the suitcase up to my shoulder before I find it, a thick wad of paper.

I vomit on the pavement outside Adam and Rose's, withdrawal taking hold again. I ask them to pass £150 to Armani, and give them a further £100 to score for us all. Adam's got his hands on the gear in fifteen and I excuse myself to the bathroom. The huge speedball I cook up explodes through my cerebral cortex like a depth charge.

Smoking and shooting up all day, so high I almost forget about Maria's suitcase. Like someone eating for the first time after a hunger strike.

Food: another word dealers use for heroin and crack. *Give us this day our daily bread.*

Explaining to Adam and Rose about the suitcase, asking them what to do. Forget what we were talking about, everything dissolving in a haze of smoke.

Home again, evening setting in. Out of drugs already. Already the post-binge whispers of suicidality. Wait ten minutes or so, wrestling with my conscience the way an adult plays at wrestling with a child, before taking another handful of cash. Can't bear to sober up, can't bear to think about what I've done. The only way is to keep going.

Back at Adam and Rose's, awake now for well over thirty-six hours. Voices in my auditory field, shapes in the corner of my vision. Too fucked to make my way home. In the front room, climbing over piles of stuff Adam's salvaged from skips – bike parts, ancient fridges, random pieces of furniture, hideous art – to reach the mould-infested sofa. Pass out for a few hours, withdrawal waking me up before dawn. Sprint to the toilet, empty my bowels just in time.

Home, grabbing handfuls of cash, not bothering to count how much, stuffing it into my rucksack before heading back to Adam and Rose's.

Calling Armani to set things straight. Apologising for what happened, trying to explain. He stops me, says we had this conversation yesterday. 'We safe, bruh. You ok, though? I swear I never heard you so pranged out.'

What was I just thinking?

Days pass like this. Three, four. I've never taken so much crack so continuously, and reality is beginning to lose focus. I'm not sure how long Maria's been gone, but the envelope in her suitcase is growing thinner. I don't sleep, just pass out every now and again from exhaustion. I don't eat. Occasionally I remember the deep shit I'm in, think about Maria's return. But my present and future selves are two people with nothing in common.

Sitting on my sofa, shirt off, seeing human figures in the corners of the room. Sometimes they talk. Blood everywhere, streaming from the wounds in my arms, hands, feet. Like stigmata. Like that figurine of Christ on the wall of Father Pete's office. Why am I thinking about Father Pete now?

Listen to you, comparing yourself to Christ!

Unmistakably my mother's voice, her Welsh accent unchanged by migration to England and the Holy Land.

Blasphemy! That's your problem! Never keeping the commandments! If only you'd honoured your father and mother! If only you'd remembered the Sabbath! If only you hadn't committed adultery! If only you hadn't coveted your neighbour's house, wife, ox, ass! Too much coveting tits and ass! Don't think I don't know what you're up to behind the bathroom door, you naughty little boy! You can't hide from me!

The only way to banish my mother's voice is a huge hit, so I empty another wrap into the spoon. Once it's ready I pull the liquid into the syringe and—

Coming to, needle still in my hand. Head pressed to the armrest. Stumbling to the bathroom to piss, works everywhere.

Pain stabbing through my foot. I've stepped on a used needle. I bend down—

Open my eyes hours later, needle still stuck in the sole of my foot. Father Pete is standing in the far corner of the room.

Moderation in all things, that's my motto! Well, it's St Paul originally of course, my dear boy. He did occasionally talk some sense. Shame about the homophobia, but we mustn't take everything so literally. That's the trouble with the non-conformist tradition. Puritans, literalists, nonces, snitches, slymongers! No, moderation in all things for me! Even in moderation! Therefore, sometimes, excess! Well, who doesn't go in for the occasional intoxicant? I like a good speedball as much as the next man of the cloth! What? Everyone's at it, my dear boy, the whole Church of England. Rife with the dark and the light! Moderation, moderation, moderation! Far be it from me to cast aspersions—

Heart galloping, I take a long pull on the pipe to make Father Pete disappear, but his voice is replaced by my father's.

Now then, boys and girls! Can anyone tell me if they've ever been naughty?

Sitting on the sofa, I raise my hand.

Good! Now who can tell me, is it bad to be naughty? That's right! It's very bad to be naughty! There's nothing naughtier than to be naughty! To be naughty is a sin. When Adam and Eve sinned against God, it spoiled his whole lovely world. It spoiled Adam and Eve, too. They became sinners. And when Adam and Eve had children, they were sinners too. All babies are born sinners. That's why little babies are so

193

naughty! *And then they grow up and have babies, and their babies are naughty, and the babies' babies are naughty, and the babies' babies' babies, and the babies' babies' babies' babies, and the babies' babies' babies' babies' babies. And so on and so forth, forever and ever, amen! Don't forget, to be naughty is to be naughty is to be naughty. And we mustn't be naughty! And we can't help being naughty! Because we're sinners! Now, that should clear up any difficulties you've been getting yourselves into!*

Phone. My brother's name on the screen.

Jonathan saying, *Matt? Matt? Are you there?*

Mmmm-hmm.

Are you ok? I hadn't heard from you in ages and—

I'm fine! Look, just—

You've been using, haven't you?

I told you, I'm—

I didn't call because I'm worried, to be honest. If you're intent on destroying yourself, I can't stop you. I'm calling because I spoke to Maria. Do you have any idea what you've done? She's got nowhere to go, she's sleeping on floors and sofas—

Tourniquet in my mouth, looking for a vein. *Nnngh.*

What?

The speedball rips through me. *I said I didn't ask her to leave.*

No, you just gave her absolutely no fucking choice. Because you were high the whole time. Just like you are now.

Why are you calling me in the middle of the night anyway?

What the fuck are you talking about? It's almost noon.

Look, I have to go.

Of course you do. You know what, Matt? I used to think you were just an idiot. Now I'm starting to think you're some kind of fucking sociopath.

Dark outside again, drugs running out, on my knees, scouring the floor for a splinter or mote of crack.

I pass out and must be asleep for hours, because when I come around I'm frighteningly lucid. I check my phone. It's Monday. Fuck. A text from Maria:

> I'll be with you at 7pm to collect my stuff. See you later.

I help myself to another £100 and make my way to Adam and Rose's. I explain my situation to them again. I've committed a serious crime, and when Maria finds out in a few hours she's bound to have me arrested.

'If only we could both be victims of a crime,' I think out loud. 'Like if my place had gotten burgled, and—'

Adam scratches his chin. 'You know, you *are* talking to someone who's clapped more houses than you've had hot dinners.'

I take a deep draw on my pipe and stare at him.

'It's easy, at the end of the day. Piece of piss. I break the lock to your gaff. I fuck the place up. Nick some stuff, plus the suitcase. We split the cash, job done.'

'It's not pretty,' says Rose. 'But right now you're looking at a stretch inside.'

'And believe me,' he adds, 'that ain't no fun.'

It's a deranged, ridiculous plan. So ridiculous Maria will surely never suspect I'd be capable of doing it.

I tell Adam to meet me at my place at 3pm.

When he arrives, he uses a drill to bust my front lock. I watch nervously for neighbours who might wonder why I'm breaking into my own flat. Once he's in, he kicks over furniture, overturns tables, throws pictures and Maria's plants to the floor. He's a professional: he's wearing black gloves so as not to leave prints. He almost seems to be enjoying himself, and I can't help wondering if all this casual destruction is necessary. Once he makes it to the bedroom he opens drawers, spilling their contents, shoves books from shelves, hurls clothes everywhere. Before making his exit he grabs the suitcase, agreeing to see me after I've dealt with Maria.

She meets me at a quiet café at the end of Belgrade Road. Sipping her herbal tea, she seems in a generous mood. 'I know you don't want to live this way, Matt. I know you don't want to be this person.'

'I don't,' I say truthfully.

'And I know there's a good person inside you.'

I'm miserable, and I know this is only the prelude to the ordeal I've arranged. 'I'm not so sure about that.'

'You've been using today haven't you? You look terrible.'

I nod. 'I'm so sorry. I meant it when I promised to stop. But I couldn't. I was using pretty much the whole time.' It feels good to tell her the truth, and I recall how much relief I always found in confessing to her. 'And then when you left—' I stop myself. 'Oh well, it doesn't matter.'

'I knew there was something wrong. I was just trying to manage. I didn't understand why you were acting so weird all the time. But listen, you're sick. You know that, don't you?'

Her kindness adds exquisite layers to my self-loathing. I'm no stranger to lying, and I know what was going on with Sinead's card was effectively stealing. But what I'm about to do is on a vastly different scale. Am I a bad person – or simply out of my mind? I was always contemptuous of my father's claim that without God there can be no morality. Once upon a time I vowed to prove him wrong by living a decent, godless life. And now look at me.

'You need help,' she says.

'I know.'

'I mean rehab, therapy, that kind of thing.'

I simply stare at the table.

'Ok, I guess you're not in the mood to talk. Let's go and get my stuff. We can chat later.'

Outside, it's a mild summer evening. 'Hang on,' I say. 'Did you pay?'

'No. Didn't you? That's embarrassing.'

'Wait there, I'll be back in a minute.'

After I've settled the bill, we walk together to the flat. I affect surprise to find the door rocking on its hinges in the breeze. When we enter and see the mess Adam made, even though I witnessed him do it, I'm genuinely outraged. 'What the fuck! This – this is madness!'

She breathes sharply. 'Oh my god. *Oh my god.*'

We make our way upstairs to the bedroom, surveying the carnage. There are books lying everywhere and our feet crunch over broken glass.

'What kind of person would do this?' I say.

'Shit, my suitcase! All my money—'

'Look, stay calm. I'm going to call the police.'

Maria walks over to the window and stares, either out into the darkness or at my reflection in the glass, I don't know which.

I dial 999 and report a burglary. A forensics officer in black boots, black trousers and a short-sleeved shirt arrives with impressive speed. He takes our fingerprints and then spreads a kind of talcum powder everywhere. It doesn't take him long to conclude the only prints are ours.

'Whoever did this was clearly motivated by drugs,' he says. 'I'm afraid there's a lot of paraphernalia—'

As he's talking, I notice my rucksack lying open beside the bed, a pile of £20 notes visible inside it. I walk over and zip it shut, but when I look up Maria's gaze is trained on me.

'It's ok, officer,' she says. 'I understand what's happened here now. You can go. I'll be in touch if I need any more help.'

When we're alone, I stand in silence for an age, staring at the floor. For as long as I can remember I've felt obscurely guilty of some nameless crime. So in a strange way it feels as though my whole life has been a premonition of this moment. I'm painfully sober, defenceless against the sensation overwhelming me now, which I can only describe as a kind of humiliation of the soul. I'm reminded of how I used to imagine the Day of Judgement: all my most pitiful, debasing moments exposed, and nowhere to hide. It occurs to me now that since childhood I've laboured under a profound misunderstanding about sin. You're not punished *for* what you do, you're punished *by* what you do. Once upon a time this might have been a valuable insight, but it's no use now.

'How much money's gone?' says Maria, interrupting my thoughts. Her voice is quiet, as though she's speaking to herself.

'Look, I'm so sorry,' I say. 'However much you hate me for this, I promise I hate myself a thousand times more.'

'I'm not interested in your feelings right now. All my savings were in that suitcase. I need to get it back.'

'I think I have a few hundred in my bag.'

'And the rest?'

'Adam's got it. Or what's left. There's a couple of thousand at least. Let me call him.'

'You know I could send you to jail for this.'

'I know.'

'Get the money first. Then we'll talk.'

I call Adam.

'Listen, the whole thing's off,' I say. 'Maria found out what happened. I need the money. Like, now.'

'Sorry mate.' There's pounding music in the background. 'It's a bit late for that.'

Dread scours my insides. 'What do you mean? Look, I need that fucking money, ok?'

He gives a throaty laugh.

'What about my half?' I say with a tremor in my voice. 'How can I get that?'

'*Your half*? Listen, you silly prick, what did you think was going to happen?'

'What the fuck, Adam. You can't do that. We had a deal.'

He laughs again. 'Didn't you and your missus have a deal?'

'You were the one who was lecturing me about loyalty the other day. Where's your loyalty?'

'Same place as yours, mate!'

'You'll fucking regret this. I know where you live.'

'And I know where you live and all. Look, I left a few hundred with Rose because I love you. Not many junkies would do that. Go and get it, and leave me the fuck alone.'

'You fucking cunt. When I see you—'

'Yeah, right. By the way, if you want my advice, you ain't cut out for a life of crime. I'd stay away from it if I was you. And look, no hard feelings, ok?'

'You fucking—'

After the line goes dead, I become aware of a decision drawing closer, making its way over the horizon of conscious thought, from the dark side of the mind.

I collect £300 from Rose. I put aside £250 for Maria, and steal a final £50 for four bags of smack to do what I need to do and a large bottle of methadone as back up, just in case. When I'm home, I hear Maria weeping in the bedroom. Instead of going to her I leave the cash and my rucksack outside the bathroom door and lock myself inside. Four wraps is by far the largest hit I've ever prepared, but I'm not afraid.

I've overdosed a number of times through carelessness, waking up with paramedics leaning over me and defibrillators on my chest. I know I'll simply experience a moment of perfect bliss before falling asleep.

I place the spoon on the toilet lid, emptying a sachet of citric acid into it. I add the four wraps until it's almost overflowing. *My cup runneth over.* Then, the spoon in one hand, I hold the lighter beneath it for a long time. My fingers start to burn but I keep going, determined not to drop the receptacle containing the only thing I still care about: my end. When all the smack is dissolved into a rich brown liquid, I draw the solution up through a needle. The moment feels oddly anticlimactic: whenever I've pictured this scene I've imagined writing eloquent notes, saying heart-rending final goodbyes to loved ones. But at this point is there anyone left who'd answer my call?

O wretched man that I am! Who will deliver me from the body of this death?

Stupid question. If you want something done properly, do it yourself.

I press the plunger, watch the liquid disappear into my arm. For a second or two I'm at home in my body, my mind, the world.

Forty Days

I woke up under a scratchy cotton sheet, damp skin stuck to my bed's plastic mattress. My clothes were in a pile on the floor, and for some reason my scuffed, filthy trainers were missing their laces. I could hear, from another room, the noise of a man crying. A dark-haired woman with a clipboard was standing at the end of my bed. Seeing me open my eyes, she smiled. But when I tried to speak my voice belonged to someone else, and the woman was a thousand miles away, and sound and sight and time and place were shrinking to a pinprick, and then there was nothing.

Over the next couple of days, in short bursts of lucidity, I tried to piece together where I was and why. I could dimly recall waking up on my bathroom floor some time after what I'd thought would be the last press of the plunger, and then finding Maria collecting her belongings from the debris in the bedroom with a tear-stained face. I must have told her what I'd just done, or failed to do, because I knew she called my mother. I had a memory of laying foetal in the back seat of the car, secretly clutching a bottle of methadone, my mother driving. The last thing I could remember was the doctor in A&E and her alarm when I told her how much methadone I'd swallowed while my mother was buying a parking ticket.

At some point I found myself able to sit up in bed. Gingerly I got to my feet, pulled my clothes on, and let myself out into a starkly lit corridor. A nurse approached, leading by the elbow a man who was weeping loudly.

'Say hello to our new resident, Godfrey!' said the nurse.

The man had food around his mouth and a large paunch that rode over his stained pyjama trousers. He stopped crying long enough to cock his head at me, snuffling and wiping his nose with his sleeve. He recommenced his wailing before being led away.

A little shaken, I walked down the hall past rows of identical doors, through a dayroom where men of all ages were slumped on sofas before a widescreen TV. Behind thick security glass there was a nurse's station, which seemed to provide the only entry and exit to the ward. Inside, a big-bosomed lady was engrossed in a brightly coloured magazine. I knocked on the glass, and once I'd caught her attention she stood up heavily, made her way over and opened the door.

'Hello darlin',' she said in a Caribbean accent. 'What can I do for you?'

'Hi,' I said, swallowing anxiously. 'I – I'd like to leave.'

The nurse folded her arms. She was, I guessed, in her fifties, and she wore a blue lanyard around her neck with a plaque that read DIANNE: DUTY NURSE.

'It's not that simple, you know. This ain't no hotel. You can't just check in and out when you want.' She smiled reassuringly. 'Give me a minute, all right? Let me just take a look at your record. What's your name?'

'Matt – Matthew – Hill.' My lips were dry, and my voice, which I hadn't used in days, sounded dry and feeble.

She sat at her desk, pulled up my notes on her computer screen, and read aloud: *'Twenty-seven-year-old male . . . presented in A&E Monday evening . . . suicidal ideation assessed as severe . . . two deliberate overdoses in 24 hours previous . . . comorbid with chronic opiate and cocaine addiction . . . patient admitted to Bevan Ward voluntarily pending full psychiatric assessment.'*

I listened to the report's description of this lost, unhappy man, knowing he was me and yet feeling somehow that he and I were perfect strangers. I remembered trying to kill myself, and I wasn't sure yet whether I was glad or disappointed that I'd failed. But I knew that, if I had to keep living, I didn't want to do it here, guarded by professionals and alongside men who walked around crying for no apparent reason.

I tried to inflect my voice with authority. 'I'd like to speak to someone about being discharged, please.'

The nurse looked at me with, I thought, a maternal sympathy bordering on pity. 'Let me go find the ward doctor. You can speak to her.'

The doctor was the same one I'd seen standing at the end of my bed. She was a bespectacled woman in her thirties wearing a cable-knit cardigan hanging loosely over black jeans. She invited me into her office, where I took a seat before a desk piled with folders and medical handbooks.

'So Matthew, we haven't met properly yet. I'm Kirsty, one of the doctors on the unit. How are you doing today?'

'Good!' I said, nodding vigorously. 'I was a bit groggy for a while—'

'You've been asleep for well over forty-eight hours.'

'Yeah. I was really tired. But I'm feeling so much better now! Anyway, I don't want to take a bed from someone who really needs it, so—'

'Tell me, Matthew. Do you know what the Bevan Ward is?'

My pulse was racing. 'It's some kind of – uh, mental health unit, right?'

'Right. It's an inpatient male psychiatric ward. People are admitted here if they might pose a risk to themselves or others.'

I tucked my feet in their laceless shoes under the chair and reminded myself to speak calmly. It was important to emphasise I was a regular person, just like the doctor herself. The fact we'd found ourselves on opposite sides of this desk was just a strange mix-up. I was, most definitely, nothing like the crying man I'd just met. I alluded to important business I needed to get on with in the outside world. Although I'd been feeling a little low lately, I was perfectly sane, and—

She bit her bottom lip. 'Nobody's questioning your sanity. But just before you came in here and fell asleep for almost three days, you drank a *quarter of a litre* of methadone. Frankly, it's amazing you're still with us.'

I stared at the floor. 'Well – I'd been using very heavily before that. So I suppose my tolerance had gotten a lot higher than I thought.'

'Are you in withdrawal at the moment?'

'Actually, no.'

The doctor explained methadone had a much longer half-life than heroin, and a dose as large as the one I'd taken would be in my system for some time. One priority over the next few days would be to stabilise me on a safe dose.

'Wait – the next few days?' I shifted in my seat. 'Look, I really appreciate you taking care of me. But, honestly, I'm not a danger to myself or anyone else.'

'I'm afraid that's something we need to keep under continual assessment. Tell me, are you having any suicidal thoughts?'

'Not really. I—'

'Not really?'

'I mean, no. Nothing out of the ordinary.'

She looked unimpressed. 'Matthew, it's very important that we know if you're thinking about hurting yourself. Your notes say you have a history of overdose.'

How could I put the truth into words? That addiction was, for me, both a way of acting out and thwarting a longing for extinction. That by dulling my pain I suspected heroin and crack had kept me alive even as they'd brought me to the brink of death. That every day of my life was a skirmish between the light and the dark, played out inside the 1ml chamber of a needle.

Instead I just said: '*Accidental* overdose. This is the first time I've ever done anything like that on purpose. I'd had a very bad day. A bad week. And look, sure, I'm the first to admit I've got a drug problem. But is that such a crime?'

'Actually, yes. Taking heroin is a crime.'

'Right. Ok, yeah, I know. What I meant was, every heroin user overdoses occasionally. It's sort of like an occupational hazard.'

'And you don't see that as a problem?'

'I know it's not ideal. But is that a reason to lock someone up against their will?'

She sighed. 'You're not here against your will. You came in voluntarily.'

'I was out of it when I came here. I hardly knew where I was.'

'You consented to be treated here.'

'Ok, well, I'd like to leave now, please. To withdraw my consent. It's not that I'm not grateful—'

'I'm afraid that won't be possible for the time being.'

'I thought I was here voluntarily?'

'You are. But if you try and leave, we'll have to keep you here involuntarily.'

'It doesn't sound like there's much difference.'

'Believe me, there is. If we're forced to section you under the Mental Health Act, it could be some time before you leave. If you comply with staff, follow your treatment plan, show you're willing to accept help, you could be out of here in a matter of weeks. So I'd advise—'

I was aghast. 'Sorry, did you say *weeks*?'

The doctor nudged her glasses up her nose and smiled warmly. 'Look, I know this isn't where you were planning on spending your summer. But was your life so wonderful before you came here? Your mother told us you're being evicted by your landlord. So you're about to be made homeless. You've been out of work for some time. You have a serious addiction to *two* Class A drugs. You're nine and a half stone.'

'*Weeks*?'

'Let me put it to you bluntly. Men in your position – with serious addiction issues, a record of suicide attempts – come and go here all the time. The same ones have a way of reappearing every few months. And each time they come in, they get closer to the point where I know I'm not going to see them again.'

The doctor paused. I could see she wanted me to ask her to spell it out, but some obstinate instinct kept me silent.

'What I'm saying,' she continued, 'is that you look like someone who's close to their last visit.'

I felt a gust of anger. I wanted to blame someone else – the doctor, Maria, my parents, God – for what was happening to me.

She stood up. 'Look, I have another meeting now. I'll find you tomorrow to see how you're feeling. In the meantime, I'd suggest having a think about what it is that's brought you here, and where you want to go next. We can support you to make the changes you need to live safely in the community. But you're the only one who can decide if you really want our help.'

I was reeling as I followed her out the door. I looked across the dayroom. Even though the staff wore casual clothes, it was obvious at a glance who worked here and who didn't. The patients were unkempt, haggard and had the atrophied movements of the heavily medicated. I slumped into a chair, wondering how my life had come to this.

'You ok, darlin'?' said Dianne, the nurse from earlier. 'Look, I made you a nice cup of tea.'

I took the steaming mug she handed me. 'Thanks,' I said dejectedly.

She sat down, and we gazed together across the ward. 'It's frightenin' here at first, I know. But you safe now. You know that, right? We gwan take care of you.'

'Look, no offence. But I'm big enough to take care of myself.'

She raised her eyebrows. 'That's what you call takin' care of yourself? Drugs and all that foolishness?' She tutted loudly. 'You know, I been workin' here fifteen year. I seen a lot a young men like you, all messed up with drugs. You still young. You skinny but you healthy. Why you wanna waste your life with foo-fool nonsense like that? Ain't nothing ever come from drugs but vexation and botheration!'

I sipped my tea. I couldn't remember drinking anything in days; warmth spread through my body.

'You do as you told in here, and we gwan get you well, you hear?'

How could I tell her that, although I hated what drugs had done to me, I simply couldn't imagine living without them? How could I explain how lonely I was, how heroin and crack felt like the best friends I'd ever had? It made no sense, but on some level I believed drugs understood me, loved me even. How could I put any of this into words without sounding so mad they'd lock me up indefinitely?

And yet it was oddly comforting to hear the matter expressed in Dianne's uncompromising terms. Whatever else heroin and crack had done for me, they'd also almost killed me. If I wanted to live – and didn't my double failure to end it all express some inarticulate desire to keep going? – then I'd have to find a way of doing so without drugs. Was it really true that, if I did as I was told, I'd get well? I realised how desperate I was to believe this. I'd tried making decisions for myself and failed ruinously. Now I wanted to submit to somebody else's orders.

'Ok,' I said.

'What's that, darlin'?'

I swallowed. 'I'll do what you tell me to do.'

She smiled broadly. 'That's right! That's what I want to hear!'

'I've reached the end of the road now,' I said, looking around the unit. From behind a bedroom door I could hear the crying man. 'If I'm not careful, the way things are heading, I'm going to end up somewhere like *this*.'

Dianne's smile turned into a look of dismay. She shook her head. Then she stood up slowly, placed her hands on the table, and leaned into my face. 'Wake up, man! Look around you! This already where you ended up! This ain't where you headin'! *This where you are!*'

The Bevan Ward was never quiet, even at night. There was the permanent background hum common to all hospital units. There was the sound of twenty-six snoring and wheezing men behind twenty-six reinforced steel doors. There was the clacking of footsteps on linoleum when the nightshift nurses made their rounds, and the scrape of the peepholes they opened and shut as they went from room to room.

For those of us on suicide watch, the shutter opened and closed every thirty minutes, twenty-four hours a day.

There was also, almost incessantly, the sound of weeping. Godfrey could be heard wailing night and day except for the odd hour or two when he fell into exhausted sleep. A long-term resident on the ward – a 'lifer', as the other patients called them – nobody had been able to discover why he'd been crying nonstop for the eighteen months since he arrived. He cried while we all queued daily for our medication – lithium for the bipolar, clozapine for those with schizophrenia, olanzapine for those suffering psychotic episodes, methadone or subutex for opiate addicts, citalopram or fluoxetine for the merely depressed, diazepam and zopiclone to regulate stress and sleep for virtually everyone – and he stopped crying only to swallow the contents of his little paper ramekin, starting again immediately after. He cried while waiting for meals, pausing to mumble whether he'd prefer halal or non-halal, before crying as he carried his paper plate and plastic cutlery to the dining area with chairs screwed to the floor. He'd perfected the art of chewing his food and bawling simultaneously. He wept while he watched – or, rather, stared at – the TV. He only ever spoke a few simple words: addressed by staff or another patient, he'd clamp his mouth shut for a moment, stare intently as though fishing around in the murky pool of his memory, and then begin wailing again. Godfrey's crying was unremitting, distressingly loud and seemingly involuntary. Nobody knew whether it was just a tic – a meaningless symptom of wrecked neurochemistry – or a signal of authentic distress. Once I'd been on the ward three or four days, Godfrey's weeping had so thoroughly permeated my auditory experience that it no longer seemed a distinct sound. It felt as though it was coming from inside my own mind.

Like a prisoner settling in for a lengthy stretch, I spent my first week on the unit in a state of numb resignation. I queued for my overcooked hospital meals. I played board games. I learned which patients to avoid, like the man who, over a game of Scrabble where he played a series of meaningless words, confided that our organs were being harvested by evil

NHS managers, before shrieking at a passing nurse who'd slightly nudged our table. I took my methadone, my diazepam and my zopiclone. Tipped off by another resident, I pretended to swallow the benzos, saving them in my room until, after a few days, I had enough for a brief, ersatz buzz. I couldn't remember the last time I'd delayed even the slightest gratification, so I decided to count this as progress.

On the fourth day, my mother came to visit. I was sitting in the canteen when a nurse led her onto the unit. I knew she saw the crisis in my life as an inevitable consequence of rebellion against God. Just as Lucifer's hubris had seen him cast out of heaven, and Jonah's had brought him to the belly of the fish, so mine had landed me on the Bevan Ward. I'd barely seen my parents since they'd moved to Nazareth, and on the way here I'd been in no condition to take my mother in. Now I saw how much older she was than I remembered, how frayed by years of stress. I steeled myself for the tirade about sin and repentance that was surely coming.

But when she sat down her eyes were shining with tears.

'Oh,' she said with an intake of breath. *'My boy.'*

She reached for my hand, but I snatched it away. I tried to think of how to steer the conversation in a safely trivial direction, but in the circumstances my options seemed few. The best I could do was to ask her to fill the gaps in my memory about how I'd ended up here. She'd been in Leighton Buzzard with Abigail, she said, when my number appeared on her phone. On the line was a panicked Maria, explaining what had happened and confessing she had no idea what to do. So my mother had driven the forty-five minutes to London, and when she arrived she told me she was taking me in to a psychiatric unit.

'I knew you'd refuse,' she said, 'that you'd kick up a fuss. *But the state of you.* I wouldn't take no for an answer.' Her voice was cracking now. 'There was *no way* I was going to leave you like that.'

Somehow my mother's compassion was more painful than her reproach. I knew how to engage her in exasperating theological debate, but I had no idea how to deal with her kindness. I answered her questions about my medication, and listened to her explain that she'd salvaged what she could from my flat before turning it over to a relieved landlord. But soon our conversation trailed off into baffled silence. When forty minutes later she hugged me goodbye, I stood with my hands at my side, flinching from the contact. She'd cancelled her return flight to Tel Aviv, she said, and would be back in a few days. Before leaving she handed me a pile of novels, a suitcase full of clothes, and an old King James Bible that was nearly slipping from its leather binding.

She'd taken a few steps towards the exit when she turned and said, 'Oh – money. Do you need some?'

Before I could answer she came back, pressed three twenties into my hand, and embraced me again.

I could hardly believe this was the same woman with whom I'd all but cut contact. She barely resembled the human storm of criticism that formed my mental image of my mother. Was it that only a genuine crisis – a double suicide attempt – was enough to elicit her care? Or was it that she'd cared all along, but hadn't known how to show it except by worrying vocally I was on my way to hell? I'd always believed I was the victim of her anger, but I wondered now if it was the other way around. Could it be that the original sin was mine – that when I'd imagined she blamed me for her unhappiness I was projecting my feelings onto her?

I was almost twenty-eight years old, and I had to admit I had no idea who my mother was. All I knew was that none of the friends or girlfriends to whom I'd cruelly joked of her that *she puts the 'mental' in 'fundamentalist'* had so far shown any desire to come and see me here. She was seemingly the only person I had left.

Or – not quite the only person. The next morning I was still unscrambling my feelings over her visit when it occurred to me that, since I no longer had easy access to drugs, there couldn't be any harm in one last relapse, for old time's sake. Pleased with this logic, I called Adam. We made up hurriedly over the debacle of Maria's suitcase: nobody could be more forgiving, more eager to make amends, than a pair of addicts determined to exchange drugs for money. I explained my predicament, agreeing to pay him sixty pounds to come and visit with two dark and two light smuggled inside some kind of gift.

But when that afternoon I watched him arrive at the nurses' station with a single loaf of supermarket white bread, my heart sank. Dianne confiscated it straight away and I watched mournfully as she placed it in a medical waste bag for incineration. Empty handed, Adam was ushered in to see me. He sat down and shrugged.

In case the nurses were watching, I smiled like someone reunited with a dear friend. Under my breath I said, 'What the fuck, man? Who the hell brings a loaf of bread as a gift?'

Joining in with my act, Adam beamed, displaying two rows of false teeth. 'I done my fucking best, all right?'

I tipped my head back and laughed heartily. 'You might as well not've bothered!'

He grinned, shook his head, and slapped his knee. 'You think I'm happy about this? You think it don't break my heart to see good gear wasted like that?'

I leaned in close and whispered. *'Is there a single thing you don't fuck up?'*

'Look, I ain't had much practice bringing gear into a fucking cackle factory, all right? Where's my money, anyway?'

'Your money? Are you serious? Where's my drugs?'

'I done what you asked me to do. Took hours out of my day and all. So it didn't work out. Your plan, your risk.'

'Here, you can have forty.' Bitterly I passed him the notes under the table. 'And you're lucky I'm giving you that.'

Adam and I had spent countless hours in each other's company, having labyrinthine conversations about whatever entered our heads. But now, sober together for the first time, our talk quickly petered out. He left before long and, when the ward's triple-locked door closed behind him, I felt my mind's escape hatch slam shut.

With surprise I noticed that the feeling passing over me wasn't disappointment but immense relief.

So I surrendered to the authority and care of professionals. I adjusted to the rhythms of institutional life. Knowing I couldn't bring myself to harm was deeply comforting. Drugs were inaccessible, my belt and shoelaces had been taken away, and to use a razor I had to request supervision from a nurse. I'd spent my life pursuing freedom even unto death, so it was with a slightly sheepish gratitude that I accepted my infantilisation.

I watched my track marks heal, turning from lurid ribbons to violet bruises to faint scars, and I tried to imagine the synapses and receptors in my brain healing too. When, after a fortnight, Dr Kirsty told me I was being taken off suicide watch and would now be allowed to leave the ward for two hours a day, I realised I longed to feel my limbs in motion. It had been years since I'd used my body as anything but a delivery system for drugs, and my first run took me no further than the perimeter of the hospital car park before I was stopped by a knifing pain in my side. But the next day I ran a little further, and the following day further still, and I held on to these little tokens of progress, telling myself I was growing stronger, no matter how slowly. Soon I was covering several miles along the towpath beside Regent's Canal, cutting north from Homerton to Dalston and all the way to Angel before turning back. It was nearly June, the sun bursting off the water, and the air felt miraculously fresh in my lungs as I weaved past pedestrians sipping coffee or walking dogs. I felt almost like a human among other humans. I'd sprint the final stretch, arriving back on the ward panting hard and collapsing onto my bed in a flush of elated exhaustion.

Not only was I staying off heroin and crack, it had been some time since I'd told a lie. I'd spent the last few years going to elaborate lengths to hide the despicable reality of how I was living, so it was liberating to talk to the other patients without evasion or subterfuge. In fact, I barely felt the need to explain myself at all, preferring just to listen to their stories. Only a few were dangerous or entirely detached from reality. Most were simply traumatised, mangled by life and tormented by misfiring brains. It wasn't long before I got to know a few of them. Abu, a Sudanese refugee who'd lost his whole family to war, heard terrifying voices and woke up screaming most nights; he had a Master's in International Relations and loved to spend hours discussing Middle-Eastern politics or African history. And I became fast friends with Gabriel, a nineteen-year-old kid who reminded me of my brother. His Jehovah's Witness parents had disowned him when he came out as gay, leading to a chronic self-harm habit evidenced by the cockled white ridges covering his arms and even parts of his face.

There was no need for me to lie to Abu or Gabriel or anyone else on the Bevan Ward. What was there to lie about anyway? We were society's emotional detritus, its psychic scrapheap. We couldn't fall any further. It hardly mattered what we thought of each other.

I began to recover an inkling of something I'd all but forgotten: hope. When Dr Kirsty suggested I begin taking a daily antidepressant, I said that instead I'd like to begin reducing the methadone, benzos and sleeping pills I was

already prescribed. Heroin and crack were the only substances I truly cared about, so I might as well walk out of
here – whenever that might be – free of drugs altogether.

The next day I was dispensed not 90ml of methadone but
80, and not 20ml of diazepam but 18. At first I barely noticed
the difference; I went running and felt almost physically lighter
for the reduction of substances in my body. Dr Kirsty, Dianne
and the other staff watched my determination to get clean
with pride, and their encouragement brought me the same
childish pleasure I'd derived from coming top in class at school.

But not long after taking my last 10ml dose of methadone
a week and a half later, I was sicker than I'd ever felt before.
My body was engulfed in a brushfire of symptoms. Every
hour or so I'd sprint to the toilet, either to vomit or to shit. I
had a malarial fever but my skin was icy cold, no matter how
many extra blankets I requested from the nurses. I was both
unbearably restless and too exhausted to move. I waited all
day for the reprieve of sleep, but all night I lay awake, waiting
for morning with a thudding heart. I couldn't snatch more
than twenty minutes of oblivion at a time. My whole body
was in revolt against what I'd done to it, and as the days wore
on I began to forget what health had ever felt like.

But the physical pain was nothing compared with the
mental anguish. The self-belief I'd begun to feel in recent
weeks drained away. Dr Kirsty explained that, since I'd been
pumping my body with artificial chemicals for so long, I'd
drastically down-regulated its ability to produce the natural
opioids necessary for positive mood. I pictured my brain as a
dried-out husk, coated in cobwebs and teeming with mag-
gots. My mind rattled with dark, frightened thoughts. I tried
to envision a future in which I was an ordinary person – kind,
sane, well – but from my sweat-soaked pillow the idea seemed
fantastically alien. Twice a day Dianne brought tea and
wrapped my arm in a plastic cuff to take my blood pressure.

Swallowing anything made me nauseous, so after a sip or two I'd place the cup beside my bed and continue waiting for time to pass.

I tried to distract myself by reading, but my concentration was shredded. The only book that held my attention was the King James Bible my mother had left behind. I hadn't read the Bible since I was eighteen, but the familiar phrases of the Authorized Version were like the pacifying food of childhood. Whenever I felt strong enough, I'd flick through the wafer-thin pages with their musty scent, telling myself that every chapter or psalm would bring me a few minutes closer to recovery:

> From above hath he sent fire into my bones, and it prevaileth against them: he hath spread a net for my feet, he hath turned me back: he hath made me desolate and faint all the day . . . Behold, O Lord; for I am in distress: my bowels are troubled; mine heart is turned within me; for I have grievously rebelled.

It was the Old Testament I preferred, with its feuding families, flawed prophets and cacophony of lamenting voices. I read and reread the story of Jonah who, commanded to do God's work in Nineveh, chose absurdly to board a ship and flee. I imagined the days Jonah spent in the cold, wet belly of the fish, wondering if he knew the darkness swallowing him was his means of rescue and redemption.

On my eighth day of withdrawal I flipped by chance to the Bible's frontispiece and found an inscription beneath it:

> Philip D. Hill 6.8.64
> This Bible was bought when first I gave myself wholly to the Lord.
> Llandridnod Wells Convention 1964

I hadn't known I was reading my father's very first Bible. He'd have been fifteen in 1964, living with his secular, working-class parents in a small town in south Wales. In the combination of his child-like scrawl and the slight grandiosity of his syntax I felt I could see directly into his past. His own father was a drinker and prone to violence. No wonder that, at the same age I'd been when I began turning against my parents, Philip Hill had wanted to be born again. With the purchase of this Bible, he was forging a new self. *For behold, I create new heavens and a new earth: and the former shall not be remembered, nor come into mind.*

How could my teenaged father have imagined that the future would carry him not only into the pulpit but all the way to the land where Jesus lived? And how could he have guessed the disappointments in store? His marriage to my mother had resembled trench warfare: every day, after swapping countless tonnes of artillery, neither side had advanced or retreated more than a few yards. And then there was the backsliding of his children, who'd each concluded their parents' dissatisfaction and perpetual conflict were the best possible arguments for atheism.

That night I dreamed I was nine years old. I was on a beach, hot sand beneath my feet, my parents lost in a crowd further along the dunes. I couldn't see them, but I could hear them arguing. The sea eddied and roiled, painted with blades of white light. I jumped into the water, trying to swim away. There was no land visible anywhere, I was in the middle of the sea, but still my parents' arguing echoed in my ears. Then I knew my mother and father weren't on the beach, they were further out, and they were drowning. I tried to swim over and save them, but the harder I tried the further they drifted. Then a giant starfish came and wrapped me in its scaly arms, everything was dark and I was being sucked into its belly. Suffocating inside thick folds of animal flesh, I tried to scream but no sound came. I grappled and writhed. Then I heard nothing but the noise, in the distance, of a man crying.

It was first real sleep I'd had in days.

The morning of my release, my mother came to see me, just as she had twice a week throughout my stay. The woman who'd brought me into the world had inarguably done everything in her power to block my exit from it.

We were watching the dayroom TV in companionable silence when I turned to her and said, 'Mum, can I ask you something?'

'Go on.'

'Why did everything feel so hard? You know, when I was small?'

She looked at me as though she'd been considering the very same question. 'I was at the end of my tether. All the time. We were poor. We were worried sick about money. We didn't know whether we were coming or going. When Jonathan was born we had three children under three years old. I didn't sleep for years.'

She rubbed her eyes, as though to remove the effects of hundreds of restless nights. 'And you were so *naughty*. You were the most stubborn little boy anyone could imagine. If I wanted you to brush your teeth, I'd say, *Don't you dare go and brush those teeth!* And you'd say, *I don't care what you think! I'm going to brush them right now!*'

I laughed. Undeniably there was more than a hint of me in this portrait.

'But none of that was really my fault, was it? I mean, I was a tiny kid.'

'You're right. It wasn't. It was absolutely not your fault. It was just – your father and I, we didn't really understand each other. We were both so tired all the time. It's not easy, being a mother to four children. We were *so tired*.'

More and more I was learning that, when my mother and I forgot to talk about God, we could communicate like ordinary people.

'I know the feeling,' I said, changing the channel on the TV. 'I'm tired too.'

I was finally discharged from the Bevan Ward that afternoon. It was mid-June, two weeks after my birthday. I'd been registered as homeless, and a place had been secured for me in a local 'halfway house' where my tenancy would depend on a clean weekly drug test. I had some time to kill before meeting the social worker who'd take me there, so I sat at a table outside a little café next to the hospital. For the last week I'd been coming here to read after my morning run, Dr Kirsty having told me when I recovered from withdrawal I could now leave the unit for three hours a day. The café was decorated in warehouse chic with exposed brickwork and reclaimed wood. It felt like the height of freedom to sit among its aromas of toasted poppy seeds and roasting beans, making my way through *David Copperfield*. All week I hadn't been able to stop myself smiling gratefully at the staff as I placed my orders. When it was time to pay, the barista brought my bill.

'Aren't you going to take your discount?' said the young woman. I guessed she was in her mid-twenties. Her arms were covered in geometric tattoos and her auburn hair was held in a bun by a pencil.

'Sorry?'

She pointed to a sign in the window that advertised 20 per cent off for NHS staff. 'I've seen you coming from the hospital on your lunch hour every day, but you never take your discount.'

'Oh, right. Well – uh, sure.'

'In that case, here's 50p. It's your lucky day.'

'Wow, I'll try not to go too wild.'

Instead of heading back inside she sat down, opened a tin of tobacco, and pulled out a pre-rolled cigarette. 'Do you mind?'

'Go for it.'

She inhaled with a little shiver, and blew out a plume of smoke. 'I keep meaning to quit. It's a filthy habit, I know.'

'There are worse habits.'

She peered at the cover of my book. 'Good read?'

'Well – yeah. I like it, anyway.'

'I've never read anything by David Copperfield.'

'Oh, well – that's not actually – I mean—'

As I tripped over my words, I wondered if six weeks on the Bevan Ward had deprived me of the faculty of ordinary conversation. How long had it been since I'd had a normal chat with someone who wasn't a psychiatric patient, a mental health worker or my mother? But then how long before that had it been since I'd had a fully sober conversation with anyone at all?

She took the book from my hand and scanned its back cover. 'I'm impressed you have the energy to read in between your shifts.'

'Well,' I said, lowering my gaze. 'Some days are more tiring than others.'

Nodding over at the hospital, she said, 'What do you actually do over there?'

'I'm – uh – I'm kind of in the area of mental health.'

'So you're, like, a psychiatrist?'

I'd fallen out of the habit of lying, and I was surprised how difficult it had already become. I was tempted just to tell her the whole ugly truth: that I'd tried to kill myself, that I'd been locked up for my own good, that I was being released today. Instead I said, 'Yeah, I guess so.'

She narrowed her eyes playfully. 'So are you or aren't you?'

'I – I'm training. It takes a long time to qualify.'

'Do you have, like, a specialism or something?'

I could feel my teeth grinding. 'Well, addiction, I suppose.'

'That's cool. I'm thinking of training to be a counsellor. Or maybe a social worker.'

'How old are you?'

'Twenty-four.'

'In a way I wish I'd waited till I was your age before becoming all grown-up. Let my hair down a bit, you know.'

'But it's a grass-is-always-greener kind of thing, isn't it? When you're making a hundred lattes a day, you envy people with, you know, a vocation.' She looked at her watch. 'Well, that's my break over.'

'Well, hey, look. If you wanted to chat more later – like, after my shift?' The absurdity of what I was doing suddenly hit me. 'Oh, then again – tonight—'

'Long hours, right?'

'Exactly.'

'Maybe another time. You get back to saving lives.'

'Ha, I'm not sure about that,' I said modestly.

Before heading to my appointment I returned to the ward one last time to collect my suitcase and say goodbye to Abu, Gabriel, Dianne and Dr Kirsty. I looked out over the day-room where men in the unit's unofficial uniform – joggers, hoodies and slippers – were lounging on sofas. If anyone had told me when I first arrived here that a future version of me would feel a little sad to leave, I'd have thought *he* should be locked up.

As I wheeled my suitcase through the streets of Hackney, I wondered whether the hallucinatory brightness around me was due to the season or my newly unfiltered consciousness. The sky was a piercing turquoise. The veins on the roadside elms were like brown capillaries. The eyes of a girl who passed were surreally green. I strolled through London Fields, taking in the pocking sound of tennis balls and the charred smell of cooking meat from makeshift barbecues. Two men, one with an accordion and the other a ukulele, played a kind of klezmer romp at the end of Broadway Market. At their feet was an open instrument case into which people tossed coins that arced and glinted in the light. I hadn't heard music in weeks; I almost broke out in a little dance.

I felt like a child, overpowered by the world in all its immediacy. But my excitement was backlit with an anxiety I couldn't quite suppress. It was just gone 3pm; there were seven or eight hours until I could put my head on a pillow and sleep. The day stretched out ahead of me. There was such a vast amount of time for me to endure without using a single substance to manipulate my emotions. It was one thing to stay clean on a secure hospital ward, but out here I wondered how anyone did it. The world was too vivid, the sensation of being alive too fierce. My phone, from which I hadn't deleted Adam's number, burned in my pocket.

No, I couldn't destroy all the progress I'd made. It had been six weeks since I'd touched heroin or crack and nearly three since I'd taken any substance at all. I'd run out of lives; I may not survive another slip. I left the park and made my way down a residential street. Inside large terraced houses I could see high-ceilinged living rooms with stuffed book-shelves, wall art and chandeliers. I'd always told myself I despised the complacency of bourgeois life, but now I found myself longing for the order and security these spaces evoked. At the end of the road I saw the social worker – bearded, baggy-jeaned, folder under one arm – waiting to take me into my new home. Once he'd gone I would grit my teeth and make it until nightfall. I wouldn't self-destruct. I'd begin – right here, today – learning how to live.

And, as I greeted him with a handshake, I understood that I'd need to start by finding some people to whom I could tell the truth.

Noble Truths

Life is suffering. The First Noble Truth seemed plausible when, at 4am, the gong woke us with a brassy shimmer from our narrow dormitory beds. I stumbled out into the halflight, a silvery moon in the sky, and made my way to the washroom. Men shaved and brushed their teeth before steamy mirrors while showers hissed behind bamboo partitions. Although we'd only taken our vow of silence after dinner the previous day, one evening of meditation had been enough to disabuse me of the idea that a Buddhist retreat might be relaxing. As soon as we'd stopped talking, my mind began churning with restless thought. I hadn't experienced the passage of time as such an excruciatingly tangible ordeal since waiting for dealers back when I was a junkie.

The gong sounded again – I could tell I'd grow to hate that thing over the coming nine days – and I walked to the meditation building. Two separate paths led up a slope towards the entrance, one from the women's enclosure and one from the men's. I removed my shoes in the lobby and padded into the hall, finding my cushion. On a dais at the front sat the Teacher, a stern-jawed man in his forties with a side parting and a headmasterly air.

When everyone had settled, a recorded voice droned from a tannoy like the low notes of an untuned organ.

'*Anicca vata sankhara, uppadavaya-dhammino. Uppajjitva nirujjhanti, tesam vupasamo sukho.*'

A few people shifted on their plastic mats. There was the sound of throat-clearing. A sniffle.

'Remain completely aware,' said the Indian-accented voice. 'Very attentive. Very vigilant. Constantly aware of the breath. As it comes in naturally. As it goes out naturally.'

I tried to focus, but within seconds I began to perceive textures in the silence around me. The room was filled with the fluttering, thrumming sound of 150 people breathing in and out, in and out.

'Remain aware at all times. You must work very hard. Diligently. Ardently. Patiently. Persistently. Continuously.'

I heard a fly zipping past on my left. I opened one eye and then another, watching it slalom through the air.

At the front of the hall was an eight-foot golden Buddha statue surrounded by jars of burning incense and vases of flowers. Buddhism was the most kitsch of religions. It was even worse than Catholicism. The nonconformist churches of my youth had been austere, almost décor-free. I recalled as a child seeing the Vatican on TV, the clergy in swishing robes surrounded by gold and marble. My father had snapped the machine off in disgust, almost spitting: *And they call themselves the Church of the Christ who was born in a stable!* I was terrifically impressed by his scorn, and even now I disliked any but muted styles. The finicky display of gloss and primary colour here was my idea of aesthetic hell.

The Teacher glared at me. I shut my eyes.

'If thoughts should arise, no matter. Simply direct your awareness back to the breath. The entire length of the incoming breath. The entire length of the outgoing breath.'

With a prodigious effort I tried to follow these instructions. Doing so felt like untangling an enormous ball of knotted twine.

The thrash and sprawl of my thoughts reminded me of a day four years ago, shortly after my release from the Bevan Ward, when a pigeon flew into my room at the halfway house. As I tried to usher it back out it panicked, diving at the window pane with a sickening thud of beak and talons. Feathers plumed everywhere and animal blood smeared the glass. I waved my arms frantically, trying to protect my face while guiding the terrified bird out of the window. After a few minutes it found the gap and swooped upward to freedom.

'Do not have prejudice or preference for any sensation. Otherwise there is danger of creating *sankharas* of craving and aversion. You have to come out of this mad habit-pattern. No more craving. No more aversion. Understanding fully well that every sensation has the same characteristic of arising, passing away. Arising, passing away.'

I wrestled my attention back to my breath. I was lost in thought, utterly distracted. The retreat was barely underway and I was already failing.

'It is necessary to experience unpleasant sensation to break your habit-pattern of aversion. Only then you get a wonderful opportunity to break out of your bondage.'

Ten days of silence: the no-talking cure. I cursed myself. It was so typical of me to try and learn meditation by coming here instead of, say, downloading an app and sitting for twenty minutes each morning at home. Why did I have to be so extreme, even in recovery? Wasn't my inability to practise any form of moderation exactly the problem?

My mind was like a tank of fish bait I'd once seen on a walkway in Guernsey, a mass of flesh-coloured worms writhing over each other.

Or it was like the Boo Box full of scorpions from the pirate film that had terrified me as a child, and I was locked inside.

Stop thinking about what thinking's like: that's precisely the opposite of what you're here for.

Loops and spirals of thinking.

A snake devouring its tail.

STOP.

'It is only when you experience unpleasant sensation that you find a way to come out of your habit-pattern of generating aversion. Good that you are experiencing unpleasant sensation. Make use of it as a tool. Otherwise how can you come out of your misery? Welcome, welcome, welcome every unpleasant sensation. *Anicca. Anicca. Anicca.*'

It was during my first week in the halfway house that it became clear to me that my mind was not my friend. My every third thought was of heroin. Only terror kept me clean. Alice, the 'support worker' with jangling purple earrings who occupied an office in the basement, administered a weekly urine test. Despite my recent truce with my mother, going to my parents in Israel wasn't a realistic option. So if I used drugs my next stop would likely be the pavements of east London.

If I'd thought drugs were my problem, those early days after getting clean showed me how wrong I was. Without them I felt crazier than ever. My body shuddered with tension. My brain crackled and blared. I cycled rapidly between feelings of mania and doom. I was living on unemployment benefit, most of which I spent on late-night sorties to local newsagents and fast-food outlets. If I devoured enough junk the hit of sugar and fat was enough to numb my skittering mind for a couple of hours until I fell into a nauseated sleep. I began to alternate the shops I visited so the proprietors wouldn't see me coming back each day to buy the same piles of chocolate or trays of fried chicken.

I quickly learned which foods were best for throwing up. Ice cream was the least offensive on the way back out. I'd buy two budget cartons, microwave them until they were a soft slurry, take them back to my cramped room, and neck them like pints of lager while sitting on my single bed. Almost instantly I'd fall into a sugary fugue. When I came around I'd go to the communal bathroom and drink warm water from the tap until my stomach swelled grotesquely. I'd stab my gullet with the index and middle fingers of my right hand, trying to poke the fleshy leaf of my epiglottis until ice cream surged back up, mixed with sour stomach juices and bilious globules of half-digested matter. It seemed I was destined to spend my whole life doing sordid things behind locked bathroom doors.

I knew there was a word for this kind of behaviour, but I shrank from uttering it to myself or anyone else. It was an illness I associated with lovelorn teenage girls, not grown men. Heroin addiction still sometimes had for me a kind of nihilistic romance. But there was nothing romantic about sitting alone in your underwear at 1am, guzzling budget ice cream you planned to puke up in fifteen minutes' time.

I was as friendless in the halfway house as I'd been at boarding school, but for the opposite reason. I'd stood out there for my relatively humble origins, whereas here I was suspiciously posh. At first the other men – who'd mostly come from prison or the streets – didn't seem to know what to make of me. My outcast status was confirmed the day I bought a carrot cake and left it in the communal kitchen with a note that read *Help yourself!* When I returned that evening I was bewildered to find the imprint of a fist where someone had punched the cake, flattening it. It was some time before I understood that my gesture had been interpreted as a sign of weakness, earning contempt from my housemates by marking me as vulnerable – and that one in particular had felt humiliated by my note, because he was illiterate and therefore had no idea what it said.

After a couple of weeks in the house I decided it was time to call Maria and apologise. Her phone rang for a long time, and I was about to hang up when she answered. I explained I'd saved a little money to begin repaying her for what had happened with the suitcase. It wasn't a lot, but it was a start. Could I see her?

'Where are you living?' she said.

'It's kind of a – a house share. With a bunch of guys. Not far from where you lived with me before.'

She took a deep breath, audibly cagey. 'I'll come and see you tomorrow, after work.'

When I answered the front door the next evening, I had a sense of déjà vu. It felt like I was meeting someone from another life, even though it had only been a couple of months. I led Maria down the entrance corridor, past a wall-mounted fire extinguisher and a notice about how to evacuate the building in an emergency. In the kitchen were four giant fridges and a rack of chopping boards colour-coded for vegetables, bread, meat and fish.

'What is this place?' she said. 'It feels kind of institutional.'

I explained to her the principles of the halfway house.

'So they test you here?'

'Every week. For drugs and alcohol.'

'I should have thought of that.'

I winced. She turned away and gazed out the window. In the yard two residents in vests were sitting in deck chairs, smoking roll-ups. At their feet was a jar of bloated fag butts pickling in brownish water. I watched her closely, trying to gauge her mood, wondering why she'd agreed to come.

'Look, Maria, I know it's not worth much at this point. But I'm sorry about – well, everything.'

'I know you are, Matt.'

She continued staring into the yard. I took a few steps forward until I was standing behind her. When I put a hand on her shoulder she leaned towards me until her back was touching my chest.

'Do you want to see the rest of the house?' I said.

She turned and looked up at me as though trying to place someone she half-recognised. 'Ok then,' she said eventually. 'Let's go.'

Half an hour later we lay curled in each other's arms. Until Maria had stepped into my room I hadn't realised how ravenous I was for human contact.

'I've missed you,' I whispered tentatively. 'Is there any way we can put the past behind us, start again?'

I felt her body grow tense. She uncoiled herself from me and folded her arms under her chin. 'I don't think you have any idea how much you hurt me.'

I tried to swallow, but my throat was full of cement.

'Even now I don't know what was true and what wasn't.' The light was failing outside, and oblong shadows slid across her back. 'Can you even imagine what that's like? It was those little blue and white wraps. Tiny scraps of plastic, everywhere. I hoovered them up every day, but they just kept coming back. Do you remember what you said when I asked you about it?'

'No.'

'You said relationships are meant to be based on trust, and if I didn't trust you there was no point in us being together. And you complained about the stigma faced by addicts – you kept saying that word, *stigma* – and how it was so unfair you were always being treated with suspicion.' She laughed acidly, her eyes narrow. 'It was quite an impressive performance. You don't remember any of this?'

'I don't lie any more, Maria. I'm done with all of that. I'm sick of having to remember what I've told who. It's exhausting. Look, I understand why you're angry—'

'That's the weird thing. I keep telling myself to be angry. I know I should be. But somehow I just feel sad. What you did – it was so pathetic. That whole business with my suitcase. It was all so shameful and stupid.'

She stood up and began getting dressed. My stomach clenched at the thought of being left alone again.

'I'm glad you're doing better, Matt. And I hope you find some way forward, I really do.'

She laced up her shoes, and told me to get in touch when I had some more money for her. Then, before leaving, she said, 'By the way, the point of being honest isn't supposed to be that it's more convenient for you. It's that lying *hurts other people*.'

The weeks after Maria's visit were the loneliest in my lonely life. All the friends I'd once partied with had peeled away. I was wary of the ones who were still using, and those who weren't were wary of me. I called George, who was back at his father's place in Leighton Buzzard. Our relationship remained frosty after the disaster our house share had become, and we hadn't spoken in months.

'Hey, how's it going?' I said when George answered.

'Oh, you know. Nothing much to report here. What's going on with you?'

'There's – um – been quite a lot, actually.'

I gave the briefest summary of my time in the Bevan Ward, as though spending six weeks on a psych unit was the kind of strange thing that could happen to anyone.

'Anyway,' I said. 'It'd be awesome to see you some time.'

'Sure. I mean, that would be great. It's just—'

'Maybe I could jump on the train up to Leighton Buzzard? Or if you'd like to come down here?'

'Look, Matt. I don't want to hurt your feelings. But, well, it hasn't exactly been easy in recent years. Being your friend.'

'I know. I understand that, and I'm sorry. But I'm clean now.'

'Right.' He let out a long, pained sigh. 'And that's great. It really is. It's just – well, I've had to ask myself a lot of questions lately about how much I can offer you. And there comes a point—'

'No, I know. I get it.'

'Listen, we've known each other since we were practically kids. We'll always be friends. It just sounds like you have a lot of stuff to figure out at the moment.'

'Right.'

'You know, I'm really proud of you. For stopping.'

It was already hard to remember why I'd taken drugs for so long – I'd taken drugs because I was a drug addict, that was all I knew for sure – but on some level it was because I sensed other people were very far away, and for a time drugs promised to bring them nearer. I thought of my early days drinking with Emma, and of those raucous parties when I'd first moved to Belgrade Road. And yet here I was, spat out on the alien shore of sobriety, without a single person to talk to in a city of millions.

It was time to take stock of things, I decided. So later that evening I sat on the single bed in my room, a grease-streaked pizza box and two ice-cream cartons, all empty, at my feet. After a few minutes of stock-taking, I came to a conclusion: that I wasn't so much a human personality as a series of morbid paradoxes. I was a loner who couldn't stand his own company. I was ruled by my feelings but had no idea how to access them. I'd do anything for freedom except tolerate the slightest uncertainty. Life struck me as one big joke, and I took it extremely seriously. The only release I'd ever found from my condition was heroin. So here was a new paradox: I loved drugs so much that I could never take them again.

One day I got a call from Sinead, who I hadn't heard from since I'd moved out of her place. To my surprise, she told me she was sober. She'd started attending meetings where recovering addicts helped each other stay clean.

'I've heard about this,' I said. 'It's a religious thing, isn't it?'

'It's not religious. It's *spiritual*.'

'I'm not sure it's my cup of tea, to be honest.'

There was a pause. 'Are you getting any help?'

'I can't afford therapy. I don't have a job.'

'So how are you managing?'

'I'm on the dole.'

'I meant, how are you managing to stay clean?'

'I don't know,' I said honestly. 'Willpower. I go running. They test me every week where I live, so if I use I'll be homeless.'

'All I'm saying is, are you sure it's not worth a try? What have you got to lose?'

I found myself missing Sinead. 'Why don't we go to a meeting together some time?'

'We can't, I'm sorry. It's not encouraged for newcomer women to hang out with newcomer men.'

Sinead had evidently joined a cult. I wished her well and hung up. But over the next couple of weeks, while I took long solitary walks around London, I found myself thinking about her suggestion more and more. It was late summer, and the city seemed overrun with people doing things together. In Dalston Kurdish taxi drivers played pool and watched football in crowded social clubs. Outside gay bars young men in sportswear shared cigarettes with drag queens. Afro-Caribbean hair salons catered to gossiping women late into the evening. The streets of Stamford Hill were thronged with Hasidic men in furred hats and women with multi-buggies, and I found myself daydreaming about joining their community, allowing my identity to dissolve in a tribe like a tablet in water. Did the Hasidim accept converts? Would I have to learn Yiddish?

I called Sinead back and asked her to recommend a meeting I could try. The next evening, I was in Newington Green, searching for the address she'd given me. Rain was falling in a gauzy mist and the roads were streaked with oily light. When I saw Sinead had sent me to a church – Unitarian, but still a church – I decided to turn around and head home. But just as I was doing so, a man detached himself from the crowd huddled by the entrance under a penumbra of cigarette smoke.

'You a newcomer, mate?' he said.

'Uh, yeah.'

He lunged at me. I flinched, thinking for a split second I was being attacked. But then I found myself being wrapped up in a firm hug.

He stepped back and gazed at me with crystalline blue eyes. He had an unblinking expression, and his neck and hands were covered in tattoos.

'The problem isn't that there's a problem,' he said. 'The problem is that we think the problem's a problem.'

What was this, some kind of riddle? 'Right. Thanks.'

'No problem.' The man smiled. 'It's a killer illness. But we're the lucky ones. It's just a case of taking it one day at a time. Today's all we've got. Have you used today, mate?'

'No.'

'That's brilliant! Incredible! And what time did you get up this morning?'

'Uh, about seven?'

'I got up at eight. So you've been clean longer than me!'

A bell rang, and people started filing into the building. The meeting room was strip-lit, with two rows of fold-out chairs arranged in a semicircle around a trestle table. Taped to the back wall were cards with seemingly random slogans, like EASY DOES IT and WIND THE TAPE FORWARD and YOUR BEST THINKING GOT YOU HERE.

Behind the table sat a goateed man with a sclerotic complexion. He cleared his throat to hush the room. 'Hello everyone. I'm Christopher and I'm an addict.'

'Hi Christopher!' chirped back fifteen or twenty voices.

'I'd like to welcome you all to the 8pm meeting at Newington Green Unitarian Church. And most especially, I'd like to welcome any newcomers to the fellowship.' A number of faces turned and smiled at me. 'For the safety of the group, can I ask anyone who's got any drugs or paraphernalia on them to stash them outside and rejoin the meeting. Thank you. Now let's have some readings.'

For a few minutes people took turns reciting liturgical language about addiction and recovery from laminated cards. The air was musty with the smell of damp clothes. Christopher opened the meeting, inviting people to 'share'.

I'd come, I supposed, hoping to hear something that echoed my own experience, and perhaps to pick up tips on how to stay clean. Instead, one person after another introduced themselves by name, identified as an addict, and spoke in a jargon-mired psychobabble about 'the Disease', 'the Programme', 'the Rooms' and 'the Steps'. There was talk of a higher power and of spiritual awakenings. And practically every speaker seemed to contradict the previous one. *Getting clean's all about learning to be selfish*, said one person; *Recovery's all about putting others first*, said another. *The Programme helps you put your feelings aside*, said one; *The Programme's all about learning to feel your feelings*, said another. *Nobody's going to help you stay sober except yourself*, said one person; *Self-reliance is the enemy of recovery*, said another.

At times I simply couldn't follow what was being said. One person opined, with an air of profundity, that the longer you hung around a barber's shop, the more likely you were to get your hair cut. Another drew nods of approval when he pointed out that the Disease was an *ism*, not a *wasm*. And then the man from outside with the permanent glare and tattoos spoke, and wound up by declaring he would get back in the saddle with his knees on the floor and his arse in a chair.

Christ, I thought: if I hadn't walked in here today with a drugs problem, hearing all this half-digested brain dross would surely send me away with one.

I eyed the exit, but I was sitting at the end of a row and leaving would mean shuffling past several pairs of knees. I resigned myself to waiting until the end of the meeting. Then Christopher spoke up again. 'We've now reached newcomer's time. This is reserved for people in their first ninety days of recovery. Please come in by raised voice.'

The room was absolutely still. Of course, I had no intention of saying anything. The silence stretched out, turned viscous. There was a cough. A clock on the wall ticked and ticked. It was 8.47pm. The meeting had thirteen minutes left to run. I tried to keep my eyes fixed on the floor, but I was aware of a number of people turning expectantly towards me.

Fuck it. If they want to hear what I think, let them.

'I'm Matt,' I croaked. Silence. 'And I, uh, I'm an addict.'

'Hi Matt!' said the room in a frightening volley of enthusiasm.

'Um, I don't know what to say.' More silence. I looked up. Every face in the room was staring at me. My heart had a syncopated beat. 'I'm nearly three months clean.'

'WELL DONE!' thundered the room.

'Uh, thanks.' Sweat prickled my forehead. My mouth was dry. I tried to think of what to say. 'I spent my childhood in churches. In a way, I can't help thinking the whole problem started in places like this. So it feels weird to be back here looking for a solution.'

I'd meant this as the plainest statement of fact, but the room erupted in laughter, as though I'd put my finger on some hilarious irony. A rash of irritation broke out in me.

'It's not just the location that bothers me, to be honest,' I went on. 'It's the mumbo-jumbo, the pieties, the groupthink. No offence to any of you, but I've had a gutful of all that shit. And as for this whole idea your higher power's been looking out for you, well, there's a hospital not far from here where children are dying of cancer *as we speak*. Do you think their parents haven't prayed? What makes you think you're so special, that your higher power's kept you alive but can't be bothered to do the same for those kids? Do you have any idea how *fucking stupid* – how downright offensive – that sort of bullshit is? *Have you ever given it a moment's thought?* If that's the outcome of your spiritual awakening, quite honestly you can keep it. In fact I'd rather be a street junkie than be infected by this kind of nonsense. I mean, no offence. Uh, I guess that's it. Thanks.'

'THANK YOU, MATT!' cheered the room. The man to my right gave my back an encouraging thump. A leather-jacketed young woman in the row in front turned and gave me a thumbs up. A couple of people even clapped.

'And that brings us to the end of a wonderful meeting,' said Christopher. A cup was passed around for donations. Volunteers were solicited for the stacking of chairs. 'And now let's close with the Serenity Prayer.'

Suddenly we were standing in a circle, my hands were being grabbed by people to my left and right, and in unison the others were asking God for acceptance, courage and wisdom. Yes, this was definitely a cult. I almost gasped with relief when I could rush for the exit.

I'd barely made it out the door when I heard a voice from behind me. I turned and saw the woman in the leather jacket.

'Hey,' she said. Her hair was a dark brown and her complexion was, I guessed, Mediterranean. 'I'm Nadia.'

'Oh, hi. Matt.'

'I just wanted to say – I *loved* what you said in there.'

'Really?'

'Yeah, I got *so much* identification from it. I just thought you verbalised the blinkered perspective of the addict so well. That whole I'm-special-and-different mentality, you know?'

What was wrong with these people? Didn't she understand I'd just savaged her most dearly held ideas, that I'd in effect called her and her 'fellowship' a bunch of credulous fools?

'And I really get it, you know,' she went on. 'The anger, I mean. The resistance to accepting help. I felt exactly the same at my first meeting. Still do, sometimes.'

Nadia's warmth was disarming. She was, I reckoned, around my age. I found myself wanting to keep talking to her. We figured out we were heading the same way home, so we set off together.

As we walked, heads bowed against the drizzle, I asked Nadia how long she'd been clean.

'Coming up to ten months. One day at a time!'

What *was* it with these people and that phrase? How else did they think you were supposed to stay clean – or do anything – for an extended period? All at once? Working backwards from the end?

And yet I couldn't deny I was impressed. Living without drugs for the best part of a year seemed inconceivable. I wondered if Nadia could be lying, but there was an ease about her, a humility, that suggested she had no need to impress anyone. We chatted while making our way towards Kingsland Road, cars lighting up gutters as they swished past, and I felt slightly forlorn when she reached her bus stop. She hugged me goodbye, asked if she'd see me at next week's meeting, and I found myself answering yes.

*

During that first year of sobriety, I found I had a manic need for order. I planned every moment of every day. I only occasionally made myself sick after meals, but I weighed each serving of food and counted my calories, never exceeding 1500 in twenty-four hours. I saved my benefits until I could afford a second-hand GPS watch to track the distance and pace of my morning runs, figures I entered carefully in a little notebook. The rest of the time, I read books. I vaguely dreamed of becoming an expert commentator on current affairs, someone who marshalled facts, knew right from wrong, spoke in tones of certainty and authority. I set myself targets for how many pages to read each day, filling margins with scribbled notes. I'd lost all the books I'd collected over the years when I was on the Bevan Ward and my mother had to hurriedly return the keys to my landlord – but I didn't care. Fiction had altogether lost its interest for me. I could no longer fathom why it had ever mattered to me what reasons Dorothea had for marrying Casaubon, or how Raskolnikov felt about Sonya, or what it was like for Gregor Samsa to turn into a giant insect. What I craved now was reality: history, politics, economics. I'd fashioned my self, such as it was, by violently subverting the roles I'd found myself playing: the preacher's son, the scholarship boy, the privileged undergraduate. So to get up at dawn and make my bed with martial precision felt like another rebellion – except, this time, against my footloose former self. Arriving on time for appointments, knowing where I'd be next Tuesday evening, promptly completing any paperwork: learning how to do these things at twenty-eight felt strangely iconoclastic.

When my alarm went off each day I'd inspect my schedule. My time was filled with exercise, reading and recovery groups. Sometimes I asked myself why, given how much I disliked meetings, I was organising my life around them. One reason was that I had little else to do. Another was, undoubtedly, Nadia, with whom I talked on the phone most days. Nadia was virtually unshockable. When, during one call, I told her what had happened with Maria, she told me about the time she'd been sent to a psych ward.

'That was kind of a turning point. I was in a lot of denial at first. Then I started getting drunk on the hospital's alcoholic hand gel—'

'And that's when you realised you had a problem?'

'Nah,' she said. 'That was just social drinking, as far as I was concerned. I finally accepted there was something wrong when I started on the hand gel *in the morning*.'

Nadia took recovery seriously, but she didn't mind listening patiently when I complained about the theology and culture of the Programme.

'Don't you hate how even the mildest coincidence in any addict's life is supposed to be the work of their higher power?' I said once. 'I'm having coffee with this guy after a meeting the other day, right? And when I say that maybe a coincidence is just a coincidence, he thumps the table and yells, *If it's odd, it's God!* And he folds his arms, all pleased with himself, as though anything you can say in rhyme must be true.'

'Who taught you to take everything so literally? Who cares whether it's true if it works?'

I pressed on with my case. 'But have you ever noticed how competitive people get in meetings about how *sick* they are? It's almost like they're boasting about their sex addiction or panic attacks or PTSD. And then there's the way everyday human behaviour gets pathologised. Loyalty's *codependence*. Self-sufficiency's *isolating*. If you're selfless you *lack boundaries*. It drives me crazy.'

'You don't have to like everyone in the Rooms, Matt,' she said archly. 'You just have to *love* them.'

Even as I passed the milestones of six months, nine months – each time going forward at the end of a meeting to receive, with a mixture of pride and embarrassment, a commemorative keyring and a round of applause – I kept finding troubling aspects of the Programme. Worst of all were its echoes of my religious childhood. It had its own sacred text, the 'Big Book', which was considered all but infallible and was spoken of in worshipful terms. The addict was expected to follow a series of 'Steps' – numbering twelve, of course – which amounted to a journey of conversion, confession, restitution and evangelism. And the whole business was presided over by a 'higher power' supposedly of the addict's 'own understanding' but who bore a striking resemblance to the God of Judeo-Christian vintage.

'Remind me how long you've been sober now?' said Nadia during one call when I listed several new objections.

'Ten months.'

'And could you have done that without the Programme? When a medicine's keeping you alive, do you complain about the taste?'

Of course I was besotted with Nadia, but I knew she respected the Programme's prohibition against regular members dating anyone under a year sober. Nadia had passed this point some time ago, and I was waiting for the moment when I could declare what I suspected she already knew.

The strange thing was that, when I spoke to Jonathan about the Programme, I'd find myself taking the opposite position. Over a year of testy phone calls, and then more relaxed coffees, I gradually repaired my relationship with my brother. He kept pressing me to find a therapist. I had a little spare money now. I did occasional work for university acquaintances who were setting up businesses and needed copy for new websites. I'd placed a handful of articles about politics in newspapers. And I'd found some work tutoring the sons and daughters of precisely the kind of families I'd once studied alongside at the Famous School. But when Jonathan urged me to speak to a professional, I insisted all I needed were my meetings.

'But do you ever talk about the past? About Mum and Dad, that kind of thing?'

'Resentment is the number-one enemy of recovery, Jon. I try not to think about all that stuff.'

'God, Matt, you're starting to sound like you've been brainwashed.'

Irked, I said, 'So what if I have? Maybe my brain needed some washing. Look, the Programme's just common sense dressed up in spiritual language. Like the whole higher power thing. All that means is, you're fucked unless you rely on something bigger than yourself. For me, that's the Rooms themselves. Put it this way, before I started going I was killing myself with heroin and crack. Now I'm nearly one year clean. Who cares whether it's true if it works?'

And then the morning arrived that marked the fact I'd somehow stayed clean for 365 days. I woke at 6am, ate my usual breakfast of chopped banana and bran flakes, and changed into my exercise clothes. As I ran laps around Hackney Downs, summer light threading through the trees, I realised I'd expected everything to feel different today. But, of course, nothing had changed. My GPS watch told me my split times were on the slow side. I went home, showered, got dressed and set out to meet Nadia for a celebratory coffee.

She was already waiting with a broad smile when I arrived at the Italian espresso bar we'd chosen. Her skin was newly sun-coppered, and her hair had a fresh lavender scent. We sat down at an oilcloth-covered table, facing each other. 'So,' she said. 'One year *clean-and-serene*! I'm so proud of you!'

I played along with a theatrical shudder.

'Sorry,' she said, 'I thought you loved that thing, with the rhymes. Seriously though, how does it feel?'

'Oh, you know—' I trailed off, unable to imagine feeling anything that wasn't connected in some way to the smell of her hair and the look of her skin. So I stared at the laminated menu in my hands and told her how much her friendship had meant to me. That if not for her I doubted I'd have gone to a second meeting. And, in that case, who knew if I'd still be clean?

'Sweetheart, if you'd never gone to another meeting, *maybe* you'd still be alive. But, no offence, your chances of being a year clean would be somewhere between nil and zero.'

Conversations with Nadia had a way of speeding around hairpin bends from earnestness to irony and back. 'So you're saying—?'

'No, you don't owe me for saving your life. You just owe me for the fact your life's worth living.'

'Nadia, I've just realised. You're my higher power!'

She jutted out her lower lip and blew some hair from her face. '*Finally*, he notices.'

'Just one thing. Where the fuck were you when everything was going to shit a few years ago?'

She nodded sagely. 'I had a feeling you'd ask that. Whenever you turn around, my child, and see our two trails become one pair of footprints in the sand, know that—'

'Oh, right. You were *carrying* me. That's beautiful.'

'Uh, not exactly,' she said, affecting a sheepish shrug. 'Actually I was in the pub, getting shit-faced. I never said I was a perfect higher power.'

'That's very . . . human of you. But seriously, I do really appreciate it. Having you around.'

'Well, *service keeps you sober*, as they say. But you know it hasn't been *pure* charity, don't you?'

I decided to take that as my cue to say what I'd rehearsed on the bus into town. 'Of course, uh, now I'm not a newcomer any more – well, I guess the terms and conditions are sort of different.'

Nadia seemed unfazed. 'Oh, absolutely. Somebody better tell the ladies to form an orderly queue.'

'Ok, there's no need to be sarcastic.'

'Sarcastic? Me? No, but honestly, is there anyone you have your eye on?'

The anticlimax of this anniversary, the sense of having crossed a threshold I'd believed would inaugurate a new life but which of course had changed nothing, the stark fact that at almost thirty I was still living in a halfway house – all led me into a mood of despair from which, I decided, only Nadia could rescue me.

'Well, there is someone.'

'Oh?'

'Maybe it's stupid.'

'Of course it's not. Is she in the Rooms?'

'Yeah.'

'Do I know her?'

I glanced at her. 'You do, actually.'

Something dawned across Nadia's face, and she looked down. She began stirring her coffee energetically. In that moment I felt the entire meaning of my life depended on what she said when she looked back up.

'Is it who I'm thinking?' she said without expression.

'I'm afraid so.'

She raised her mug to her lips with both hands, took a long sip, and set it back down. Then she was saying something about how she was still deep in her Steps, that her sponsor had advised her not to date until she'd worked through her old romantic patterns, how she valued our friendship but had never seen me in that way, and anyway I was vulnerable and still figuring myself out. She carried on talking for a long time, and after a while I no longer heard her words but instead the message hidden inside them: that I was tainted, defective – and that not even a hundred years of recovery could make me worthy of anyone's love. Then we were hugging goodbye, and then I was walking alone back to the tube, and then in Dalston I was opening the door of The Kingsland pub. I was hit by the thick scent of stale beer and male bodies as I pushed my way to the bar.

When I had a pint of lager in front of me, I reminded myself I was doing something momentous, that I was trashing a year's hard work. I wasn't sure if I was trying to dissuade myself or intensify the sense of occasion. I felt like turning to the man next to me, who was engrossed in his phone, and telling him this would be my first intoxicant for a year. I considered calling Jonathan. I considered calling Nadia. Instead I raised the glass to my lips, tasted the sour foam, sucked on the fizzing liquid. Just like the first time I'd broken my promise on my word-as-a-Christian, nothing happened. Perhaps sobriety had been yet another superstition I'd fallen prey to, and I'd been denying myself for nothing. Alcohol had never really been my problem anyway. Had quitting it represented a cowardly submission to the Programme's dogma that all addicts were 'powerless' over all substances forever? And hadn't I survived my youth by pitting my own reason against the irrational faiths of others?

I decided to be sensible. I'd have two drinks and tomorrow I'd call Nadia, confess all, apologise for making her feel awkward, and begin counting from day one again. No harm done.

I had the two drinks I promised myself. Then, feeling much more cheerful, and seeing what a superb idea this had been, I had two more. Then I had two more. At some point I lost count.

When I woke up the next morning I was so ashamed of what I'd done that, instead of calling Nadia, I called Armani.

I didn't get clean again for almost two years.

There was half an hour until breakfast at the meditation centre, so I wandered off in the direction of the woodland encircling it. A trail threaded through a wildgrass meadow into a copse of pine and fir trees sparsely covered in green. Ahead of me walked a female student with platinum-blonde hair and grey leggings that clung to her hips and thighs. I sped up, but as we entered the wood the path forked and a sign directed men and women down different trails. Sullenly, I veered left. The branches made a fretwork above my head and cast chainmail shadows on the floor. In a clearing at the bottom of the wood, someone had carved ten notches into the silvery bark of a birch. My breath turned to steam in the cold air.

As I rounded the bend at the far edge of the grounds I saw Gus, a man I'd fallen into conversation with on the train down from London. When he'd discovered we were both heading for the Vipassana retreat, he told me excitedly about his daily meditation practice – one hour in the morning and one in the evening – and how his 'life goal' was to 'transcend suffering'. *Good luck with that*, I'd said, but he hadn't noticed my irony, and went on to explain how microdosing LSD helped him in his work as a cryptocurrency trader. Now Gus, hair in a topknot and wearing harem pants, sat on a bench with his eyes closed and his palms turned upwards, thumbs and middle fingers touching.

Irritation curdled in me. As if the morning session hadn't been arduous enough, here was Gus snatching an opportunity to squeeze in some extra meditation before breakfast. It was blatantly performative of him to do it out here, renouncing the ego in full display. Gus could go fuck himself. They could all go fuck themselves – not just the sanctimonious students with their *sankharas* and habit-patterns but the Teacher and, especially, that Indian guru with his fatuous instructions and love of adverbs.

But immediately remorse stole up on me. Was I really in a position to sneer at the likes of Gus? Was I so wise? I'd come to a retreat based on the principle of universal compassion and I was already generating petty resentments against people who were doing nothing more than sitting quietly with their eyes closed. Either that or I was eyeing up women in lycra. Even my feelings towards other people swung like a pendulum, it seemed, between aversion and craving. What the hell was wrong with me?

During the terrifying relapse before I entered the rehab that saved my life, my renewed drug use was more destructive, more overtly suicidal. Gone were my attempts at self-reform, my oaths that this would be the Very Last Time. I had some money now, so before I could be kicked out of the halfway house I moved into a small one-bedroom flat, quickly turning the place into a crack den. With a key to my own front door, free to use unseen by anyone, all bets were off. I was the ruler of my own two-room kingdom of squalor and self-loathing. It was some months before I was finally sacked from my last tutoring job, when midway through a lesson with an A level student I excused myself to the bathroom, passed out with a needle in my arm, and woke to find the boy's father breaking down the door. The money I'd earned was enough, I knew, to keep me going for some time.

I began to feel I was living a posthumous life, and I didn't care. I had tried getting by without drugs, I'd thrown everything I had at it, but the task had defeated me. It was time to accept that there were those who could cope with existence and those who couldn't. My year of sobriety had afforded me enough clarity to perceive what was valuable: purposeful work, service, honesty, love. But now I saw more clearly than ever how far out of my reach such things were. For a time I'd fooled myself into imagining I belonged among the sheep, but I'd been a goat all along.

One morning a year or so after my relapse I was waiting for Armani when I received a call informing me that Gareth Lloyd, an old university friend, had died, most likely from an overdose. Gareth and I had found our way to hard drugs separately, but we'd used together a few times over the years, and we'd bonded over our common Christian upbringing and Welsh roots. All day at his funeral I had the vague sense that something inside me was trying to make itself known, something about the connection between past and present. But it was ultimately drowned, along with any grief I may have felt, by the chemicals flooding my system.

Back when I'd started using drugs, I associated them with adventure and excitement. Now my life was an endless loop of mundane repetition. Every day was the same. I called dealers, I waited on benches or in stairwells, I cooked up, I injected. Frequently, I'd OD. On the rare occasions I ate, since I refused to spend money on anything but drugs, I shoplifted sandwiches from local supermarkets. I wore the same clothes for well over a year, and when the button snapped off my threadbare black jeans I began tying them up with a piece of rope. My tentative reconciliation with my family stalled; I resumed ignoring calls from my parents and even my brother.

Now and again the monotony was interrupted by some lurid drama. One night I found myself wandering the streets of Bethnal Green at 4am, looking for a way to score, and ended up at a flat used as a base by a group of wraithlike, glassy-eyed young women I soon learned were sex workers. We sat on two filthy mattresses on a concrete floor. Although we had enough spare needles to go around, there was only one spoon. So I cooked up a huge speedball and passed it around the room, inviting everyone to take a hit like a priest conducting a diabolic Eucharist. We continued taking drugs, most of which I supplied, while dawn rose outside the window. Every now and again one of the women received a call on her mobile, left for an hour or so, and returned with enough cash to score again. At around noon I decided to make my way home but, as I was leaving, the resident pimp – an acne-mottled man with a docker's physique – appeared in the doorway, claiming I owed him several hundred pounds for use of his premises. I considered what to do. If I was going to die, I wanted it to be by my own hand, not thanks to a beating from this hooligan. I allowed him to march me to the nearest cash machine and handed over the money.

Time passed. There was nothing new. Days bled into weeks, weeks into months. My flat was on the third floor of an old Victorian terrace, and I'd lie on the sofa for hours on end, sitting up only to prepare another hit, before slumping back to stare out at the rectangle of sky framed by the living-room window. I made occasional forays outside for drugs and other things – works, cigarettes, lighter fluid – before rushing home to keep using.

I no longer had any use for clocks or calendars. My flat – needle-strewn, soot-blackened – was like some ghoulish afterlife, an eternal present on the quiet limit of the world.

Just two drinks. A recent change in the quality of light through my window signalled that those two drinks had become almost two years. By now I rose each day – or, rather, jerked awake wherever I'd passed out – mildly irritated to find I was still alive. I couldn't remember when I'd last washed my clothes, which were mainly now a supply of tourniquets. One day I was sitting on my sofa, a bloody jumper sleeve wrapped tight around one arm, when I heard a sound so rare I was briefly startled.

My phone was ringing. The screen showed a familiar name. I finished my hit and answered.

Sinead had spoken just a few words when the speedball landed. *Fuck, that's strong*, was all I could think before not only her voice but my thoughts were drowned out by a noise like a jet engine roaring to life. Each time I thought my pleasure had peaked, it kept escalating, and then it was too intense, it was alarmingly pleasurable, I could feel my heart rattling with adrenaline, I didn't think *I'm dying* because I couldn't form thoughts, but in some visceral way I felt myself nose-diving towards nothing.

Then the rush passed and I was weightless, aloft.

I picked up my phone from where it had fallen to the floor.

'Hey, are you still there?' Sinead was saying.

'Sorry, I was just – uh – trying to find something.'

'Right. And did you?'

'Don't worry, I'll find it later. One way or another.'

There was a pause. 'Are you ok?'

'*Ok* is a *very* strong word, Sinead,' I said with a bitter laugh.

'It's great that you find your own jokes so funny. Seriously though, Matt. Should I be worried?'

'Of course you should! Life's nasty, brutish and short. Nature's red in tooth and claw. And that which is crooked—'

'Jesus. Just shut up and listen a minute, will you?'

I tried to sound serious. 'I'm all yours, I promise.'

'Lucky me! So, like I said, I'll be in your area tomorrow. And I want to see you, ok? It's important.'

When it became clear Sinead wouldn't take no for an answer – and she knew enough about my circumstances that I didn't insult her by claiming to have plans – we fixed a time and place.

The next day, in the most presentable clothes I owned, I entered a Turkish café on Kingsland Road and scanned the room. Sinead was at a corner table in her work uniform – black-rimmed glasses, grey shift dress – absorbed in her phone. I walked over and pulled out a chair.

She looked up. Before she could reset her expression, I said, 'You could at least pretend not to be *quite* so appalled by the sight of me. You're looking well, anyway.' It was true. Now several years sober, Sinead somehow appeared younger every time I saw her.

When she spoke, I could tell she was choosing her words carefully. 'I mean, I love the whole swim shorts and knitwear look, Matt. But you *are* a bit on the skinny side.'

'It could be worse. I had my first shower in a week this morning.'

'You really know how to make a girl feel special.'

'Anyway, I better pop to the toilet and—'

'Freshen up, sure. Have fun. I'll see you in a minute.'

After my hit, I returned to find an application form for a London rehab on the table. Sinead explained that she'd already filled it out. All I had to do was add my signature, and she'd deliver it. My annoyance was tangled with melancholy affection for this woman who persisted in denying what everyone, including me, had now accepted: that I was a lost cause, a no-hoper. This woman who repeatedly behaved as though *she* owed *me*, in spite of the material and moral facts.

But I was in no mood to pick a fight with Sinead and her formidable lawyerly brain, so I signed the form. When we stood to leave, she held on for a couple of extra beats, and there was something oddly formal – almost ceremonious – about the way she said goodbye.

A few days later my phone rang again. This time it was a man with an Estuary accent, who introduced himself as 'Harry from Grace House'.

'Grace House?'

'Yes, Grace House Drug and Alcohol Rehabilitation Centre. We got your application form. As it happens, a place just came up. Can we get you in for an interview? Say tomorrow?'

I put a glass bottle to my mouth, lit one end and inhaled until it was full of opaline fumes.

'Hello?' said the man. 'Are you still there?'

Exhaling a cloud of caustic smoke, I said, 'Uh, sorry. I'm busy tomorrow.'

'How about the day after?'

I thought, guiltily, about Sinead. It would be best, I decided, to show up for the interview and fail it deliberately. That way I could at least tell her I'd done everything possible to get help. I made an appointment with the man, promised not to use before coming, and said goodbye.

Grace House was a complex of nondescript buildings behind large ironwork gates off a busy high street. When I arrived – an hour late – Harry showed me into an admin office full of wall charts, filing cabinets and boxy computer monitors. The room had the odour of instant coffee. I couldn't see how anywhere as utilitarian and uninspiring as this could help redeem a situation as abject as mine.

Of course, I'd never had any intention of showing up sober. Although it wasn't yet midday I'd already had a couple of major hits, and I'd stowed a crack pipe in my jacket's inner pocket. Harry gestured to a chair, and I sat down.

'So, your application form said you're in a spot of trouble.' He was a wire-thin, owlish man with a thatch of white hair and a preternaturally gentle manner that belied his no-nonsense style of speaking.

'Did it?'

'Well, you wrote it.'

'Actually, my friend Sinead wrote it. I don't know what it says.'

He peered at me and sighed. 'From where I'm sitting, I'd say your friend has a point.'

'I'll try not to take that personally.'

'Take it any way you like.'

We sat silently for a moment. Harry eyed me with his arms crossed.

'Tell me something, Matt. Have you ever had a spiritual experience?'

I almost choked. 'Oh God. So this is a Christian place? You want to heal me by getting me to believe in Jesus?'

'I don't give a monkeys what you believe. I'm just looking at someone who's going to be dead in a year, and I'd like to see if there's anything we can do about it.'

'I've been in more churches than I've had crack pipes. And I don't know which did me more damage.'

Harry chuckled. 'I wouldn't necessarily disagree with you there. Certain forms of organised religion can do an awful lot of harm.'

I explained that I knew all about recovery, that I'd previously been clean for a year and attended meetings every week.

'Meetings are a good start,' he said. 'I'm not knocking meetings. But – tell me, Matt. Did you have a happy childhood?'

'Oh, I get it. This is all about therapy. Look, I've read my Freud.' This wasn't strictly true: at university I'd chosen a module on Freudian readings of modern literature, and failed to show up. 'I know it's all about proving how traumatised I was as a kid.'

'It always fascinates me how hard some people find it to believe that our upbringing has quite a lot to do with how we turn out as adults. It'd be strange if that wasn't how it worked, don't you think? So, yes, there *is* a heavy emphasis on childhood in our programme' – that word again – 'but we also believe the addict needs to have a spiritual awakening to really change.'

'A spiritual awakening? Seriously?'

'You've read your Freud, but what about your Jung? He said recovery can only be achieved through *a higher education of the mind beyond the confines of mere rationalism.*'

'I'm sorry. That's just not something I believe.'

'Well, can I suggest that whatever you do believe doesn't seem to be helping? How about trying something different?'

I couldn't decide if I was talking to a tambourine-slapping charlatan or a man of rare insight.

'So you're saying if I came to you for – what, a few weeks?'

'Six months.'

'Six months . . . then I'd come out the other side no longer a drug addict?'

'I'm afraid not. You'll always be an addict. But in six months I hope we'll have taught you to love yourself. So if you keep on doing the right things you won't need to take drugs any more.'

I groaned. 'Love myself? *Christ.* What does that even *mean*? It's like you're asking me to split myself into two people, one of whom loves the other. It doesn't even make sense.'

'Well, I get the impression you've already split yourself into two people, one of whom hates the other.'

I froze in my seat. I had to admit, he had me there.

As we'd been speaking, a realisation had come to me: that even in the nuclear fallout of my last two years a little cockroach of hope had survived. Hope that things could be different, that life might be worth living. It was the hope you had to watch out for. At least with despair you couldn't be disappointed. With despair you knew where you were. My deadliest addiction wasn't to heroin or crack, it was to hope. I'd tried giving it up so often, and of late I'd really believed I was done with the filthy habit. But I just couldn't seem to quit.

So I found myself saying, 'Ok, I'll come. I'm afraid I'll disappoint you though. I know the whole point of therapy is to get people weeping cathartically about how they weren't loved properly as children. The thing is, I'm not an especially emotional person.'

Harry leaned back in his chair, folded his arms behind his head, and smiled. 'Well, we'll have to see about that.'

Whatever else you could say about Sataya Narayan Goenka, the guru whose voice and image presided over the Vipassana retreat, he was not someone who could personally claim to have defeated craving. The recorded 'dharma talks' we gathered to watch nightly in the hall revealed an immensely fat man who always sat perfectly still, except when he took a handkerchief from his shirt pocket to dab his forehead and sandbag-like cheeks. The other students watched these rambling soliloquies with rapt attention, evidently believing they were full of transcendent wisdom.

'It is said that the truth will set you free,' said Goenka. 'Therefore let us now talk sense.'

So what were you talking before?

He wiped his brow. 'Open are the gates of the deathless state to those who renounce their lack of faith.'

A tensile force spread through my body. I should have seen this coming. Here I am again: back, to all intents and purposes, in a church pew, being asked to succumb to a puerile fantasy of eternal life, and to do so *on faith* – that is, by leaving my mind at the door. I was overcome by physical discomfort, just as I'd always been in those wooden pews. Every way I tried to arrange my limbs felt wrong.

In a ponderous and highly repetitive style, Goenka went on to explain the philosophy behind Vipassana. 'Many people begin this technique by complaining of this discomfort, that discomfort. Entirely natural. This is because your body and your mind have become prisoners of their own habit-pattern. They start revolting: *I don't like it!* Thanks to this technique, you have begun to experience the physical and mental structure in its pure form.'

My mind began to drift. There was nothing here but the same spooky waffle of which I'd heard a thousand different versions in the past. I began mentally composing an acceptance speech for this year's prize of UK's Most Spiritual Man. I wasn't motivated by awards or acclaim, I explained to my imaginary audience, only the unglamorous work of transcending the ego. If I'd learned one thing on my journey, it was that—

'The final goal of Vipassana,' said Goenka, interrupting my thoughts, 'is to purify the mind at the deepest level. Let us say something unwanted happens in the life. *I don't like it!* You start generating negativities, tensions. You become a prisoner of your hatred, animosity, ill-will. Tying up in knots all the time. So tense. So miserable. You are always craving, craving, craving, for things to be different.'

This was an infantile image of the self, and yet how could I deny its truth in relation to me? Hadn't I spent my life tied up in knots of craving – not just for drugs but for the love of one or another woman, for events to work out precisely according to my plans? And when reality had refused to cooperate, hadn't I revolted like a mewling child, trying to hurl away my discomfort like an unwanted toy? Hadn't my behaviour shown that, on some level, I believed life ought to be one long uninterrupted series of pleasant sensations? Was *that* my whole problem?

'You don't want to multiply your misery. And yet you remain miserable.'

This was true. I'd spent most of my life more or less unhappy, and I longed to be free. As Goenka spoke, I began, despite myself, to hang on his words. The old desire reared up in me: to spring the trap of myself, to be saved, reborn.

Then I caught myself. Wasn't this just the same renunciation of the world I'd been taught in church? How were you supposed to follow these teachings and still exist? I thought of my father. He'd returned with my mother to Swansea for retirement, and we'd been trying to revive our dormant relationship. He'd quit the cigarettes and codeine, but nowadays food was his drug. Every time I pleaded with him to lose weight for the sake of his health, he replied with the same breezy assertion: *When the Lord decides it's my time to go, it'll be my time!* In these moments my father's faith seemed very much like nihilism: an inability to see any point in life before death.

Goenka's philosophy was, at root, little different: the promise that, with enough meditation, we could enter a realm of non-attachment where nothing mattered. Was I supposed to have no preference at all – no 'craving' – for joy over suffering? Was I never supposed to 'crave' the wellbeing of people I cared about? Goenka seemed to want to turn me into some kind of airy spirit, floating through the universe with no feelings about anything at all. Around me, faces gazed at the screen with expressions of placid reverence. There was no end to the snake-oil peddlers of the world, I decided, and no end to the human desire to sidestep the human condition.

There you go again, I thought. Finding fault in everything. What exactly was the point in coming here if you're going to do nothing but spend ten days in a tantrum of resistance? If anybody needs to learn to live in the moment, it's you. Is it so inconceivable that the people in charge of this retreat – which, by the way, nobody forced you to attend – may know something you don't? What exactly have you got to lose by giving the process a try and seeing what happens?

If I'd learned anything since getting clean again at Grace House – since the Bevan Ward, even – it was this: doing things my own way never, ever worked. My belligerent scepticism of other people's ideas – which was both the product of, and the only means of escape from, my parents' faith – had long outgrown any use it had once had. Like drugs, what had once been a crude way of coping, even surviving, had turned monstrous, become an addiction, and ended up threatening to destroy me.

Yes, that was it, the single piece of wisdom I'd gained. You can't live your whole life in a state of insurrection against everything around you. In the end, you have to come to terms with existence. When you're losing badly, the only way to achieve peace is to stop fighting – in other words, to surrender.

It was eighteen months now since I'd arrived at rehab trailing a single battered suitcase. After being shown to my room, I immediately collapsed into unconsciousness. Harry had told me to quit heroin and crack before coming, warning there'd be a drugs test on entry. I'd succeeded thanks to a combination of diazepam, methadone, and reserves of willpower I didn't know I possessed, focusing my mind on the moment Grace House's ironwork gates would clang shut behind me.

My bedroom led out to a quadrangle of identical doors overlooking a balcony, beneath which lay a fish tank containing silver and reddish trout swimming in light-dappled water. The building had a faint eucalyptus odour and was homely in a monastic way. Everything worked: if a tile cracked or a plug socket needed rewiring, Harry or one of the other counsellors would quickly arrive with a tool kit. Grace House was the first place I'd ever lived where nothing felt like it could go drastically wrong.

The six men in the rehab programme had our time organised according to a strict schedule. Breakfast was at 8am, then chores before prayers at 8.50am, group therapy from 10am until lunch at 1pm. In the afternoons there was either one-to-one counselling or 'spirituality workshops', and dinner at 6pm. By the evening, I was usually exhausted.

Not that there was anything physically taxing about life at Grace House. It was the constant emotional labour that was so demanding. Addicts, our counsellors explained, were people who'd spent their lives in flight from feeling. Getting well would mean rewiring our brains to embrace, not evade, emotion. Our task here was to feel *everything*. Each weekday we sat in a circle, or rather a heptagon – six seats plus one for the counsellor on rota – for 'group'. These punishing, hours-long sessions took place in what was, unmistakably, an out-of-use chapel, with a boarded-up baptismal font under foot. An annex to the main rehab building, it had vaulted windows on all sides that let in every variegation of outside light. It was difficult, at first, to find words for what happened in there. Each visit felt less like entering a chapel than some outlaw pharmacy that dispensed random combinations of exotic drugs. You could never predict what state you'd leave in, or how long it would last.

But slowly, as though mapping the coast of some unknown continent, I learned to trace at least the outline of my inner life. In group one morning of my second week I noticed, pinned to the wall, a chart headed IDENTIFYING YOUR FEELINGS. It had colour-coded boxes: blue for SAD, yellow for HAPPY, green for ENVY, and so on. Christ, I thought: what is this, a rehab or a fucking nursery? In that moment a burning sensation raced along my shoulders and up my neck.

The counsellor turned to me and said, 'Are you ok, Matt?'
'Sorry?'

'I'm just sensing there's a lot coming up for you today. Do you want to check in with yourself and share what's going on? We're all here for you, aren't we, guys?' Nodding at me were five men of different ages in trackies, shorts, flip-flops and vests: one unwritten rule of rehab was that nobody ever got fully dressed. 'Remember what we said about honouring every feeling like a guest?'

Oh, fuck off, I thought. Then my whole body was aflame. My eyes burned, I couldn't speak. I looked up at the wall and saw a square of dark, fiery red and the word ANGRY.

I shook my head wordlessly until the counsellor sighed and moved the conversation along. I seemed to be *feeling* a *feeling* – not as a sudden shift in worldview or a compulsion to act, but as a bodily event – for the very first time I could recall. So that's *anger*, I thought to myself with curiosity. Yes, I hated it when they spoke to me like that, as though I were a child. But what I hated even more was how pathetically – how childishly – I craved such tokens of kindness. Why was it so hard for me to admit that I wanted to be cared for? I felt a raw, scathing sensation, and then a kind of inner dissolving, and when I looked back at the chart my moist eyes darted between blue (SAD) and bright, scarlet red (ASHAMED).

In group we emoted over our families, our histories of using, our hopes for the future. And afterwards we continued emoting: about our sleep or lack of it, the weather, the food we ate in the canteen. Our feelings were so novel that no amount of description or interpretation could exhaust each day's material. The old pool table with scarred green baize in the recreation area was also our confessional. A miscue might prompt a disclosure about the fear of failure, a long pot might lead to an admission of toxic pride. Usually we kept talking well after the game had finished, until neither player remembered who'd sunk the black, but one knew all about how his opponent, say, was coming to see that his mother had always had this way, any time he really needed her care, of quote-unquote empathising by bringing everything back to *her* feelings, which were mostly related to the hardships of motherhood, insisting she was only saying this to illustrate that *Mummy knows exactly how you feel*, and that anyway she didn't mind sacrificing her happiness for him, *because that's how much Mummy loves you*, which was actually pretty fucked up now he thought about it, because all his life deep down he'd believed he was a burden, impossible to love, that it'd be much better if he didn't even fucking exist to be totally honest, but all he felt for his mother was gratitude mixed with guilt that she'd had to put up with him for so long, spending every day of her life feeding and clothing him, getting him to school, the way she spoke about it was like she was doing him some incredible favour and not, you know, fulfilling the basic tasks of parenthood and, by the way, if she wasn't doing those things social services would be round pretty sharpish with a few fucking questions, wouldn't they, and of course nobody was saying parenthood's a walk in the park, but was it really fair to put all that on a *kid*, a tiny child for fuck's sake, we're talking six, seven, eight, and it was obvious now that that's where it all started, even before his sister's diagnosis and the divorce and custody battle, well anyway it wasn't long before the expulsion and the whole armed robbery thing, which by the way, we're talking a Swiss army knife that wasn't even open, *I mean give me a fucking break*, his counsellor had helped him see the whole thing was an unconscious acting out of the aggression and powerlessness he'd always felt around you-know-who, and even though his lawyer literally begged him to appeal, he fucked the guy off, actually accepted years of bird, which made sense now because he'd come to see that on a core-belief level he'd always felt guilty, not for that bullshit with the not-even-open Swiss army knife, he meant for the crime of even breathing, oh and by the way, guess who showed up every single week for three years to repeat her quote-unquote empathy number, except now her complaints revolved around getting the cold shoulder at bridge club, *because word's got around about the kind of people I'm related to*, so after all these years he was still the problem, and by the way, did she ever once, in three fucking years, ask him a single question beyond *how are you*? Did she fuck. Anyway, whose turn was it to break?

We were floating on a permanent emotional high tide. We were wide open. We were learning habits of 'active listening' and affirmation. A great deal of hugging took place. This was, the counsellors assured us, the route to wellbeing.

Teaching myself to look inward without the colour-coded chart, a replica of which I pinned up in my mind, took so long it made me feel faintly *orange* (EMBARRASSED). Then came an exhausting period in which my newly identifiable emotions seemed like sudden, violent onslaughts that required me to maintain a constant state of high alert.

But after a while, my image for how I aspired to live with feeling was the way the counselling room instantly caught and held every changing shade in the sky's light. I loved to sit alone in there through the evenings of the autumn I turned three and four months clean, hoping to watch the bright air take on a drowsy amber glow, then an ecstatic roseate flush. There was even a plaintive beauty in the fast-fading dusk, which caused the room to dim and sent numberless shadows creeping across the walls, until I couldn't see my wallet and room key at my feet.

In these moments I realised I'd spent my life in a defensive crouch against emotion: that even in my previous clean year I'd been trying to manage discomfort with a few crude methods: self-discipline, positive thinking, a support network largely comprised of a woman I had feelings for, and what I was no longer afraid to call an eating disorder. Now it seemed obvious that a large part of mental wellbeing meant accepting, even welcoming, whichever feelings came your way. This required honing a state of receptivity. And I learned that you couldn't pick and choose: if you wanted pleasure, you had to make room for pain. Hope, serenity, even wonder and delight, would all come and go – albeit not on your schedule. And only if you were willing to sit in the dark.

And, of course, like a maze in which you endlessly find yourself turning the same corner, everything always led back to childhood. Addicts, our counsellors said, contained a wounded 'inner child' who once upon a time hadn't received enough love, or enough of the right kind of love, and as a result had spent their lives on a frantic search for love-substitutes. The drugs to which we'd been so passionately and insanely devoted were, they explained, surrogate mothers and fathers.

Part of me railed against this simple story. It was so obvious, so reductive, so *inartistic*. It was, frankly, embarrassing. When I looked in the mirror, I saw a thirty-one-year-old man, not a wounded child. Whenever a counsellor stopped me in group and asked how 'little Matt' was feeling, I wanted to be sick. In any case, didn't I have a degree in English Literature? Hadn't I read *Middlemarch* not once but *twice*? What had I been doing during those thousands of hours immersed in novels and poems except gaining expertise on the inner life? What did these people with their counselling diplomas have to teach me about the self, the mind, the heart and the tangled threads between them?

I felt sure there was another, more complex story of my life – one that didn't exclude my counsellors' interpretation but that was open to others – but I didn't know what it was yet. Anyway, these people were feeding me three times a day and keeping a roof over my head. Moreover they were showing me a generosity I hadn't known existed and which I'd done nothing to earn except nearly slaughter myself with brown and white powder. And I couldn't deny I was learning more about myself from therapy and 'spirituality workshops' than I ever had by reading books. When a counsellor pointed out that my anger was usually a defence against sadness, or that my bouts of florid self-disparagement contained a paradoxical core of narcissism – *I am the chief of sinners* – I had to admit that, if such insights had been hidden in the pages of Jane Austen or James Baldwin, I hadn't had eyes to see them or ears to hear.

So I stayed, I submitted, I did more or less as I was told. I panned through my childhood in search of pain as if it were a precious metal to present to my counsellors. Unlike many Grace House residents I hadn't suffered any obvious abuse or neglect at home, but even so I didn't have to search far for my very own trauma. If you inspected anything closely enough, I found, it began to resemble scar tissue. For instance, I'd always told the story of my parents' conflict, with their ridiculous trading of Bible verses on car journeys, as a kind of black comedy. But – like someone who, squinting at an optical illusion, perceives an entirely new image – I now saw these scenes as frightening dramas in which the two huge people I depended on for life and security turned into hateful warring spirits. And whereas I'd learned to relate my adolescence as a series of ribald anecdotes about wanking into flower beds and in church car parks, I now understood it as a phantasmagoria of self-hatred.

As for my loss of faith, I came to see I'd all but forgotten the long ordeal of cognitive dissonance and self-reproach of my teenage years. When the topic came up in group, I claimed the experience had been no more protracted or painful than the day I'd woken up and realised I'd outgrown my childhood haircut. One of the other men gently suggested I may be in denial, a notion I vehemently denied. But the more I denied I was in denial, the more deeply buried in denial it became clear I was. Eventually, over several gruelling sessions, the group coaxed the true experience out of me.

And yes, despite what I'd told Harry in our interview, I wept. I didn't always know why I was weeping – for the entire six months of the rehab programme I wasn't entirely sure I believed the story about my life I was learning to tell – but I wept anyway. And when I did so, I felt freer, as though I'd been weighed down by a poisonous load of feelings that could only be purged through my tear ducts.

Some Grace House residents proved less susceptible to help than others. One who didn't last was Ricky, a coke dealer who'd broken the golden rule of his trade: *don't get high on your own supply*. The first time Ricky had met his father was when he arrived home from school one day to find a strange man in the living room with a present: his very first gun. Gangs came to provide for Ricky a camaraderie and identity sorely missing at home, but a life of crime came with its own perils. One day in a 'spirituality workshop', Harry stood before a flipchart and asked the group for examples of times we'd *faced our fears*.

'I got one,' said Ricky, leaning back in his chair, legs spread wide. 'This one time – yeah? – I was being held against my will. You know, for a ransom.'

That caught our attention. Every face in the room turned towards him.

'Anyway, cut a long story short, I got away,' he said. ''Course, when I get back to my yard, I'm bare vexed. But a few days back on road and I'm so busy making paper, I ain't even thinking about it no more.'

'Do you know what's the most dangerous kind of resentment?' said Harry. '*Legitimate* resentment. So I think it's to your great credit—'

'Anyway,' interrupted Ricky, who'd been scowling at his cuticles. 'About a week later I'm cotching near my block, bunning a zoot, yeah? And guess who I clock coming up the street towards me? Yeah, exactly. Man's like, a few feet away before *he* clocks *me*. He stops, stares right at me, close enough I can see the diamond grillz in his mouth.'

He paused for dramatic effect. Harry's magic marker was usually poised, mid-air, to extract a moral from any story. But now it was capped and hung limply at his side. 'So,' he said. 'What did you do?'

'Not gonna lie, boss, I thought about cutting. What you got to understand, this ain't just some wasteman, yeah? Man's sort of a big name in the ends. Same time, it's not every day you see a brer like that just rolling solo, no posse. So I think about it. And then I'm like – ok, time to *face my fears.*'

'That's wonderful!' said Harry. 'So, uh, how did the two of you resolve things?'

'Well, I run man down till he ducks into this chicken shop, yeah? But I'm after him, mad quick, and I've got him up against the window, and I've got my skeng, and I'm dipping him under the ribs, and—'

'Let me stop you there,' said Harry gently. 'We're supposed to forgive our enemies, Ricky.'

He looked perplexed. 'I thought we was allowed to smite our enemies?'

Harry's face turned pink. 'No, Ricky! No, no, no! Absolutely not! You're not allowed to smite anyone! Not even your enemies! Has everyone got that?'

Ricky nodded and scribbled something in his notepad. I leaned over and saw, underlined, the words:

In the end Ricky was asked to leave – not because he'd relapsed, but because it was judged that for a Grace House resident to keep thousands of pounds in his room while using it as the base for a drug-dealing operation was against the spirit, if not the letter, of its rules.

Grace House was Christian, but not in any way I'd previously understood the word. Hell was never mentioned. Harry and the other counsellors didn't seem especially exercised by what we were doing with our genitals. Homosexuality bothered them not at all. They quoted from the Bible, but to encourage rather than chastise. Scripture here was more like the ultimate self-help book than an iron maiden of doctrine designed to restrain any unauthorised movement of mind or body. This was a Christianity stripped of punishment or intolerance, and repackaged as a message of all-embracing love with a faintly gnostic flavour. Harry and his colleagues had searched through a collection of religious texts from the ancient Middle East and found a set of values roughly approximating those in a Liberal Democrat election manifesto.

I didn't know what to make of this, but to my surprise it hardly seemed to matter to the counsellors. My parents' churches had been obsessively focused on an individual's *beliefs* – salvation came by faith, so believing the right things was a matter of eternal destiny – but the staff at Grace House seemed more interested in my feelings and behaviour than my opinions. Provided I was staying clean and growing in the direction of serenity and kindness, they made it clear I could believe whatever helped. My occasional attempts to spark a theological debate in group led nowhere except into a discussion of which difficult feelings I was trying to ignore by doing so.

One morning, out for my usual pre-breakfast run, I almost collided with Harry, who was walking the opposite way to work. Head bowed and eyes closed, he was obviously praying. How did anyone dare ask God for anything in a world of grieving, traumatised people? Prayer always made me think of those heartbreaking news clips of aid workers hurling grain sacks at crowds of sunken-eyed men and women.

But as I skipped around Harry, who didn't look up, I realised I couldn't imagine him doing any special pleading before the Lord. He could only be asking for more compassion, patience and wisdom to carry out his work – which happened to include, among its tasks, saving my life. For the first time, I saw that a certain kind of prayer could be its own answer. And I felt a swelling of gratitude not just for this man, who each day laboured thanklessly to reform society's most fucked-up specimens, but for the faith that was so clearly his motivation.

Now Harry's image blurred into that of another religious leader who'd once been responsible for keeping me safe and well. I pictured my father in the moments before his Sunday sermon, head bent so low it almost touched his knees, lips moving just a little. He, of course, was my first object of worship. My childish awe of him had been like a summer so glorious I'd never imagined it could end. But then the air had turned cold so fast, and the frost and dark were now so thick, that it was the old warmth that seemed unimaginable. Why was it only his sermons about judgement and sin I recalled, rather than the ones – there must have been some? – about compassion and mercy? A fundamentalist believer, his world had a binary logic: *he that is not with me is against me.* Rejecting it was impossible without rejecting it *all* – including the people from whom I'd learned it. I'd had no choice but to become a fundamentalist *un*believer. I'd abandoned my childhood faith, but by tacitly accepting its all-or-nothing terms, I saw now I'd failed to outgrow it. Wouldn't finding freedom, and becoming myself at last, mean recognising not just where my mother and father had been wrong, but where they'd been right? Counting not just their debt to me, but mine to them?

Just forming these thoughts was painful. Did I hate my parents and their faith so much that viewing them in shades of grey – rather than through the dark and the light they'd weaned me on and to which I'd ever since been addicted – was intolerable to me?

But no, that wasn't it. Over the years I'd tried so hard to hate them I'd sometimes succeeded, or believed I had. But the familiar ache under my ribs – which I felt even now as I picked up pace, weaving between yawning commuters who streamed towards tubes and buses – felt nothing like hatred. No, the problem with my parents had never been that I hated them, not really. The problem was that – despite everything, despite my better judgement, despite our intractable differences – I was still half in love with them! Drugs had helped me outrun that love and all the hurt, guilt, fury and pity that came with it. I'd stopped taking drugs, so wasn't it time to stop running too – whatever that meant?

I'd come to Grace House with the vague notion that I'd stay six weeks, eight at most: long enough to get back on the straight and narrow. But the experience was like climbing a series of peaks where each one only revealed more clearly how far away the destination was. After completing the six-month rehab programme, Harry asked if I'd like to stay on at a next-door block of flats that housed a community of recovering addicts. I instantly said yes. Getting through the day without drugs no longer felt difficult. But it was increasingly clear to me that staying clean wasn't the ultimate purpose of recovery; it was just a precondition for growth – emotional, psychological, or (the word always came with quote marks in my mind) 'spiritual'. When I asked Harry how much longer he thought I'd have to stay, he responded with his usual homespun mysticism: 'When the time comes for you to leave, you'll know.'

So when, six months later, I turned a year clean, I was still at Grace House – but in a spartan bedsit-plus-kitchenette next to the rehab proper. Twice a week I made the short trip to the main building for counselling – which I knew was helping rearrange me in some fundamental way, though I didn't know what the outcome was supposed to be. At least there were tangible signs of progress, like the fact that this time I didn't celebrate one year of sobriety by embarking on two years of suicidal using.

But the best proof was my spontaneous response to other people. Not long ago the world had seemed filled with dim forms representing the threat of rejection and humiliation – or, occasionally, the hope of rescue. But twelve months of talking almost incessantly about myself in counselling had produced an odd side effect: *other people* had come alive to me. By comparison with characters in fiction, the human beings I'd previously known had often seemed pale, rough-edged, thinly drawn. But now I frequently found myself talking to someone no less engrossing than Jay Gatsby or Jane Eyre. The recovery meetings I still sometimes attended were packed with perfect strangers who were hardly likely to prove useful to me outside the room, and yet I found myself *wishing them well* – instinctively and sincerely. Every meeting was a gathering of people who differed by gender, class, race, age, you name it, but who were united by their broken-ness and a longing to heal. At times I had a euphoric sense of the borders between us collapsing, and every face around me seemed to radiate beauty. If, in those moments, my turn came to speak, I had an urge to stand up and testify that I'd escaped bondage, finished wandering the desert, and entered the Promised Land! *I once was lost, but now I'm found*: it was the corniest of plot structures, but there were days I believed it was true.

Then there were the other days, when living without drugs felt like living without skin. Every now and again I made myself sick late at night after a second dinner. And the future filled me with fear: how would I manage outside the cocoon of Grace House, where I could devote myself full-time to staying clean? Although I'd resumed, for the first time in years, grooming and dressing smartly, I felt a piercing self-consciousness I'd never known as an unwashed, dishevelled junkie. I wondered if things would feel different if I had the 'spiritual awakening' that had so far eluded me. I'd watched other Grace House residents profess one by one to having felt the brush of a 'higher power', secretly envying the brightness in their eyes when they said God's love had helped them love themselves. At some point I'd lost or abandoned most of the intellectual self-confidence that had sustained my atheism since I was eighteen. The best principle I knew for how to live was to do the opposite of what my instincts told me. In any case, I was hardly in a position to disdain anything that might help. It was sentimental, it was trite, it was undignified, but I didn't care: *I* wanted to love myself too!

I thought of Jesus's words: *Come unto me, all ye that labour and are heavy laden, and I will give you rest.* The truth was that, although I was no longer a suicidal malefactor, and although things were much better than they'd ever been, I was still heavy laden, and I still longed for rest. And what was the burden I was carrying except myself, myself, myself? Could anyone tell me how to slough off this ugly, damaged, boring, resentful, trivial, frightened, stupid thing altogether – this irreducible *me*?

I even tried prayer, one night when I was sixteen months clean, agonising once again over whether to throw up the food in my stomach. I remembered Mark 9:24 as I got on my knees and closed my eyes. *Lord, I believe*, I lied; *help thou mine unbelief.* But when I saw and heard nothing, I got up, let myself into the bathroom, and knelt a second time – over the cistern, jamming my fingers down my throat as tears burned my cheeks.

The next day I was reading about Buddhism: I only ever bought books from the Body, Mind and Soul shelves nowadays. The author argued that the self didn't require redemption or even reform, because it wasn't there. The key was, simply, to know this – not intellectually but at the level of intimate experience – and then the self would float away like a dandelion head on a breeze.

After thirty minutes online I found a ten-day silent retreat where participants paid what they could afford, booked my place and a return train ticket to south-west England, where the centre was based. That done, I decided to practise sitting down on the floor, crossing my legs and closing my eyes.

From that first attempt at meditation, I'd been amazed by how difficult I'd found it. The image it brought to mind wasn't of a dandelion on a breeze but of two dogs with their tails tied together, an accelerating whirligig of panic and confusion. How could something so ostensibly simple – just sitting there and breathing – be so laborious, and what did that say about me? I couldn't sit in the lotus position, for one thing; I was so unflexible that after a few minutes my whole body would begin to feel like a clenched fist.

But on the ninth day of the retreat, with the end in sight – though I reminded myself again and again that I was here to be present, not to long for the experience to be over – I concluded there was simply no way I could subdue the endless babble in my mind. And it wasn't even productive: it was babble about the babble, a self-defeating, self-abrading, self-pitying commentary on the self. I'd come here hoping to transcend my ego, but instead I'd had a head-on collision with it. On the whole the experience had been like spending nine days watching an ultra-slow motion video of a vehicle crashing into its own reflection.

Then again, that wasn't the whole story. As the retreat had worn on I'd found these long stretches of frustration interspersed with stranger moments. At times my breathing would slow, the internal babble would ease just a little, and I'd feel I was skirting some profound devastation, an unbearable pain lying just out of sight. At other times I thought I could feel a brisk sparkling sensation across my skin; it was a pleasurable, almost joyous feeling, like bubbles bursting everywhere. But no sooner did these feelings arise than I would, as Goenka said, attach to them with craving, and then I'd be cast back into my familiar pain and irascibility.

Peculiar things had been happening in between meditation sessions too. One afternoon I was striding through the meadow when I saw Gus mooning idiotically at a spiderweb on the ground, no doubt pretending to be transfixed by its beauty in an ostentatious display of spiritual transport. I walked past him, seething. The whole route through the grounds took about five minutes to complete. When I'd finished my lap and was approaching Gus a second time, I noticed he was bent even lower. Now he was actually gazing like a lunatic at a lump of cow shit; he had his face inches from it. Was he actually inhaling deeply, smelling it?

The woolly-minded cretin was asking for it. If I were to lose my footing – purely by accident, of course – just as I passed him on the trail, nudging him off balance . . . well, then we'd see how much he loved being 'present' in nature. I approached quietly, careful not to break his reverie with the sound of my footsteps. Not that I had any definite intentions of course. It was just so slippery out here—

As I drew level with Gus, his backside pointing skyward, I was seized by a mad impulse – to embrace him. Grabbing him by the elbows, I pulled him towards me. He straightened, froze for a moment, and stood limply as I hugged him from behind. Then he turned and wrapped his arms around me. We stood there clasped together in the wildgrass for a full minute or so. Then, at the same moment, as though we both knew what the other was thinking, we let go and walked off in different directions. Whenever Gus and I passed each other afterwards we made no acknowledgment of our moment of passion, connection, whatever it was. But every time he was near, I felt a deep current of love passing through me. And, strangest of all, I was certain he felt it too.

But now it was the third meditation session of the penultimate day, and if anything I was struggling more than ever. My problem, I saw, was that I'd been trying too hard. Whatever happiness is, I thought to myself, it can't be pursued directly. Doing so is like seeking a shadow with a torch – the search itself banishes what you're looking for. Happiness can only be approached obliquely, and achieved as a by-product of some other pursuit.

That's quite good, I went on thinking to myself. Had I had a spiritual insight? So that I wouldn't forget to write it down later, I began mentally repeating the words: *happiness cannot be pursued directly – doing so is like seeking a shadow with a torch.*

Oh, I was an idiot. I was simply devising a new way to render this retreat a failure: reciting to myself a neat formulation about the failure of the retreat, dressed up as wisdom. And it wasn't even clever. It was no doubt precisely the kind of thing you could find in a thousand self-help books. Forget it, and return to the present, the sensation of the breath moving in and out.

Then I felt as though I were falling into an abyss, falling and falling with nothing to catch me. I opened my eyes to break the illusion, closing them again only when the Teacher stared me down. Next I found myself being visited by hideous memories – a kind of showreel of every repellent and degrading thing I'd ever done. Stealing the money with Sinead's debit card. Breaking into Maria's suitcase. Exploiting the cab driver in Bethlehem. Every lie I'd ever told, every person I'd disappointed or harmed. Further back, before I'd been a drug addict, lying to Rana about Emma, and to Emma about Rana. Fights with my siblings, aping our parents' conflict, redirecting our anger at each other – and me the biggest, the most aggressive. I thought I saw the story of my life, the person I'd been, and it showed that I'd started as a mean little bully and, catalysed by drugs, grown into a pathetic, nasty loser. All the talk at Grace House about self-love and self-forgiveness was sentimental trash. I was a vile person. No wonder my mind was so inhospitable: living inside it was an entirely apt punishment for the sin of being myself.

And then, just as suddenly as it had begun, this state of torment passed and my mind was absolutely blank. I was both absent from my body and aware of every inch of skin, every hair on my head. I felt a great tension passing out of me. As in a dream, I was somehow certain that the bodies around me belonged to people I knew. On my left, I could hear my father's slow respiration. To my right was my mother's tight, quavering breath. Ahead of me were Rachel, Abigail and Jonathan. The six of us had not been present in the same room for years, but here we were, meditating serenely together. There was no conflict, only a deep ease. For a long time I'd seen my family through a dark glass of blame; I'd believed they owed me, that they were somehow responsible for my problems. But now I saw that we each carried our pain, that we'd each given and received hurt. We hadn't desired each other's suffering. We hadn't lacked love, only skill. I felt now – though my eyes were shut – that I was at last seeing them face to face. I was no longer attempting to follow the sensation of my breath or to avoid attachment or aversion. I understood that I'd probably later think I'd lost my mind due to nine days of silence, or that I'd generated this hallucination to persuade myself the retreat had been capped with a profound moment. Never mind. For now I believed I was experiencing something outside the confines of reason, and I was absolutely at peace.

Gradually I became aware, with annoyance, of an intrusive noise. Somebody in a far corner of the meditation hall was crying. My concentration ruined, the vision evaporated like mist. I sighed. How selfish, how embarrassing – simply to allow yourself to weep unrestrainedly in front of 150 people.

Then I felt a hand on my shoulder. I opened my eyes, and saw the Teacher standing above me with a look of concern. He looped his other hand under my arm and pulled.

'Up you get,' he whispered. 'Let's get you some fresh air, shall we?'

Suddenly I was aware that my face was wet.

He helped me to my feet, and began gently leading me to the exit.

Once we were outside he said, 'It's all right, it's perfectly common actually. There's really nothing to worry about. Why don't we go to my office and have a little chat?'

TRESPASSERS WELCOME: The large blue sign hangs above the entrance to Open Doors Baptist Church at the north-east corner of Hackney Downs. From the bench where I'm sitting, I watch an exuberant crowd of bright-hatted ladies and sharp-suited men milling outside before the service. It's an unseasonably warm March day, and the trees are already frosted with little panicles of colour. In past years I sat here waiting for countless hours, unable to think about anything but the passing seconds and minutes. I'm twenty-one months clean today, but this spot is still a busy artery in the local drugs trade: if you wait here long enough some bottom-feeder of the illicit economy will approach you, hoping to pick off a customer who's grown impatient with their dealer. Like the kid on the BMX with the hi-top trainers and Avirex jacket who keeps passing, trying to catch my eye. He rolls past me now, turns his head, brakes.

'You waiting for something, fam?' he says over his shoulder.

'Not me.'

He wastes no time cycling off.

Twenty-one months during which I've had nothing stronger than coffee. Twenty-one months with no damper pedal for my emotions. Twenty-one months of my own consciousness, neat. This is by far my longest period of sobriety since getting drunk before school on Emma Bosworth's parents' vodka. Coming here is my little private ritual to mark the day, an act of remembrance. After all, the nightmare of addiction is already starting to feel unreal, the way even the most frightening dreams dissolve in the sane routines of morning. Sometimes it's not just addiction but my whole past that seems dreamlike, with its restless scene shifts and transitory characters. Not to mention the several selves I've been: son of a preacher and born-again atheist; valleys-born Welsh boy and schoolmate of the super-rich; student to whom every door seemed open and patient behind a triple-locked exit.

But now I'm plotting my most dramatic conversion yet: from a smack-sunk, crack-cracked delinquent, spiralling towards death, to an ordinary citizen. I've begun looking for work with a view to moving on from Grace House soon. I don't make a habit of lying, or harming other people. I've repaid my debts, to Maria and Sinead among others, and done what I can to make amends to those my addiction harmed. As a result I've reconciled with friends like George, who I see every week now he's living back in London. I'm thirty-two years old, and I'm a gentler, softer person than the one I was at thirty. The desire to make myself sick after meals seems, for now at least, to have gone. Most importantly I'm no longer at imminent risk of waking up in a psychiatric ward, or going the same way as poor Gareth Lloyd. However long twenty-one months feels, I still can't consider my luck – or grace, if you like – without gratitude.

A breeze rocks the bough above me with the noise of a creaky hinge. Spring light spangles the grass. Have I had my spiritual awakening? Sometimes I think if the man I was two years ago woke up in my skin today, he'd be convinced a miracle had occurred. On the other hand, wouldn't most people say all I've done is gained some minimal – and belated – maturity? Is the definition of a spiritual awakening when a person grows the fuck up a decade behind schedule?

But what was my vision on the Vipassana retreat, if not a spiritual experience? I felt sure in that moment I'd been granted a profound epiphany, and as I caught the train back home I carried the image of the six members of my family meditating together like a priceless vase that could slip and smash at any moment.

Not long after I arrived back in London, my mother asked if I'd come to Swansea for her sixtieth birthday. After protracted negotiations she'd arranged for all my siblings to be there; it would be the first time we'd met as a family for some years. I hadn't been to Wales since Gareth's funeral, but my counsellor at Grace House suggested that returning to the scene of my childhood might be useful for my 'therapeutic process'. So with Jonathan I boarded a train at Paddington, and ignored the anxious feeling in my stomach as we rode it westward through the Severn Tunnel.

One by one my siblings and I entered my parents' house, just a ten-minute walk from Sketty Avenue where we'd lived two decades ago. We sat down at the dinner table like mob bosses arriving warily for a summit, wondering who'd brought a gun. There were six of us here, which meant fifteen complex dynamics; I'd counted them with my counsellor. Never mind the endless configurations of threes and fours in which tension could be reflected and multiplied – a funhouse hall of resentment. Once my father had served his signature chicken curry, he hushed us and said:

'Right then! Everyone quiet while I thank the Lord for our food!'

I folded my arms. 'Sorry – you go ahead, but I don't pray.'

'Oh, for God's sake,' said my brother.

'Jonathan!' said my mother, rapping him on the arm. 'Don't you dare take the Lord's name in vain!'

'I'm just telling Matt to get over himself.'

'Look,' I said. 'There are people in this world dying of hunger—'

'Off he goes,' said Abigail.

'If we thank God for our food,' I continued, 'we're implicitly holding him responsible for famine elsewhere. Do we really want to—'

'Why do you have to be so literal-minded all the time!' said Jonathan. 'Why can't you just see prayer as adopting a sort of – a posture of gratitude?'

'Oh, so *I'm* the one with a literal-minded approach to religion now, am I?'

'What the fuck are these boys talking about?' said Abigail.

'*Abigail*!' said my mother.

'Anyway, you're not even religious!' I said to Jonathan. 'And neither are you, Rachel! How about the people who want to pray, pray, and those who don't, don't? That's the thing about religious people—'

My father, who'd been burying his face theatrically in his hands, sat up straight. 'And that's the thing about liberal humanists! You're always talking about tolerance, tolerance, tolerance. But there's nobody less tolerant than a liberal humanist when someone else wants to—'

'Look, enough of the philosophy debate,' said Rachel. 'The point is, Dad's cooked a lovely meal for us, and we've come all the way down here to spend time together.' She glanced pointedly at me. 'So how about everyone just being *nice*?'

Chastened, I muttered, 'Who said I'm a liberal humanist anyway?'

'Well, what are you then?' said my brother.

Everyone stared at me. I cleared my throat.

'You're right, Rachel,' I said at last. 'Look, I'm sorry. I was making a fuss about nothing. Let's pray.'

'Did I just hear that?' said Abigail. 'Did Mr I-Know-Everything just say somebody else was right for once in his life?'

'*Why does everybody always have to argue?*' said my mother. 'I'm at my wit's end with all of you!'

It was good to be home.

After dinner I found my mother watching TV in the lounge. The walls were hung with old family photos and music exam certificates, most of them my brother's.

'I'm sorry about that,' I said as I sat down next to her. 'I was being childish.'

She smiled at me. 'Thank you, Matthew.'

'Jon was right. There's more than one way to look at prayer. Not just prayer, other religious practices too. I've actually been thinking a lot about the way aspects of religion embody all kinds of universal wisdom, if you see what I mean. You know, since the meditation retreat. I actually had this really strange experience there I've been wanting to talk to you about. Kind of like an epiphany or something, I guess.'

My mother listened patiently as I tried to explain my vision and the meaning I saw in it.

'The way we were all just sitting there, together. Without words,' I said, surprised to hear a little catch in my throat. 'It was just so *peaceful*. Like the sort of peace – I don't know exactly what I'm trying to say, but—'

'A peace that passeth understanding,' she said, visibly softening.

'That's *right*! That's exactly it! All this trying to *under-stand*, to fit things into words, concepts, doctrines. And this need to be *right* all the time – it's just a total waste of our lives. Who cares if we call it God or a higher power? Or

Metta, or love? Isn't that Paul's whole point when he talks about love? Even if you speak like an angel, understand everything, have enough faith to move mountains – without love, you're nothing. In the end, love's all that matters. That's what it says in *your* book, Mum! So can't we just love each other, without caring who's right and who's wrong? Without words always getting in the way?'

My mother looked thoughtful. I'd presented my spiritual experience to her like a supplicant before an Old Testament Pharoah. It suddenly struck me how desperately I hoped it would win her approval.

Finally, she spoke. 'Do you know what else Paul says? *Love rejoiceth not in iniquity, but in the truth.* That's right, Matthew: *the truth*! Call me old-fashioned, but I still believe there's a difference between fact and fiction, honesty and lies, right and wrong. That's what those Buddhas have been filling your mind with, is it? *Oh, up is down, black is white – what difference does any of it make?* Are you sure there's nothing satanic—'

'Mum, will you just *listen to me*!' I had the familiar sense of shouting at my mother across a vast, bridgeless chasm. I felt ferociously alone. 'I'm just saying that we all want the same thing in the end. We're all trying to find our own way to the same place. Mum, *please*! *Can't you hear what I'm saying?'*

'*I am the way, the truth and the life: no man cometh unto the father except through me.* That's what Jesus said. And he didn't say anything about sitting around meditating for days on end, I can tell you that now. How much did the ticket to the retreat cost anyway? Did you get the super off-peak return?'

I sighed. 'Yes, of course.'

'And by the way, there's only one word I'm especially interested in. It's called God's Word. And wherever you think you're going, excuse me if I trust God's opinion rather than yours. The Bible teaches that if you accept Jesus as your Lord and Saviour, you'll go to be with him for all eternity. And if you don't—'

'Ok, Mum. I know,' I said, standing up to end the conversation.

It wasn't long after I'd arrived back in London that I saw my mother's number flash up on my phone. When I answered she told me, tripping over her words, that my father had had a stroke. After preaching the morning sermon at a village church in mid-Wales he'd gone for Sunday lunch at an elder's home. Then, on returning to his hotel, he'd collapsed next to the bed. The telephone had been within reach, thank the Lord, so he'd managed to call an ambulance from where he lay on the floor. He'd been taken to a specialist stroke unit in the Midlands where his condition was 'critical'.

Within forty-five minutes I was sprinting through the closing doors of a northbound train at Euston. Dripping with sweat, I took my seat. My relationship with my father had never fully recovered from my loss of faith, though I couldn't say for sure whether the coolness had been more on my side or his. He never uttered the word, but he'd grown more and more depressed with age. The cause was hardly mysterious: already reeling from the mortal combat of his marriage, the knockout was delivered via four pitiless blows: his children's rejection – one by one by one by one – of everything he'd ever stood for. He'd grown distressingly fat in recent years; the stroke was no surprise. For a long time I'd been angry at my father – but why? As a grey industrial landscape beyond the train window gave way to green meadows and farmland with grazing cattle, I considered that my resentment was not primarily to do with the irrational faith he'd imposed on me as a child, nor the painful spectacle of his conflict with my mother, nor even the growing distance between us which I'd interpreted as rejection. No, it was his unhappiness, and the agony of bearing helpless witness to it, even at a distance, that most enraged me. For years our relationship had comprised long stretches of silence punctuated by bursts of jaunty bonhomie that guarded against meaningful and therefore painful conversation. I'd formed closer bonds with men who'd cut my hair or whose cabs I'd hired in recent years than I had with my father.

It was too late now to say what we'd left unsaid, or repair what the years had broken. But if this was goodbye, I was determined to recover – even if just for a moment – the love that had once knitted us together. I'd spent my time at Grace House resisting the counsellors' doctrine of the 'inner child'. And yet the man who was now pushing through the stroke ward's double doors felt no less need of his father than the nine-year-old boy on Guernsey. Except this time I was on dry land and he was, I feared, drifting over the horizon.

A nurse led me by the arm, explaining my mother would be back shortly from the canteen. Then she pulled back a curtain, and I saw him. He lay in his bed, sallow-skinned, dark bruises under his closed eyes. His mouth was wide open, as though he'd somehow mistaken this experience for a routine dental checkup. Tubes sprouted from him everywhere, and he was surrounded by the electronic chirruping of medical equipment.

'Hello, Dad,' I said, holding his fingers gently. 'How are you?'

He furrowed his brow and closed his rheumy eyes. 'Errything . . . dizzy.'

'You're going to be ok. You're in the best place. Do you need anything?'

Very slowly, he shook his head no.

'I'm just going to find someone to ask what's happening. Promise you won't run off while I'm gone?'

I intercepted a doctor on his rounds, a man in pale blue scrubs with the hurried patience of someone who didn't have time for all the ways in which he was direly needed. He explained that my father had suffered a bleed in the region of the brain governing, among other things, balance. That's what was causing his sensation of dizziness. Recovery was possible, but it was too soon to predict to what extent. The current priority was to stabilise his blood pressure to mitigate the possibility of another stroke.

'What's the outlook?'

'Like I said, it's too early to be sure.'

He began moving away, but I blocked his path. '*Please*. I want you to tell me how likely it is my father's going to die.'

He frowned. 'We're certainly doing everything we can to make sure that – uh, well – look. All I can say is, he's not out of the woods. The next twenty-four hours are going to be crucial.'

When I got back to my father's bedside, my mother was there. We hugged and then sat on opposite sides of the trolley, half obscured from each other by my father's huge green-gowned belly. My mother was pale with worry. After decades in which my parents had found it increasingly difficult to exchange civil words, it surprised me to see her so distraught. My parents' fighting, I thought, must have expressed a primitive intimacy binding them together more closely than they or I had suspected.

I took a deep breath. 'Shall we pray?'

I hadn't seen my mother look so shocked since I'd shown her my first tattoo, but when I took my father's right hand she placed hers on his left where it rested on the guardrail. Reaching across the bed around my father's stomach, I grasped my mother by the wrist.

I knew what I wanted to say; I'd planned everything on the train. 'Dear Lord Jesus, I want to thank you for Mum and Dad. Thank you too for Jonathan, Rachel and Abigail. Please bless Dad in his suffering. We know you have promised that our light affliction, which is but for a moment, worketh for us a far more exceeding and eternal weight of glory. May you lighten Dad's affliction now, Lord, and may you show him your glory. Most of all, may he know he's surrounded by love – yours and ours. In Jesus's name. Amen.'

'Amen,' said my mother.

'Ahhhm,' croaked my father.

'Now then,' I said, opening my rucksack. 'How about a hymn?'

I'd brought my portable speaker for just this moment. I played 'Nearer, My God to Thee', 'Be Still, My Soul' and 'Guide Me, O Thou Great Jehovah', the warbling harmonies of a Welsh male voice choir ringing through the ward. Finally I played 'Gwahoddiad', the tune I recalled from Gareth Lloyd's funeral. I'd found a translation, which I read aloud from my phone:

> *I am coming, Lord!*
> *Coming now to thee!*
> *Wash me in thy precious blood*
> *That flowed at Calvary!*

When the final chord faded I couldn't immediately look up from the floor. When I did, I saw we were all at pains not to catch each other's eye. But there was a moment when I glanced at my mother, who was gazing at my father, who in the corner of my trembling vision I saw gazing at me.

I excused myself and wandered down a long corridor in search of a bathroom to compose myself. I was pleased. I'd put aside my qualms and helped create a moment of spiritual consolation – and of authentic connection – my family only ever seemed to discover together on hospital wards. It wasn't much to set against a lifetime's baffled hurt, but it was something.

So when after a few days the doctor informed me my father would pull through after all, my relief was faintly tinged with disappointment that the perfect deathbed scene I'd choreographed had been spoiled.

My father spent weeks in hospital, and he'd need months of rehab. When I next visited Swansea, he walked with a cane, and the baritone that had resounded from the pulpits of my childhood was replaced by an elderly rasp. It was as though the emotional erosion that had rendered my father spectral and tame in recent years had happened all at once to his physical being. And in a way his theology had now been fulfilled: his body was not only the afterthought he'd always treated it as, it had become a burden he was carrying like the temporary weights grounding an air balloon before it soars skyward.

My thoughts are interrupted by the squeak of brakes. The kid with the BMX is back and looking me over with appraising eyes. 'You sure you ain't waiting for nothing, bruv?'

'I'm sure.'

''Cos I swear down, you look like you waiting for something.'

'Honestly, I'm fine. Thanks.'

I've always been one of those people who peer in fascination over a fatal drop, spooked by the thought a crazy urge might send me hurtling to the edge. I'm beginning to wonder if I quite trust myself today, whether I came here not in a spirit of serene reminiscence but reckless experiment. And the kid's right: I *am* waiting for something. During a routine GP check-up some time ago a nurse, on discovering I was a former IV drug user, persuaded me to submit to additional tests. A week later the doctor called me into his office and told me. Hepatitis C: a blood infection that slowly attacks the liver and, if untreated, causes cirrhosis, cancer and finally death. I was booked in for an ultrasound at Homerton Hospital, the place where four years ago my recovery from addiction had made its first faltering start on the Bevan Ward. I lay nervously with gel smeared across my abdomen, watching my ghostly organs on the monitor. The gastroenterologist gave me the good news: my liver was unscarred, meaning the virus hadn't yet begun its slowly murderous work.

All that's left to discover is which treatment the doctors will deem I'm suitable to receive, based on factors including my lifestyle and which genotype of Hep C I have. There are two, starkly different, possibilities. One is an old drug, Interferon, which has a fearsome reputation among recovering junkies for its uncertain outcome and six months-plus of withdrawal-like effects. The other is a new drug, Sofosbuvir, which would clear up my Hepatitis C in twelve weeks with absolute certainty and with no side effects. The real world is never as simple as God/Satan, heaven/hell, good/evil – except, I suppose, when it is. Interferon/Sofosbuvir. I find out tomorrow which I'll receive, and I'm afraid.

As I sit here now I believe – though I know it's irrational – I can feel the illness pulsing in my veins and arteries, moving stealthily through my organs like a thief in the night. It occasionally strikes me with disgust that my *blood itself* is laced with a deadly virus, that I'm awash in poison. It feels like a bitter irony that after all the effort of getting clean I remain, in a grotesquely material sense, dirty.

The poison in the blood. This is, of course, what I was taught from infancy: the doctrine of Original Sin. Evil passed down from Adam through the human lineage, condemning each of us to hell unless we seek salvation in Christ. It took me eighteen years to reject this notion. And it was only thanks to the counselling I received at a Christian rehab that I came to see how insidiously the idea had distorted my view of myself by convincing me I was tainted, filthy. Over the last twenty-one months I've made real progress in rooting out this idea from my psyche. And now – I could almost laugh; it's a good, nasty gag – I've made it a biological fact by contracting a real blood infection. Talk about biblical literalism!

I look over at Open Doors Baptist Church. The forecourt is clear now; the service has started. Fear makes you your most primitive self, and despite all my efforts to move on from the past I can't deny the pull such buildings still exert on days like this. Faith isn't the kind of thing you can just *lose*, not when it's passed to you through the umbilical cord. I've often envied people whose passage to adulthood didn't involve a savage tussle with superstition and moral brutalism. But then again, maybe my case isn't so uncommon. Isn't everyone's childhood an indoctrination in the more or less deranged outlook of the people who raised them? And isn't growing up for everyone a more or less successful attempt to overcome their conditioning and see clearly, with their own eyes?

So what do my eyes tell me? Well, here's one thing. To the extent that I've been restored to health, it's undeniably been thanks to several kinds of religion. As an evangelical atheist in my early twenties I enjoyed pointing out some striking resemblances between the religious and the very mentally ill: both heard voices, saw things invisible to others, discerned patterns in everyday life pointing to hidden forces at work. Meanwhile I sought replacements for God in a hundred different places – in women, or the fantasies of salvation I projected onto them; in the books I mistook for holy writ;

and, most of all, in the transcendence of drugs. In the process I learned a thing or two about real mental illness: not as snarky metaphor, but as the way into a hospital ward from which there was no immediate way out. Soon afterwards, I found spiritual life support on plastic chairs in church halls and basements. But after my pilgrim's progress faltered, it was religion again that saved me – this time via the ministrations of Christian counsellors in a Christian rehab, and gurus in meditation halls. In time, I took up my bed and walked.

So isn't the moral of my story obvious? Doesn't narrative logic demand that I swap spiritual half-measures for God himself, straight, no chaser? I've always had a taste for harder stuff; it was, after all, my mother's milk. Give me, any day, a fire-breathing zealot who'll tell me I'm headed for damnation, over some radio-friendly liberal who'll happily split the difference between our views – because, deep down, he's just an agnostic with a taste for robes and evensong. So is that how my story's shaping up after all, as a replay of the parable of the Prodigal Son? And is that my father I see a great way off, waiting at the roadside for my return with a cane and the fatted calf?

The major advantage of my parent's theology is that it brooks no ambiguity: every important question comes with an emphatic heavenly answer. And doesn't Joel 3:21 say, *For I will cleanse their blood that I have not cleansed*? It would be so easy to wander over to the church, seek out the minister, confess how frightened I am – and pray for the purification of my blood, my self, my soul. Purity: the mirror image of addiction. Instead of more more more, less less less.

Then again – I can see the kid at the far end of the park now, making a wide loop that's bringing him back towards me. And I wonder whether the problem isn't that I'm not enough of a Christian but that after all these years I'm still too much of one. How long have I spent waiting? Waiting on park benches for dealers. Waiting to arrive home and begin cooking up. Waiting for the hit to cross the blood-brain barrier. Waiting for the woman who'll redeem me. Waiting for the next drink, the next cigarette, the microwave with the ice cream inside to ping. Waiting to be one year sober. Waiting to be two. Always waiting to cross some threshold in the future when my pain will vanish and my real life will begin. Haven't I been like my father, neglecting this world, this body, for the hereafter? Haven't I, in short, spent my whole life waiting in one way or another for salvation?

And what would it mean to stop waiting? To say: this is my life. Here is the person I am. To hell with higher powers and transitional objects. It's my responsibility, using whatever crooked tools I have at my disposal, and whatever help I can find from other imperfect humans, to build a life worth living.

The sky is a huge blue dome, off which the shouts from a nearby football match glance with a dull echo. A passing runner's headphones emit music like the quiet roar of an inner sea conch. The kid is cycling up the path towards me again; a few more seconds and he'll be here. There's the old anxious energy, the gut-slackening anticipation. I tell myself: it would only take a single word, and you'd have it in your hand, the portal to another realm. And then, in a moment, in the twitch of an eye, everything would change.

He slows down, stops.

He opens his mouth to speak.

Tell him. Tell him you're not waiting for anything.

Afterword

I began writing *Original Sins* in October 2017, when I was just short of two and a half years clean. From the outset I knew the book would end with the moment in March of that year when, faced with a choice over whether to use drugs again, I'd briefly hesitated.

I'd come through that moment, and a few others, by the time I sat down to write. Over the next two years my progress on the book was slowed only by the rewards of successful recovery: finding work, my own place to live, even beginning a new relationship. In October 2019 I had enough material to share with publishers, and before long came to an agreement with Chatto & Windus to turn my story into a book.

At that point I'd been clean almost four and a half years. Choosing not to take drugs had long begun to feel automatic, academic even – the same way I chose, every day, not to drink toilet bleach. I was healthy, and happier than I'd ever thought possible. I was on the verge of realising my lifelong goal of publishing a book. Best of all, my relationship had led to a series of declarations, promises and plans. If, after many years of ODs and institutions, I'd concluded my book here, it would have read like a Hollywood ending.

In other words – though I still attended meetings, reciting the mantra of *one-day-at-a-time* – the book's final scene felt so far removed from my current life that I'd begun to view it as an elegant literary conceit as much as a serious warning about the contingency of recovery. For myself, at least.

But, as we all know: *tragedy is comedy plus time.* In my case, the *time* part was so short it proved I'd been guilty of a different kind of conceit. Two weeks after agreeing to revisit my past on the page, I revisited it in a different way. After making the right choice for 1614 consecutive days, I made the wrong one.

There's another story to be told about the reasons why, about how my slip became a spiral of trauma, chaos and the kind of darkness I'd believed would stay confined to my book's pages. At times, I flirted with an altogether different ending to my story. One reason I resisted was the desire to finish *Original Sins*.

Over late 2020 and early 2021 the gloom began to lift – slowly, falteringly, but sufficiently to enable me to work. And when I came at last to write my final scene, I didn't doubt my early instinct to set it in March 2017, any more than I had when I thought I had my Hollywood ending.

And as I wrote the conclusion I'd been drafting in my mind from the very beginning, I saw it had been wiser, in a sense, than I was. It understood what I'd begun to forget: that recovery, unlike a story in a book, has no final page. There's no arrivals terminal, no victory lap, no closing credits with swooning strings.

So, clean a little while again as I write these words – though, I regret, nowhere near the six-plus years I hoped and expected to be by now – I'm grateful, at least, that I have my story.

That is, my two stories: the one with the ending that was there all along, and the one that keeps on going, because it's made of nothing but a string of todays.

London, September 2021

Acknowledgements

My main debt of gratitude is to the power-greater-than-myself that is Britain's National Health Service. Without it, this book could not have been written because its author would not be alive. Homerton Hospital's Gastroenterology department treated, and cured, my Hepatitis C; and its Bevan Ward cared for me during a crisis recounted in these pages. Several paramedics whose names I never learned averted what would otherwise have been fatal overdoses. Thanks to all the NHS workers who have cared for me over the years with tireless compassion and skill.

It's no exaggeration to say that the programme at 'Grace House' changed me fundamentally, and turned me into the person capable of writing this book. Though its staff can hardly be blamed for my remaining blind spots and short-comings, whatever maturity or perspective I possess is largely due to their help. I'll always be grateful for the model of Christian charity they showed me in my time there.

Thanks to St Mungo's for providing me a room in the 'halfway house' described here when I had nowhere else to go. Thanks to the River Rehab in Chiang Mai, Thailand, for helping me through a difficult period. Thanks to Ciconia Recovery in Harrow. Thanks to Caspian and Peta James for being there when it mattered. Thanks to Mark Goss and Sofie Heien. Thanks to everyone in the Rooms.

I'm immensely grateful to Sophie Lambert for her dedication and brilliance as an agent. She showed remarkable kindness and professionalism during what was not always a smooth project. Thanks to Meredith Ford, Kate Burton, Alexander Cochran, Jake Smith Bosanquet, Matilda Ayris and everyone else at C&W. And thanks to Anna Stein at ICM Partners.

Huge thanks to my editor Poppy Hampson for improving my writing in a thousand big and small ways. With patience and ingenuity she coaxed a better book out of me than this would otherwise have been – even if I'm solely responsible for the flaws that remain. Thanks to Clara Farmer, Greg Clowes, Tom Atkins and the whole team at Chatto & Windus, and Rachel Cugnoni at Vintage. Thanks also to Jim Gifford at HarperCollins Canada and John Glynn at HarperCollins USA. And to Jon Elek, whose early support helped bring the book into being.

A number of people read sections of the book and provided valuable feedback. Thanks to Paul Abbott, Sally Bayley, Emma Bosworth, Emily Carlton, Jenn Catterall, Liam Cotter, Stuart Forbes, Georgie Fozard, Lara Haworth, Jonathan Higgins, Karina Jakubowicz, William Kraemer, Allegra Le Fanu, Abel Matondo, Julia Minnear, Will Orr-Ewing, Amy Raphael, Michael Russ, Nahid Samsami, Jasleen Kaur Sethi, Anna Tosh, Allegra Van Zuylen, Lily Walker, James Watkins, Gloria Willis and Adam Yeh.

Being turned into a supporting character in someone else's story can be an invasive and disorienting experience, especially given the fallibility of memory and the wicked subjectivity of point of view. A few people allowed me to write about them despite my having harmed them in the past. Their doing so required a special form of what I can only call grace. I'm enormously grateful to everyone who allowed me to write about them, whether disguised or under their own name.

I'm hugely indebted to my family – Philip, Angela, Rachel, Jonathan and Abigail Hill – for selflessly giving me permission to tell this story in my own way, even when it touched on painful or intimate material, and even when our perspectives differed. My love to them all.

My younger brother Jonathan, who I loved more than anyone in the world, died suddenly at the age of thirty-four while I was writing these pages. I'm grateful I was able to show him the early chapters, but it pains me that he'll never hold a published copy in his hands. For a time after his death I lost the will to keep going, but recalling his loving support for this project ultimately gave me the strength to finish it. I'll miss him forever. This book is for him.